CORVETTE

Illustrated Encyclopedia

by Tom Benford

BentleyPublishers.com

[Left column — partially legible]

Corvette. Chevrolet supported the program ... build the option B2K to the program. ... outrageous of these cars was the Callaway ... turer, a joint program with John Lingenfelter. ... ngheimmer was driven from Callaway's ... d Lyme, Connecticut, to the TRC track in ... le it was clocked at over 250 mph. It was ... a home.

... way companies consist of three operating ...

... way Cars produces and markets high- ... mance automobiles and marine engines.

... way Advanced Technology designs high ... mance engines and components for ... way Cars and automotive, industrial, and ... ft clients worldwide.

... way Competition, GmbH, builds sportscars ... durance racing cars such as the ... way Corvette LM, the Callaway C7— the ... ny's first complete in-house designed and ... actured automobile— and the Callaway C12, ... y high performance sportscar for both road ... .

... way Cars and Callaway Advanced ... logy entities are located in a new building, ... -square-foot facility in Old Lyme, Connecticut. ... Competition, based in Leingarten, ... is the competition affiliate of The Callaway ... a. See also *Lingenfelter Performance* ... ng.

... y, Reeves (1947–)
... he Callaway III is the founder of Callaway ... ng and overseas operations at Callaway ... Connecticut and at Callaway Competition in ... Reeves ... projects and products of the Callaway ... a.

... y Sledgehammer
... way Sledgehammer is a highly modified ... vette. Callaway added twin turbos, a six- ... anual transmission and other modifications ... in an 880 hp car with a top speed of 254 ... o 0–60 time of 3.9 seconds. The $400,000 ... nmer was 50-state street legal and very ... erful track driving.

... y Speedster
... way Speedster is a limited edition of twelve ... built to order. The Speedsters are based ... laway SuperNaturals introduced in 1992 ... owered by the SuperNatural LT5 (490 ... at pounds) built to racing specification by a ... g engine development company, Callaway ... Technology. They are 50-state emission ... automobiles, meeting all requirements ... eral Clean Air Act and the California Air ... es Board. For off-road use and exhibition ... builds the unregulated SuperSpeedster with ... a Turbo LT5 horsepower.

... y SuperNatural
... way SuperNatural Corvette was conceived ... oped as a complete car, incorporating ... d improvements in power, handling, ... ppearance and comfort. Performance of ... Natural is optimized without sacrificing ... or durability, resulting in an outstanding ... , equal to or better than European exotics ... on of this cost. The SuperNatural 383 ... elivers consistent 0–60 times of 4.4 ... and runs the quarter mile in 12.7 seconds at ... in street tires with factory gearing.

... y Twin Turbo
... way Twin Turbo option was first offered in ... ough it was not a factory-installed option. ... ordered in advance through Chevrolet ... fully assembled Corvettes were shipped from ... ng Green factory to Callaway Engineering ... icut for engine conversion and final ... ons. The special engine was rated at 345 hp ... take the car to a top speed of 177.9 mph ... -mile gearing. All Callaway's had manual ... orts and none were certified for sale in ...

In 1987, 184 Twin Turbos were built and ... way option cost approximately $20,000. In ... Twin Turbos were built, the option cost ... 6,000 and the horsepower rating was 382. In ... were produced at a cost of almost $27,000. ... 86 were produced and the cost of the option ... same as the previous year. In 1991, the ... 82 were produced at a cost of $35,000, ... ion.

... efers to a wheel's inward or outward tilt ... ertical; camber is measured in degrees. ... camber is present when the wheels are ... the top (viewed from the front or rear); ... front or the rear); positive camber is present ... wheels are further apart at the top.

... Rod
... monly called the strut rod, this rod is part ... 3 to 1982 independent rear suspension ... controls the camber of the rear wheel. It ... directly below the half-shaft. The same ... s used and on the ½—in fact the camber ... of both ends. See ...

[Center-left column]

parallel carbon strands. The resulting fibers are ... 92–98 percent pure carbon, exceptionally strong ... and weigh significantly less than metals. A graphite ... fiber—which is 99-percent carbon—has the stiffness ... and strength of steel at ¼ its weight. Carbon fiber and ... graphite fiber are so similar that the two names are ... interchangeable.

Carburetor
A carburetor is a device that meters vaporized fuel ... and engine intake air, maintaining an approximately ... consant air-fuel ratio. The carburetor increases ... the rate of fuel to air in response to varying engine ... operating conditions such as starting, idling, transient ... acceleration and maximum power.

Three single-barrel carburetors were used on the ... 1963, 1964 and 1965 Corvettes with the Blue Flame ... Special six-cylinder engine. From 1955 through 1961 ... four-barrel carburetors were used on Corvette V-8 ... engines (in 1956–1962 dual four-barrel–optioned ... engines were available). Starting with the 1982 model ... year, carburetors were replaced with electronic fuel ... injection, first as the unit injector Cross-Fire Injection ... (CFI) then in 1985 as the multi-injector Tuned Port ... Injection (TPI), and in 1992 as Multi-Port Tuned ... Injection (MTI).

Carlisle Events, Inc.
Carlisle, Pennsylvania, is the site of a series of car ... swap meets produced by Carlisle Events, Inc., during ... the year at its 82-acre fairgrounds. Chip Miller and ... Bill Miller are the co-owners of both Carlisle Events, ... Inc., and the Carlisle Fairgrounds. The all-Corvette ... show, Corvettes at Carlisle, is held every year on ... the third weekend of August. There is also a large ... show in the spring and fall for general car parts and ... several specialty car events throughout the year. See ... *Supplier and Service Appendix*.

Carter AFB
The Carter AFB was a high performance four-barrel ... carburetor built by Carter in the early 1960s. It was ... used on the 327 cid/300 hp and the 327 cid/340 ... hp engines. Typically, the Carter AFB was rated ... at 800 cfm.

Carter WCFB
The Carter WCFB was a four-barrel carburetor used ... on Corvette engines both in single- and dual-quad ... configurations from 1955 to 1963. Typically, they were ... rated at 450 cfm.

Casting Number
When a part is cast the mold has a ... part number and a date code set so ... that the part is forever identified. Most older Corvette ... parts such as heads,

blocks and manifolds, usually have a seven-digit ... casting number beginning with 3 to identify the part. ... On most Corvette blocks the casting number is ... located on the bellhousing flange ... behind the driver's-side head. See ... also *Matching Numbers*.

Castle Nut
This is a type of nut with notches cut across its face ... to accommodate a cotter pin driven through the ... notches and through a hole in the bolt which locks ... the nut in place. Castle nuts are typically used on ... mission-critical components such as the rear shock ... hangers on Corvettes. They get their name from the ... fact that they look like turrets on a castle.

Catalytic Converters
Catalytic converters are exhaust emission control ... devices that by virtue of their very large surface ... area in contact with the exhaust gas help drive ... partially oxidized products of combustion to their ... completely oxidized state. A coating of trace amounts ... of platinum, palladium or other rare earth metals ... is used to extend the effectiveness of the catalytic ... converter to lower temperatures, thus making the ... converter effective during starting and warmup where ... most of the regulated emissions occur. Converters ... were first fitted with catalytic converters in 1975. As a ... result of the catalytic converters, the use of unleaded ... gasoline was mandated. Early catalytic converters ... were of a high backpressure, single-stream design ... and required the exhaust merge via a 'Y' pipe ... into the converter and then split back to dual mufflers. ... Starting in 1982, horsepower was increased by the ... use of a single, low-backpressure, monolith converter. ... On 1992–1996 Corvettes, individual converters were ... used close to each exhaust manifold, and an 'H' pipe ... containing a resonator was positioned between the ... converters and the exhaust pipes. Starting with the ... C5 Corvette in 1997, (the first year of OBD II) discrete ... catalytic converters were used for each exhaust ... manifold and the exhaust pipes ran straight back from ... the converters to the mufflers.

CE Block
CE is often defined as Chevrolet Engine, and it ... designates the motor as a warranty replacement ... engine installed by the Chevrolet dealer's service ... department as an alternative to rebuilding a badly ... damaged original-equipment engine that failed under ... warranty. The engine part carries a CE code instead ... of the traditional code on production engines. The ... last number indicates the year and the next five digits ... are a sequential numbering for the unit that year; ... 20,000 to 49,999 is for Flint-built V-8s; 60,000 to ... 79,999 is for Tonawanda-built V-8s. The VIN is usually ... not stamped in the pad, but is often misaligned and of ... irregular depth, due to it being hand-stamped by the ... dealer, if at all. These are relatively rare in Corvettes, ... as they indicate that Chevrolet warranty work was ... performed and the original engine was destroyed. ... These are the only cases of Chevrolet intervening ... in the life of a Corvette once it left the factory, since ... engine replacement required Chevrolet management ... authorization and most warranty work was simply ... handled by the dealer.

Central Office Production Order (COPO)
During the late 1960s and early 1970s Chevrolet dealers ... would contact the Central Offices in Michigan ... to request deviations from regular production ... options that were available for the model year. For ... instance, special color paint could be requested ... for an additional charge in the case of a fleet order. ... Generally, options that were requested had to be ... in current production for other models. Chevrolet ... engineering then had to grant approval for these ... vehicle parts combinations. These types of orders ... eventually became the groundwork to build factory ... race cars, and it was a convenient way to order ... competition-ready Corvettes directly from the ... assembly line.

Centrifugal Advance
This is a mechanism within the distributor that ... consists of two weights that rotate with the distributor ... shaft. As the rotational speed increases centrifugal ... force causes these weights to move outward against ... spring tension. The movement of the weights is

[Center-right column]

Vehicle. Zora Arkus-Duntov designed a single seat, ... open-wheel racer data dubbed CERV I. It was used to test ... suspension and powertrain components as well as ... for demonstrating the performance and engineering ... capabilities of GM to the public. Its rear suspension ... was the basis for the 1963 Corvette rear suspension. ... The CERV I is now owned by Mike Yager.

CERV II
The CERV II was Zora Arkus-Duntov's most exotic ... experimental car. Like the CERV I, this car was ... built to do research on suspension and drivetrain ... components. For many years the CERV II held the ... ... Group ...

[image area — title overlaid]

The CERV III was a mid-engined, fully functional ...

... 348 cid and the 409 cid (the first big-block engines) ...

... by Larry Shinoda's concept Mako Shark and powered by ... Chevrolet engines. Chapanaak used many visual cues ... that would later be incorporated into the Mako Shark ... and the 1968 Corvette. See also *Ground Effects*.

Cheetah
The Cheetah was a race car built in 1963 by Bill ... Thomas based on the 1963 Corvette fuel-injected ... engine and rear suspension. The front-engined ... Cheetah weighed less than 2,000 pounds and had ... a 40/60 weight ratio front to rear. Thomas wanted ... to build a car to beat the Cobra and he had ... hoped to get support from Chevrolet. Chevy did ... not officially support him and, after a factory fire, ... Cheetah production ended after approximately 40 ... cars were built. Most Cheetahs ran C-Modified in ... SCCA racing and some actually entered the first year ... Can Am races.

Chicago Corvette Supply
Chicago Corvette Supply is a major source of ... Corvette restoration parts ... and accessories. See the *Supplier and Service ... Appendix*.

Chip
See *Microchip*.

Clamshell
A hood design that incorporates the front fender and ... is hinged at the front is sometimes called a "clamshell ... hood." When it opens it exposes the entire ... top of the engine, suspension and tires. The C4 ... (1984–1996) Corvette uses a clamshell hood.

Clift, Bob (1920–)
Clift was one of the Corvette engineers of the 1950s ... and 1960s who drove many of the Corvettes in ... testing. He was an avid SCCA racer in the 1950s, ... racing a modified 1954 Corvette. Clift was also ... heavily involved in the development and testing of the ... Bricklin. He currently resides in Hollywood, Florida.

Clutch
In an automobile with a manual transmission the ... clutch connects the engine's flywheel to the gearbox. ... Smooth coupling and uncoupling of the engine to the ... drivetrain is made possible by the gradual slipping of ... the clutch's friction discs and the cushioning effect of ... springs incorporated in the clutch disc facing.

Clutch Pressure Plate
A clutch pressure plate assembly bolts to the flywheel ... and contains the springs, levers and throw-out ... bearing that disengage the clutch.

Cobra, Shelby Cobra
The Cobra came about when Carroll Shelby mated ... a Ford 260 cid V-8 (later a 289 cid Ford V-8) with ... an English A.C. Ace body and chassis. Weighing ... around 2,300 pounds, the somewhat crude Cobra ate ... Corvettes alive due to its light weight and superior ... acceleration. Later Cobras had various versions of ... the Ford 427 cid motor in a re-designed chassis and ... were only named when SCCA began to equalize the ... weights on the cars. Ford saw a good thing and used ... the Cobra as a means to give its cars a performance ... image while only having to mildly support Shelby.

Coil
See *Ignition Coil*.

Coil Bind
Coil bind occurs when a coil spring is compressed so ... tightly that one winding touches another winding and ... cannot close any more. In valve springs, this usually ... results in a broken spring.

Coil-over Shocks
When a coil suspension spring surrounds the shock ... absorber and is mounted to it, it is referred to as a ... "coil-over." Typically the mounting is threaded making ... the spring height adjustable. The 1957 Corvette SS ... used a coil-over shock front suspension. Coil-over ... shocks are a popular performance modification for C4 ... and C5 Corvettes, since they allow easy adjustment ... of ride height.

Cole, Edward (1909–1977)
Ed Cole was president of GM and former Chief ... Engineer of Chevrolet. The Corvette was already a ... clay model when he first saw it. But he recognized it ... instantly as the ideal symbol of a soon-to-be-reborn ... Chevrolet marque. What really excited Ed Cole ... was the bizarre notion that such a car—two seats, ... plastic body, six months from drawing board to ... driveway—could come from GM's most conservative ... car division. He also saw it as a great way to launch ... his Chevrolet renaissance.

For all the 4 years at General Motors, only ten were ... spent at Chevrolet, but they were Chevy's postwar ... growth years and they cemented the foundation ... for the division's long domination of the American ... automotive market. His stated task when he ... became Chief Engineer in May 1952, was to ... bring a lightweight, low-cost V-8 into the Chevrolet ... engine lineup. He did and it was called the Chevy ... small block. For the next 50 years it would reign

[Right column]

... keep its members informed and aware of ... ideas breaking news in the Corvette hob ... *Supplier and Service Appendix.*

Corvette Enthusiast Magazine
A monthly magazine devoted to Corvette ... *Enthusiast* is published by Amos Automo ... Publishing. See the *Magazine Appendix*.

Corvette Fever Magazine
This is a monthly magazine devoted to e ... published by Primedia Specialty Group. ... *Magazine Appendix*.

Corvette Hall Of Fame & American ...
... won the breechblock ... bugat who was once ... dgot who was once ... of the now-defunct ... the museum was to estab ... ... through 50 years of ... this sports cars as the N ... enters ... in Cooperstown, N ... howover ... Corvettes in period docu ... 1960s ... and memorabilia from the ...

... Built in 1985, the Corvette Indy was first ... '86. Dubbed ... owatased C ... ar, built by L ... Lotus techni ... t owned by ... a mid-ship ... 32-valve ... ins based o ... he was nicke ... racing engine ... it is estima ... nd drive, four ... on were a b ... cused on th ... the dash provi ... neva. Indy incorpo ... became standard ... iomer, including electronic throttle con ...

Corvette Magazine
Corvette Mike is an Anaheim, ... California-based dealership and facility to ... sells, trades and services used and vinta ... Corvettes. See also *Vintro, "Corvette Mi* ... *Supplier and Service Index*.

Corvette Museum Delivery
Listed as option R8C, the National Corv ... Museum's in-house delivery program is a ... feature that lets buyers of new Corvettes ... cars under the golden 140-foot-diameter ... Skydome in the midst of Corvette's histor ... in 1994, it must be specified at the time ... finalized and a special ship code of '186 ... also be used to identify the Corvette for ... Delivery.

Corvette News Magazine
In the 1960s, amazed at the growth of Co ... clubs, for Pike became the editor of a fre ... magazine produced by Chevrolet that wa ... to every Corvette owner. Due to Chevrol ... organization, the number of subscription ... too large to manage, often due to mailing ... *News* to people who had not owned a Co ... years. Chevrolet canceled the subscriptio ... early 1980s and made the publication av ... only through general paid subscription. S ... exclusivity was lost, many readers did no ... subscribe. Within a few years the magazi ... Later, *Corvette Quarterly* would be on a ... being back ON on a subscription basis.

Corvette Postage Stamps
Several countries have recognized the C ... their postage stamps over the years. Am ... are the Marshall Islands, Republique du ... Tajoristan, Liberia, Nicaragua-Tavalo, Re ... Federativa Islamique des Comoros, Kam ... Dagestan, Guyana, Ajman, St. Vincent, ... Netherlands Antillas and others.

Corvette Q Car
See *Q Car, Q Corvette*.

Corvette Quarterly Magazine
Dubbed "the official journal of America's w ... sports car," *Corvette Quarterly* is publish ... a year by Campbell-Ewald Publishing, a di ... Campbell-Ewald. See the *Magazine Appe*

Corvette Rubber Company
The Corvette Rubber Company is a major ... of Corvette weatherstripping, pedals, pott ... parts, heater hoses and other restoration ... accessories. See the *Supplier and ... Service Appendix.*

Corvette SS (Super Sport)
The Corvette SS was a race-only Corvet ... to run endurance races at Sebring and L ... 1957 The light magnesium body covered ... space frame featuring a deDion rear axle ... the brakes and the potential to be a winn ... due to a bushing failing at Sebring, it rati ... GM's decision to stop active factory part ... in motorsports brought the car's career t ... before it could accomplish anything. The ... 'mule' built to test the chassis showed th ... enormous potential in the design. The mu ... scrapped and the car later resurfaced as ... *Stingray Race Car.*

Corvette Stingray Race Car
Built on the chassis of a Corvette SS m ... Stingray race car was initially based on ... of GM design chief Bill Mitchell. Never a ... Corvette race car, the Stingray was raced ... by privateers at numerous events nationv ... For Dr. Dick Thomps ... the new 1963 str ... production car.

Corvette Summer (the Movie)
Released in 1978 and directed by Matthe ... *Corvette Summer* starred Mark Hamill, an ... Danny Bonaduce. Ken (played by Mark H ... built a customized Stingray in shop class ... for cruising for girls. When the car is stol ... of car thieves, his relentless search take ... Los Angeles to Las Vegas. There he me ... aspiring hooker (Annie Potts) who helps ... hot wheels down.

Corvette! The Sensuous American
The first product offering from Michael B ... Associates, *Corvette! The Sensuous Ame* ... a series of nine hardbound Corvette boo ... were published at the rate of three per y

To Kurt

This book is dedicated to my best friend,
buddy, soul mate and wife, Liz, who
truly is the wind beneath my wings.

"Save the Wave!"

Best Wishes —

Tom Beyfus

CORVETTE Illustrated Encyclopedia

Blue Flame Special: See page 18.

Collector Edition: See page 44.

Dave Hill: See page 90.

Knock-Off Wheels: See page 107.

Contents

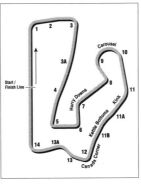

Road America: See page 162.

Waterfall: See page 202.

B **BENTLEY PUBLISHERS**™ | Automotive Reference™

Bentley Publishers, a division of Robert Bentley, Inc.
1734 Massachusetts Avenue
Cambridge, MA 02138 USA
800-423-4595 / 617-547-4170   Information that makes
                                     the difference®
BentleyPublishers
                  .com

Copies of this book may be purchased from selected booksellers or directly from the publisher. The publisher encourages comments from the reader of this book. These communications have been and will be considered in the preparation of this and other books. Please write to Bentley Publishers at the address listed at the top of this page or e-mail us through our web site.

Since this page cannot legibly accommodate all the copyright notices, the credits listing the source of the photographs or illustrations used constitutes an extension of the copyright page.

Library of Congress Cataloging-in-Publication Data

Benford, Tom.
  Corvette illustrated encyclopedia / Tom Benford.
     p. cm.
  1. Corvette automobile--Encyclopedias. I. Title.
  TL215.C6B4497 2004
  629.222'2--dc22
                         2004012578

Bentley Stock No. GCEB

ISBN 0-8376-0928-3

08 07 06 05 04   10 9 8 7 6 5 4 3 2 1

The paper used in this publication is acid free and meets the requirements of the National Standard for Information Sciences-Permanence of Paper for Printed Library Materials. ∞

Corvette Illustrated Encyclopedia, by Tom Benford

Manufactured in the United States of America

Foreword

by Mike Yager

Corvette passion hit me early and has stayed with me all my life. As a boy, when I first saw my older brothers drive their Corvettes, I knew I had to own one. My Corvette dreams have come true beyond my wildest expectations. I purchased my first Corvette when I was 20 years old. Over the years, I estimate I've owned 200 Corvettes. Today, I own more than 30 Corvettes, including very rare and one-of-a-kind models. I am especially blessed to be the founder and "Chief Cheerleader" of Mid America Motorworks, a leading supplier of parts and accessories to Corvette enthusiasts.

Like all Corvette lovers, I enjoy sharing my passion for America's sports car with other enthusiasts. I never pass up an opportunity to talk about Corvettes with other owners. Tom Benford is one of the enthusiasts I especially enjoy talking to because I can learn so much from him about cars in general and Corvettes in particular.

Now, with the publication of the *Corvette Illustrated Encyclopedia*, everyone can tap into Tom Benford's knowledge the way I have been able to do. Whether you are a veteran of the Corvette hobby or a newcomer to Corvettes, the book you are holding in your hands is a valuable resource.

I thought I knew a lot about Corvettes, but just browsing through the pages of this encyclopedia, I discovered many new Corvette facts that I didn't know before. I've already made a promise to myself to never again get into an argument with someone about a Corvette fact without first consulting the *Corvette Illustrated Encyclopedia*. I can just imagine the delight this book will bring to someone learning about Corvettes for the first time.

After more than 50 years on the market, the Corvette has compiled a rich and diverse history. Many people would be surprised at how much you can learn about Corvettes. The casual observer would ask: How much can there be to learn about a car that has always been a two-seater, always had a fiberglass body and has only undergone a major design change six times in its history?

This *Corvette Illustrated Encyclopedia* shows there is a lot to learn because the Corvette has continually evolved. The 1953 Corvette was a first attempt by General Motors to capture some of the new, post-World-War-II sports car market that was the exclusive domain of a small group of British car makers. Fifty years later, the Corvette has become not only a world class sports car, but also one of the best bargains in the performance car market. I honestly believe no other sports car in the world matches the performance, comfort, and reliability of the latest Corvettes.

Most encyclopedias are strictly reference books you use when you want to find an answer to a question. You will miss

a lot if you use the *Corvette Illustrated Encyclopedia* only as a reference guide. The *Corvette Illustrated Encyclopedia* is a book to be read and enjoyed. On just about every page, I find something that makes me stop and say to myself, "Wow, I didn't know that."

It is a lot to ask to fit 50 years of exciting history and knowledge into one book. But Tom Benford has done an amazing job of doing just that. Tom invested a lot of time and effort into writing this book, and I am glad he did. The *Corvette Illustrated Encyclopedia* is a valuable addition to the library of every Corvette enthusiast.

—Mike Yager
    Chief Cheerleader
    Mid America Motorworks
    June 2004

Preface

by Tom Benford

About a decade ago I purchased my first Corvette, a pristine 1963 Split Window Coupe. I read everything I could get my hands on to learn more about the '63, as well as the origins of the Corvette, its developmental milestones, technical developments, people responsible for the development and evolution of the car—in short, I wanted to know everything about the marque.

Over the years, in addition to building a stable of six Corvettes (two Mid-Years and four Sharks), I've read scores of books, hundreds of magazine articles and visited countless web sites all dedicated to the Corvette. Whenever I'd find something interesting that I hadn't come upon before, I'd make a note of it and do research to confirm that it was factual and correct.

I know I'm not alone in my thirst and quest for information on these cars. I've spoken to dozens of other Corvette owners and participated in lots of internet chat rooms in the interests of sharing knowledge. It was from these conversations that it became clear that the time for the *Corvette Illustrated Encyclopedia* had come.

I've been privileged to have become friends with several important people in the Corvette world. Among these are the late Larry Shinoda and fellow Bentley authors and colleagues Jerry Burton and Dave McLellan. These individuals, as well as numerous other book authors, magazine editors, and professionals involved in both the automotive industry and Corvette world, have freely given their advice, suggestions and support in the interests of making this book a better and more complete work.

The Corvette is unique. It has its own jargon and nomenclature. Such terms as "solid axle," "stinger hood," "split window," "washboard hood" and "tanker" are but a few of the words that are used in "Corvette speak." You'll find explanations of these terms as well as other automotive terms and lots of other information herein.

I've endeavored to make this as complete a resource as possible and it will be revised to include information on new Corvettes and additional entries that are deemed pertinent. That's where you, the reader, can be of help. If you have any suggestions or comments on how to make the *Corvette Illustrated Encyclopedia* better or would like to see additional entries added, please don't hesitate to send me your suggestions, entries and comments at:

Corvette Illustrated Encyclopedia
Bentley Publishers, Attn: Tom Benford
1734 Massachusetts Avenue
Cambridge, MA 02138-1804

I sincerely hope you find this book to be useful, informative and enjoyable, and I also hope it helps you to have a richer and more fulfilling experience in the wonderful world of Corvettes.

—Tom Benford, October 2003

A is for...

Arkus-Duntov

Zora Arkus-Duntov changed the
Corvette from a turntable darling into
one of the most respected sports cars in
the world. See the full entry on page 8.

ABS (Antilock Braking System)

ABS is an abbreviation for Antilock Braking System. The ABS debut on the 1986 Corvette was the first time it had been offered as standard equipment on an American passenger car. Corvette used the Bosch ABS II system. This system was controlled by a digital microprocessor. Bosch's first ABS system, ABS I, was a much simpler analog computer based system. It was launched in the early 1980s in Europe and used by Mercedes-Benz and BMW as optional equipment on their top models. ABS II consists of an Electronic Control Unit (ECU), hydraulic modulator, pump, accumulator and various valves and sensors. The normal braking system consisting of master cylinder, vacuum booster, calipers, pads, rotors, etc., is retained.

ABS takes advantage of the observation that a tire slips measurably on the road before it slides and this slip can generate the maximum braking force available between the tire and the road. A rolling tire, even if it is slipping (but not sliding), gives the driver directional control of the vehicle. A sliding tire gives no directional control. A car sliding on all four tires gives no steering wheel control and goes wherever the dynamic forces take it.

With ABS, incipient wheel lock is sensed by the computer, which closes off brake pressure to the locking wheel. If the wheel continues to head toward lockup, brake pressure to that wheel is reduced. A pump returns the dumped brake fluid to the master cylinder so that the pedal does not go to the floor over several ABS cycles. The ABS system actually controls all four wheels as a system so that vehicle stability is maintained.

ABS must act effectively over a wide range of coefficients of friction from wet ice to dry roads. A driver practiced in making controlled stops on a particular road surface can equal ABS performance but given the uncertainties of any given stop, ABS consistently produces the shorter controlled stops.

AC

See *Air Conditioning*

AC Cobra

See *Cobra, Shelby Cobra*

Active Handling

In the mid-1998 model year, active handling was introduced as an option (JL4) on Corvette. Active handling gives the driver directional control of the car even in the most demanding control circumstances. The system effectively forces the car to go where the driver steers it. Working on all four wheels in conjunction with a yaw rate sensor, lateral accelerometer and a variety of other sensors, the antilock braking system (**ABS**) and traction control system (TCS), active handling assists the driver in maintaining control under a variety of driving circumstances on wet or dry road surfaces. In 2001 active handling became standard for all Corvettes. This second generation of active handling was significantly improved, with a more seamless operation and less intrusion under enthusiastic driving conditions.

Active Keyless Entry

Introduced on the 2000 model year Corvette, the active keyless entry system replaced the **Passive Keyless Entry** system that had been used since 1993. The active keyless entry system uses a key fob with buttons for unlocking the doors, whereas the passive system automatically unlocked the doors whenever the key fob came within a few feet of the vehicle.

Active Suspension

Active suspension was never offered on the Corvette. At one time it was considered as a special package option available only with the **ZR-1**. According to **Dave McLellan**, Jack Turner of Chevrolet R & D worked with Lotus to adapt their hydraulically controlled suspension system to the Corvette, but the project was cancelled when it was realized the technical problems were too great. The **National Corvette Museum** has the prototype on display.

Adams, Noland (1933–)

Noland Adams is a well-known author and Corvette historian whose works include a series of technical books— *The Complete Corvette Restoration*

Noland Adams

& Technical Guide, (Volume I, 1953 to 1962; Volume II, 1963 to 1967), *Corvette, American Legend*, covering the original dream car prototype and 1953 production, and the follow up series, *1954 and 1955 Production, 1956 Production, 1957 Racing and Production Details*, and *1958 to 1960 Variations*.

Adams has hosted a series of restoration videotapes, written hundreds of articles for Corvette-related magazines, and has given numerous presentations on Corvette restoration all over the United States, plus seminars in Canada, Sweden and England. A consultant to the model car industry, Adams was the technical advisor on Monogram's 1953 Corvette model car kit and the **Franklin Mint**'s 1953 Corvette model.

He is known worldwide for his knowledge of Corvette development heritage and technical understanding and is a longtime member of the National Corvette Restorers Society (**NCRS**). Adams has been involved with Corvette for over 45 years and is president of the Solid Axle Corvette Club. He attends many Corvette shows and functions each year sharing his Corvette expertise and knowledge with Corvette enthusiasts. Noland was inducted into the **National Corvette Museum**'s Hall of Fame in 2003.

Aerovette/Four-Rotor Corvette/ XP-882

A close relative of the original steel bodied mid-engine Corvette show car and the **Reynolds Aluminum Corvette**, the Aerovette was essentially a rebodied XP-882. Initially powered by a four-rotor **Wankel Rotary Engine**, it may have offered the best chance ever for a mid-engine Corvette to make it into

The **Aerovette/Four-Rotor Corvette/XP-882** showcar

production, since GM was an active Wankel licensee and was pursuing several possible production programs. The Aerovette/Four-Rotor/XP-882 featured a dramatic almond shape and a smooth fastback roofline. It also featured bi-fold **gullwing doors**, inspired by the Mercedes-Benz 300 SL.

Photographed in the GM Design Staff viewing court just before its public debut in early 1970, the experimental XP-882 looked production-ready and hopes were high that the next new Corvette would have a similar mid-engine design. With its low vee'd nose and four-lamp tail treatment, it definitely looked like a Corvette. It was shown earlier than planned to counter Ford's introduction of the Italian-built DeTomaso **Panteras**. GM built two XP-882 chassis for evaluation, but only the first one had the bodywork shown in the photo above.

In 1973, under the aegis of company design chief **Bill Mitchell**, the original XP-882 chassis was modified to carry a pair of GM's experimental two-rotor engines bolted together and producing a 420 hp "super Wankel." The four-rotor

powerplant—built by **Gib Hufstader**—designated the RC2-206, was supposed to be the replacement for the V-8 in Corvettes since it was light, powerful and had few actual moving parts.

General Motors president **Ed Cole** wanted a rotary engine vehicle in production before he retired in September 1974, and **Zora Arkus-Duntov**, chief engineer for the Corvette, had championed the idea of a mid-engined Corvette since the late 1950s. The biggest problems to overcome with the Wankel were fuel consumption and emissions. In 1973 the Environmental Protection Agency revised its regulations and allowed the door to be opened for rotaries as the emission controls were eased somewhat, which put further development of the RC2-206 back on the front burner. The fuel crisis of 1973–74 also worked against the Wankel.

GM found that having two **spark plugs** closely spaced produced cleaner emissions but fuel economy suffered. With the relief of the new emission standards GM went back to an earlier layout. The leading plug was placed normally just past the pinched waist or

minor axis (15 degrees) of the engine's trochoid. The other 'trailing' plug was moved in the other direction and would be uncovered very early (34 degrees). The quad rotor engine was 50 degrees. It was the largest displacement Wankel engine ever installed in an automobile.

By the time the Four-Rotor showcar—designed by **Jerry Palmer** under studio chief Henry Haga—was ready to be publicly displayed, problems with the Wankel engine such as poor fuel economy, leaking seals, a tendency to run hot and higher unit cost doomed it.

The four-rotor XP-882 received a V-8 transplant in 1976 and was rechristened the Aerovette, which came close to production four years later. It's a dynamic design even when viewed from overhead and in profile it displays a strongly triangulated "mound" shape, deftly balanced proportions, and artful surface detailing. The gullwing doors were articulated for easier operation in tight parking spots and the interior was more fully engineered than is the norm for showcars, another indication that the Aerovette was indeed a serious production prospect. Unfortunately, the Aerovette never made it into actual production. See also *XP-897 GT*.

AFB
See *Carter AFB*.

AIR (Air Injection Reactor)
This stands for Air Injection Reactor. Air is pumped by the "smog pumps" through air injection manifolds into the exhaust manifolds to complete the oxidization process of the unburned hydrocarbons in the hot exhaust stream. Not to be confused with **American International Racing**.

Air Box
In the late 1950s one of the available racing options (**RPO #684**) from the factory for Corvettes included a box for channeling air through the body to the rear brakes for cooling.

Air Conditioning (AC)
Air conditioning, **RPO #C60**, was introduced in the middle of the 1963 model production run. With only 278 Corvettes so equipped, cars with this option are the third-most rare of the 1963s (36-gallon tank cars and **Z06** being fewer). In later years the number of factory-air-equipped Corvettes grew. No 1953 to 1962 Corvette had factory AC. In 1963 RPO #C60 cost a whopping $421.80, which was almost 10 percent of the $4,257.00 base price for the coupe. On air-conditioned mid-year Corvettes (1963–1967), the battery was located on the driver's side (rather than on the passenger side) to make room for the additional plumbing required by the AC. Air conditioning became standard equipment in Corvettes starting with the 1980 model. In 1994, R-134A refrigerant replaced the less environmentally friendly R-12 refrigerant that had been used previously. Dual zone air conditioning, which permits the driver and passenger to set individual comfort levels, became an option with the 1997 Corvette.

Al Knoch Interiors
Al Knoch Interiors is a major manufacturer and supplier of 1953–1967 Corvette interior components. See the *Suppliers and Services Appendix*.

Albert, Jon (1953–)

Jon Albert was the GM Interior Design Chief responsible for the Corvette **C5** passenger compartment. Previously, he was the Assistant Chief Designer responsible for the Sting Ray III, as well as the Chief Designer for the 1994 **C4** airbag interior.

Alcoa Aluminum

Alcoa Aluminum was originally contracted by GM to cast the Gen III (LS1) cylinder blocks for the alpha versions (production roadtest prototypes) of the C5; however, due to casting problems the early alpha cars were equipped with iron-block versions of the motor.

Alembic 1

During the post-World War II years many companies experimented with new materials that were developed for wartime use. One of these companies was Glasspar, a boat builder, which constructed a single prototype Willys-based fiberglass-bodied sports car, originally known as the **Boxer**. The Naugatuck Chemical Division of U.S. Rubber acquired Glasspar's fiberglass sports car prototype shortly thereafter, and renamed it the Alembic 1.

General Motors also experimented with fiberglass and other resin-cured materials. In early 1952 a prototype full-sized fiberglass-bodied Chevrolet convertible was accidentally rolled during a test run. Because the body survived with very little significant damage, the decision was made to adopt fiberglass for the production body material for the company's upcoming sports car, code named **Project Opel**.

In March 1952, the Alembic 1 was loaned to GM for a short while, where it was displayed in the company's private viewing auditorium.

Alternator

An alternator is a belt-driven device that converts rotational energy to DC current. The alternator provides the energy for the vehicle's electrical system and also recharges the battery. The alternator uses the principle of electromagnetic induction to produce voltage and current. It differs from the previously used DC generator in that it produces its electrical output in the non-rotating stator. The stator actually produces an AC current that is then changed into an oscillating DC current by a solid state diode bridge. Electrical output control is achieved by regulating the field strength of the electromagnetic rotor. Corvette converted from a generator to an alternator starting with the 1963 model year.

Aluminum Radiator

See *Harrison Radiator*

AM Radio

A Corvette option starting with the 1953 model year (option 102B), the AM radio continued to be offered through the early part of the 1963 model year (option U65), until it was replaced by the AM/FM radio (option U69) in the later part of that year.

AM/FM Radio

Originally offered as an option (U69) in the later part of the 1963 model year, it continued to be offered through the 1968 model year as a monaural-output radio. In 1969 a stereo AM/FM radio (U79) was

also offered as an option. Both monaural (U69) and stereo versions (designated as option U79 through 1972, then becoming option U58 in 1973) were available through the 1978 model year.

American Custom Industries (ACI)
ACI is a major supplier of Corvette parts and accessories. See the *Suppliers and Services Appendix*.

American International Racing (AIR)
The American International Racing team was founded by actor James Garner, Donald Rabbitt, **Dick Guldstrand**, Irwin Sandin and **Bob Bondurant**. Although the funding of the team is somewhat clouded, Garner was supposed to have invested $65,000 into a start-up fund that purchased the three 1968 L88 Corvettes the **St. Louis** factory had produced in time for the 1968 **Daytona** 24 Hours. Herb Caplan supplied front money and the GM connections to buy the L88s. Goodyear also put in some sponsorship money, and the team was supposed to live on sponsorship money.

The original L88 drivers were Dick Guldstrand, Scooter Patrick, Ed Leslie, Bob Bondurant and Herb Caplan. Bondurant was seriously hurt in a **Can Am** McLaren at Watkins Glen and Davey Jordan was hired to fill in for Bondurant. (James Garner never drove any of AIR race cars in competition but he was active driving a Bill Stroppe-prepared Bronco in offroad racing!)

The AIR team only raced the L88s at Daytona in 1968 and their only claim to fame was having the two fastest GT qualifiers at that event in 15th and 16th

The 1968 L88 Corvettes of the **American International Racing** team were prepped in Dick Guldstrand's shop.

places. The Guldstrand/Leslie/Caplan car was the fastest with a time of 2:04.05/110.613mph; the Patrick/Jordan car time was 2:05.02/109.553mph. The Patrick/Jordan car led the GT category for 262 laps, then a headgasket/headstud problem put the car out—it was classified 35th. The other car soldiered on and finished 29th despite changing three rear ends. As the car crossed the finish line it was running on seven cylinders and had another leaking differential (the cars were not allowed to use differential coolers and the overheated oil blew out the differential seals).

American Stamp Collectibles
American Stamp Collectibles offers Corvette 50th Anniversary Collectible Stamp plaques, both featuring Corvette photo collages and actual uncancelled

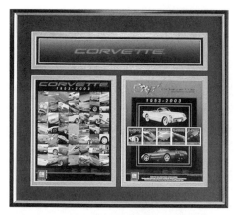

Framed postage stamp plaque from **American Stamp Collectibles** commemorating Corvette's 50th Anniversary

Corvette Stamps from St. Vincent. See the *Suppliers and Services Appendix.*

Anti-roll Bar
See *Sway Bar.*

Antonik, Michael (1944–)
Michael Antonik is the owner, president and C.E.O. of Michael Bruce Associates, an Ohio corporation founded in 1975 that specializes in publishing books about Corvettes, Camaros and titles related to general automobile detailing and photography. He is also the author of numerous Corvette books published by his company, as well as by Motorbooks International. Antonik is best known for the 18-volume *Corvette! The Sensuous American* series, *Corvette! America's Only* and the perennial *Corvette Black Book,* which is updated and published annually. See the *Suppliers and Services Appendix.*

A-Pillar
The foremost roof support of a Corvette or any fixed-windshield automobile located between the outer edge of the windshield and the leading edge of the front door upper. Also known as an A-post.

Arkus-Duntov, Zora (1909–1996)
Zora Arkus-Duntov was a General Motors engineer known for his many contributions to the Corvette's evolution.

He was born in Belgium, raised in Leningrad, and educated in Berlin. He hip-hopped through wars and revolutions in Europe and along the way, married a dancer from the *Folies Bergère.* After World War II broke out, he joined the French Air Force and later arranged for the escape of his family from occupied France. He then came to America and established Ardun Mechanical, a war munitions company that eventually employed 300 people. In the postwar years, Zora shifted gears into the high performance arena, designing a cylinder head conversion for the Ford flathead V-8 that became a favorite performance modification for hot-rodders.

After joining GM in 1953, Zora changed the Corvette from a turntable darling into one of the most respected sports cars in the world. The transformation started slowly, beginning with a suspension tweak, some aerodynamic work, the 265 cid V-8, then the V-8 high-performance camshaft, fuel injection and eventually independent rear suspension, purebred race cars and daring prototypes. For the first time, Corvettes began to appear in racing paddocks at places like Pebble Beach and **Sebring** alongside Mercedes, Jaguars and Porsches.

Duntov had a vision for what an American sports car ought to be. His vision was was heavily influenced by his European racing background.

A

Zora Arkus-Duntov
December 25, 1909–April 21, 1996

Named engineering coordinator for the Corvette program in August 1957, Duntov was appointed director of high performance vehicles at the same time. He became Corvette engine and chassis designer in 1963, and was promoted to chief engineer for the Corvette in 1968, a post he held until his retirement on January 1, 1975, after 22 years with Chevrolet engineering.

Among his many accomplishments were the Chevrolet Experimental Research Vehicles (**CERV I** and **CERV II**), created in the early 1960s. CERV I was an open-wheel, single-seat experimental car and CERV II was a mid-engined car with full-time four-wheel-drive.

He was also chiefly responsible for the introduction of such items as four-wheel independent suspension, disc brakes, four-speed transmissions and limited-slip rear ends on Corvettes.

After his retirement Zora worked as a consultant to several companies including **American Custom Industries,**

Holley and DeLorean. It was his work with ACI which ultimately led to the limited edition, "Duntov Turbo" Corvette. This customized convertible came equipped with a turbocharged 350 cid V-8 and upgraded suspension. Zora became disappointed with the poor performance and sales figures of the car; only 86 Duntov Turbos were made.

Zora Arkus-Duntov quietly passed away on Sunday, April 21, 1996, at St. John's Hospital in Grosse Pointe, Michgan, at the age of 86 due to cancer-induced kidney failure. *See additional photo on page 1.*

ASR (Acceleration Slip Regulation)

ASR is an abbreviation for Acceleration Slip Regulation and is commonly known as a form of traction control. Created by Bosch and developed in cooperation with Corvette engineers, the acceleration slip regulation system, integrated with the **ABS**, engaged automatically with the ignition but could be turned off with a switch on the instrument panel. The system used engine spark retard, brake intervention and throttle closedown (that actually made the throttle cable go limp) to curtail wheel spin during acceleration. It was introduced in 1992 as a standard feature on all Corvettes.

Assembly Instruction Manual (AIM)

Also known simply as assembly manuals, these books are available as reprints of the manuals used on the assembly line at General Motors and are a tremendous aid when restoring a Corvette. There is a separate manual created and printed for each model year, although coupe and convertible assembly instructions may be combined in a single manual. These manuals typically contain detailed

The **Astro II/XP-880** showcar

assembly drawings, original part numbers and more. They are readily available from numerous Corvette parts and accessory suppliers. The last printed factory assembly manuals were produced for the 1982 Corvette. As of 1984, all assembly instructions were computer-based.

Assembly Manual
See *Assembly Instruction Manual.*

Astoria Chas.
See *Snyder, Charles.*

Astro II/XP-880
Though it wasn't called a Corvette, the 1968 Astro II showcar spurred rumors that a mid- or rear-engined Chevrolet sports car might soon see the light of day. Developed as project XP-880, it was a follow-up to the previous year's Corvair-based Astro I, but carried a Corvette V-8 and conventional doors. The entire rear half of the body was hinged to tilt up for engine access. **Zora Arkus-Duntov** was categorically opposed to creating a rear-engined sports car, understanding full well the unsolvable handing problems

it would cause. The decision to scrap the mid-engined Corvette program also sealed the XP-880's fate.

Astro-Vette
Although the Corvette Astro-Vette was Chevrolet's other big auto show star in 1968, it was, in reality, merely an exaggerated version of that year's all-new **Shark** production design. The showcar allegedly had excellent aerodynamics, although this was never proven.

Autocrossing
Autocrossing is a motor sport in which a driver races against the clock on a course usually marked with pylons on a parking lot. Only one car at a time is on the course, unless the event is a Pro Solo contest where one driver runs against another driver on a mirror-image course. The fastest time wins. Speeds are generally close to what you can experience on a public road and the sport is considered very safe for both driver and car. Autocrossing is a very popular event at many Corvette car shows and club gatherings.

A

The **Astro-Vette** showcar

Automatic Transmission

This is a transmission that automatically shifts gears based on the vehicle's speed without the use of manual shifting linkage, a **clutch** or driver intervention. See *Powerglide, Turbo 350, Turbo 400*.

Axle Ratio

This is the ratio between the rotational speed (rpm) of the driveshaft and that of the driven wheel. Gear reduction in the final drive is determined by dividing the number of teeth on the ring gear by the number of teeth on the pinion gear. Simply put, the axle ratio is the number of times the driveshaft makes a full revolution to produce one full revolution of the rear axle(s). For example, with a 4.11:1 axle ratio, the driveshaft makes 4.11 revolutions for every one complete revolution of the rear axle(s).

B is for...

Baldwin Chevrolet

Baldwin Chevrolet was a dealership
in Long Island, New York, that had a
reputation for stocking and ordering
high-performance Chevrolets, including
Corvettes. This Baldwin Motion Vette
by Motion Performance featured a
balanced and blue-printed 427 cid L71
engine producing 435 hp. See the full
entry on page 15.

13

Baker, Kim (1956–)

Kim Baker was one of the first to race the C4 Corvette. In the early years of the C4 Baker set the standard for performance. In 1984 Kim Baker won the **SCCA** national championship, which then led to the 1985 Escort Endurance series. He won so many races that Chevrolet asked him to stop racing in 1988 and help develop the cars for the upcoming **Corvette Challenge Series**. He once pointed out that, "Those were not showroom stock cars; '85, '86 and '87 were more like prototype racing." Once the Corvette Challenge cars were developed Baker moved on to new ventures.

Corvette racer **Kim Baker**

Balancing

A rotating device is balanced when its center of mass is rotating coincident with its center of rotation (defined by bearings). Conversely, a rotating device whose center of mass is not coincident with its center of rotation will be unbalanced and it will vibrate. On close examination what you will find is that the device is actually rotating about the center of mass of the rotating element and its rotational center will be following an elliptical path about the center of mass. Unbalanced forces increase directly with mass and unbalance offset and with the square of rotational speed and can be very destructive to rotating machines as speed is increased.

In balancing an engine, or actually its crankshaft, metal is ground off or added until the assembly, spun up in a balance machine runs smoothly. The machine tells the operator where and how much material to add or remove. A crankshaft is a particularly difficult component to balance because its mass is distributed along its length and when it is not supported on its main bearings it is quite flexible. To achieve the best possible state of balance the equivalent rotating mass of the connecting rods is added to the **crankshaft** in the balancing operation. **Pistons**, pins, rings and rods are static balanced so each weighs the same as the others. The counterweights on the crankshaft should exactly counterbalance the oscillating mass of the piston, pin and upper end of the rod. Certain engine configurations such as inline-six, 90-degree V-8 and 60-degree V-12 are inherently balanced, i.e., all the internal unbalance forces due to pistons moving up and down cancel one another. All other arrangements are unbalanced to one degree or another and must add balance shafts or go unbalanced. OEM factory balance, today, is generally very

good. To achieve an even better state of balance the engine must be removed from the car and disassembled. For ultimate smoothness, the flywheel and the clutch pressure plate should also be balanced, as should the driveshaft.

Baldwin Chevrolet

Baldwin Chevrolet was a Chevrolet dealership in Long Island, New York, that had a reputation for stocking and ordering high-performance Chevrolets including Corvettes. Baldwin Chevrolet had a working relationship with Vince Piggins, Chevrolet's director of promotions, who helped get high-performance parts and engines for the dealership, including the L88 "crate engine." Baldwin's parts manager, Bill Maher, ordered two L88s in mid-summer 1967 to be installed in cars destined for the drag strip in partnership with **Joel Rosen**'s speed shop, **Motion Performance**. One was a Corvette named **Ko-Motion**, owned and driven by "Astoria Chas" **Charlie Snyder**. Baldwin also offered its own modified high-performance Camaros. See *photo on page 13*.

Balsa Wood

As part of the overall design mandate of the C5, saving weight wherever possible was a major focal point. One of the more interesting and innovative solutions that found its way into C5 construction was the use of balsa wood sandwiched between composite sheets for the passenger compartment floor. This composite construction yields a floor that is light weight, ten times stiffer than the composite skin alone and an excellent insulator of noise and heat.

Barker, Alan (1935–)

A Corvette racer of the 1960s, Alan Barker won the SCCA National championship for 1969 and 1970 in B-Production.

Base-Coat/Clear-Coat

Base-coat/clear-coat refers to the paint system currently used on Corvettes that adds a final clear-coat paint layer over primer and enamel color coats to provide a deep, "wet-look" shine that resists fading. The base-coat/clear-coat system was first used on 1981 Corvettes produced in the then-new **Bowling Green**, Kentucky, assembly plant.

Basket Case

A vehicle that has been taken apart (or torn apart as in a wreck) and has its pieces scattered about in baskets or boxes, waiting to be put back together is often referred to as a basket case. While the price of a basket case is often cheap, the labor required to put a car together can be overwhelming to many, which is usually why the owner sells a basket case to begin with.

BBC (Big Block Chevy)

BBC is an abbreviation for "**Big Block Chevy**"—the 396, 427 and 454 cid Corvette engines. See also *Rat Motor*.

Bedding-in Brakes

Bedding-in is a procedure of heating new, "green" brake pads to purge gases trapped during the manufacturing process and to quickly wear the pad to match the detailed surface of the disc. Bedding is accomplished by making about 20 stops of increasing severity from around 30 mph. It should be done away from traffic because a succession

of low speed stops without allowing time for the brakes to cool down will cause brake fade. See also *Brake Fade* and *Green Fade*.

Benchmark Award

The Benchmark is the **Bloomington** award for Corvettes achieving both Gold certification and **Survivor** status.

Bias-ply Tires

At one time bias-ply tires were the standard automobile tires. The cords in the bias tire's layers of structural fabric are at an angle (the bias) to the circumferential centerline. The typical passenger-car bias tire had two plies of fabric with cords running at a 30- to 40-degree angle to the circumferential centerline. Bias-ply tires have shorter wear life and lower cornering limits as compared with belted tires. Corvettes were equipped with bias-ply tires and/or bias-belted tires from 1953 through 1972; radial tires became standard equipment on Corvettes starting with the 1973 model year.

Big Block

The large displacement engines, including the 396, 427 and 454 cid engines that were available as options in Corvettes from 1965 through 1974, are known as big block engines.

- The 396 cid/425 hp big block engine was only available on the 1965 Corvette.

- The 427 cid engine was the big block used in 1966 through 1969 Corvettes in various horsepower ranges starting

This 427 **big block** has been fitted with chrome valve covers and Vintage Air.

at 390 hp and going up to 435 hp, depending on configuration.

- The 454 cid big block engine was available in Corvettes from 1970 through 1974.

See also *L Series Engines, Rat Motor.*

Big Brake
Big brake refers to the optional (**RPO 684**) package that included larger, heavy duty brakes as part of the overall package from 1957–1959. This package also included air scoops known as "elephant ears" to assist in cooling the brake drums by directing air onto them. In 1960 this brake package became known as RPO 687 and remained available through 1962.

Big Tank
Big tank refers to the optional 36-gallon fuel tank that was available from 1963 through 1967 or the 24-gallon fuel tank optionally available for 1959 through 1962 Corvettes. See also *Tanker.*

Billy Bob
The 1999 fixed-roof coupe originally intended to be a less-expensive Corvette model was known deridingly as the Billy Bob model. Due to its light weight and stiffness, this coupe body style became the basis for the high-performance **Z06**. See also *Fixed Roof Coupe.*

Bilstein, Delco-Bilstein
The Bilstein company was founded in 1873 and since then has produced hardware, lifting devices and automotive components. In 1954 the company entered the automotive shock absorber business and perfected a new design which was the result of their development of the monotube, high-pressure **shock absorber**. The company soon began enjoying success in the racing and off-road market segments.

After expanding its aftermarket and replacement shock business with a network of distributors and retailers in North America, Bilstein entered the domestic original equipment shock market in 1984. Working with General Motors, Bilstein shocks were chosen as an option for the 1984 Chevrolet Corvette and the Chevy S-10 four-wheel-drive truck models. In 1990 Corvette introduced **RPO FX3**, **Selective Ride and Handling**, featuring an electronically controlled variable orifice high pressure

The **Billy Bob** coupe

damper. This system was standard on the **ZR-1**. Delco-Bilstein shocks and the association with GM blossomed into a program that now finds Bilstein shocks used as standard or as optional equipment on numerous models of General Motor vehicles in three separate GM Divisions. A Bilstein engineering and marketing office was opened in the Detroit area to coordinate the GM business. In 1995, Bilstein of America set up its first production facility in this country in Hamilton, Ohio, to supply original equipment customers.

Bleeding, Bleeding Brakes

Bleeding is the process of opening a valve in the brake line to purge air bubbles or an air pocket. The brake pedal is usually pumped slowly during bleeding to force out the air-contaminated brake fluid. The system is then refilled with clean hydraulic brake fluid. Bleeding is also performed with hydraulic clutches and cooling systems.

Bloomington, Bloomington Gold Award

Bloomington Gold is one of the oldest Corvette shows in the United States. Starting as a club event in Bloomington, Illinois, at the McLean County Fairgrounds, it quickly grew to be the largest Corvette show in the country and became a commercial operation of Bloomington Gold Enterprises, a privately held corporation. In 1992 the show moved to the State Fairgrounds in Springfield, Illinois. Interestingly, both sites are on what was **Route 66**, furthering the association between Corvettes and Route 66. Bloomington Gold has traditionally been held on the

last weekend in June. In 2002 the show came under the aegis of Dana Mecom (of Mecom Auctions), who currently sponsors and administers the event, and it was held at The Pheasant Run Resort & Conference Center in St. Charles, Illinois, where, in keeping with the tradition, it was again held on June 26–29, 2003. The certifications from the show have become very important to Corvette owners interested in original or restored cars, as the awarding of a Gold or Silver certificate can greatly increase the value of the Corvette. Other Bloomington awards include the Benchmark and **Survivor** certificates. The accompanying huge swap meet has traditionally boasted "if you can't find the part here, it doesn't exist."

Blue Flame Special

The Blue Flame Special was the name given to the 235 cid inline six-cylinder engine used in Corvettes in 1953 and 1954 and a few of the 1955 models. This motor was based on Chevrolet's standard 105 hp six-cylinder engine. After outfitting it with three single-barrel side-draft **carburetors**, a more aggressive **camshaft** and some other performance modifications, the Blue Flame Special produced 150 **horsepower**.

Blueprinting

Blueprinting is originally a drag racing term which refers to the practice that made an engine as good as possible while still being technically stock and thus being eligible for certain racing classes. Blueprinting is, essentially, the art and practice of selecting and hand-finishing engine parts to the most favorable dimensions, weights and other

The inline six-cylinder **Blue Flame Special** powered 1953–1955 Corvettes.

specifications within allowed production tolerances.

The best way to describe blueprinting is by way of example. If the engineering drawing (the blueprint) specifies a **piston** diameter of 90.00 mm ± .05mm, and optimal performance is obtained with the piston at the minimum diameter, then the pistons of a blueprinted engine would be custom machined to 89.95 mm. In another example, if the piston's weight is specified as 190 grams ± 1 gram, all pistons would be trimmed to 189 grams.

Blueprinted engines are as powerful, smooth, free-running and reliable as possible within production tolerances. See also *Balancing*.

Body Mounts

Body mounts are bushings that are placed between a body and a separate chassis. Corvette used body mounts through 1982. Body mounts are typically made of synthetic rubber, although polyurethane body mounts are available for replacements. The function of the body mount is to isolate noise and vibration in the chassis from reaching the passenger compartment. Hardened steel bolts are used to secure the body to the chassis, running through the body mount bushings.

Boiling the Brakes

Over time brake fluid asorbs moisture from the air. This lowers its boiling temperature, which is important

under heavy braking where the high temperature at the pads can migrate into the brake cylinders. The resulting steam bubble in the brake fluid acts like a very soft spring in the brake system. To the driver it feels like the pedal has become a sponge, often going all the way to the floor without braking effect. Competition cars use brake cooling devices such as air ducts and cooling fans. Early Corvettes also ran insulators on the brake pistons to isolate the heat from the fluid. See also *Brake Fade*, *Green Fade*.

Bolt-ons, Bolt-on Wheels

Optional cast aluminum bolt-on wheels were used in 1967 after changes to the law prohibited wheels with eared hubnuts. Bolt-ons appeared to be similar to the optional knock-off wheels of 1963–1966 but were actually bolted onto the same hub as standard steel wheels. They had "starburst" centers that concealed the lug nuts rather than the knock-off spinner hubs of the original knock-off wheels.

1967 Corvette **Bolt-on wheel**

BOM (Bill of Materials)

BOM is a GM abbreviation for bill of materials. The BOM is used at prototype build sites as the part number list for each vehicle.

Bondurant, Bob (1933–)

Bob Bondurant is a southern California racer who drove—among many other types of cars—Corvettes in the early 1960s. Today Bondurant operates the Bondurant School of High Performance Driving at Firebird Raceway in Arizona. The Bondurant School is sponsored by GM and features Corvettes as school cars.

Boneyard

Boneyard, like junkyard, is a slang term for an automotive salvage yard.

Bore

The bore is the inside diameter of an engine cylinder, bearing or bushing. In most cases, the bore refers to the diameter of an engine's cylinder, usually measured in inches or millimeters.

Bore can also refer to the diameter of a master brake cylinder, wheel cylinder, clutch master cylinder, etc.

Bored, Boring

Boring is the machining process in which the diameter of the cylinder (the bore) is enlarged (overbored). Overbores are typically .020, .030, .040 and .060 inches. The most common are .030 and .060.

Bored and Stroked

In an engine that has been "bored and stroked," both the cylinder bore diameter and the crankshaft stroke length have

been increased to enlarge the engine's displacement, thus increasing power.

Borla Performance Industries

Borla is a manufacturer of high-performance after-market stainless steel exhaust systems, including those for **C3** through **C5** Corvettes. See the *Suppliers and Services Appendix.*

Bose, Delco-Bose

In 1984 Corvette offered an optional stereo system designed by Bose for use exclusively in Corvette (UU8). Known as the Delco-Bose Stereo System, it was considered one of the finest factory stereos available in any car at the time.

Bottom Dead Center (BDC)

Bottom dead center is the position of a piston at its lowest point of travel, at the end of the intake and power strokes.

Bowling Green

Bowling Green, Kentucky, is the home and sole manufacturing facility for the Corvette. Corvettes have been built at this plant since 1981. It is visible from Interstate 65, and can be reached by exiting at the 28-mile mark exit. The **National Corvette Museum** is at the same exit.

Boxer

In 1950 Air Force Major Kenneth Brooks contacted the Glasspar Company and asked company founder Bill Tritt, a boat maker, to fashion a car body from fiberglass. Major Brooks wanted to give his wife a Jeep for her personal use, but he wanted it to look more stylish

than the ugly but utilitarian Jeep. Tritt accepted the job and completed the car body in early 1951, naming it the Boxer. It attracted quite a bit of attention, owing to its smart looks and light green color. Glasspar and the U.S. Rubber Company's Naugatuck division began a joint collaboration and produced four more Boxer bodies in mid-February 1952. One of these prototypes was loaned to the General Motors Styling Division after being renamed the **Alembic 1**. Upon seeing this prototype in his own styling auditorium, **Harley Earl** put his efforts into high gear to make a fiberglass-bodied sportscar a reality for GM.

B-Pillar

The B-pillar is the vertical body support structure behind the front door of a vehicle. B-pillars are also sometimes referred to as "B-posts."

Bracket Racing

Bracket racing is a form of **drag racing** in which cars of unequal abilities can race. The winner is determined via a handicap system. Each driver determines his estimated elapsed time or "dial in." The start lights on the "Christmas Tree" will run so that one driver is started before or after the other driver so that each will reach the finish line at exactly same time. The winner is then the first across. To prevent using slower dial in times than you can actually run, which would let you leave the starting line earlier, a break out system is incorporated so that if the driver runs faster than his dial in time, he "breaks out" and loses automatically. See also *ET.*

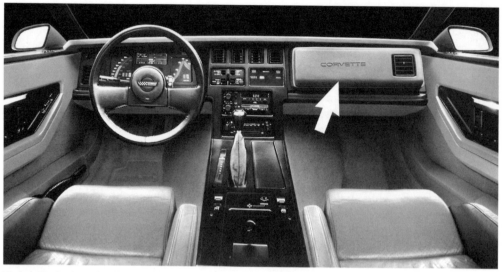

The **breadloaf** safety pad on the passenger side of 1984–1989 Corvettes was unsightly and unpopular.

Brake Booster

A brake booster is a device that is usually operated by air, vacuum or hydraulic power to reduce the effort on the brake pedal normally required to slow and stop a car. Cars equipped with booster-assisted brakes are commonly said to have **power brakes**. Power brakes became standard on Corvettes in 1977.

Brake Fade

When brakes get extremely hot they lose their stopping effectiveness. Two reasons for this brake fade are that the overheated brake pad material loses its ability to grip (lower coefficient of friction) or moisture in the fluid actually boils, creating steam bubbles which make the pedal so spongy that it can go to the floor without braking effect. See also *Boiling the Brakes, Green Fade.*

Brake Horsepower (BHP)

Brake horsepower is the power produced by an engine when measured at the output end of its **crankshaft**; this is the **gross engine horsepower** available for powering a car. The power at the shaft is usually measured by a brake **dynamometer**, which is how the term got its name.

Breadloaf

The proposed federal regulation Motor Vehicle Safety Standard (MVSS) 208 for driver and passenger safety in a front-end collision mandated that the 1984 Corvette be equipped with a collapsible steering column. In order to give the unbelted passenger similar protection, the passenger side received a padded structure nicknamed the "breadloaf" because of its appearance. The interior of the 1990 Corvette was redesigned and it included a real, working glove compartment that replaced the long-lived and unloved breadloaf.

Breaker Points

There is a mechanical switch with two contact points in early Corvette **distributors**. When closed, these two points supply current to the primary windings of the coil; when they open, the coil's collapsing magnetic field induces a very high-voltage electrical current in the secondary windings which is then distributed to fire the **spark plugs**. Corvette's optional **transistorized ignition**, introduced in 1964, did not utilize breaker points; with the introduction of **HEI** as standard equipment on Corvettes in 1975, breaker points were eliminated.

Breaker points were used in Corvette distributors from 1953–1974. HEI ignition made them obsolete with the 1975 model year.

Breathless Performance Products, Inc.

Breathless is a manufacturer of performance and appearance enhancement products for **C4** and **C5** Corvettes. See the *Suppliers and Services Appendix*.

Bricklin

The Bricklin was a **gullwing** sports car that was manufactured primarily from existing domestic running gear in 1974 through early 1976 in New Brunswick, Canada, for exclusive sale in the United States. There were 2,854 cars built before Bricklin went bankrupt, and an estimated 1,500 still exist today. The single model built was given the designation SV-1, for Safety Vehicle 1. It had a built-in **roll cage**, side guard rails and shock-absorbing, five-mph bumpers that receded into the car. It was not only safe in an accident, but had the power and handling to avoid one. The Bricklin exceeded safety requirements of the time and was considered a futuristic vehicle, well-liked by owners and the automotive press. Though some thought that, with its thick pillars and small side window, it looked too much like a tank.

The **Bricklin** SV-1 in "safety orange"

It was never produced in large enough numbers to be profitable

The second distinguishing design feature of the Bricklin (besides the gullwing doors) was that it used a color-impregnated acrylic first surface instead of paint. A heat and vacuum forming process was used to make all these very thin and fragile acrylic panels. They were then introduced into the mold that would produce the **fiberglass** panels. The fiberglass panels were actually molded to the backside of the contoured acrylic sheet. The acrylic panel had to match the tool perfectly or it would crack under the strain of the fiberglass compression molding taking place below it. Minor scratches could be buffed out within the acrylic layer. The Bricklin was a natural to be in competition with Corvette in the mid-1970s. The Bricklin used V-8s from AMC or Ford, depending on availability. Since performance of the mid-1970s Corvette was poor, the Bricklin was able to put up a good showing. It only lasted a few years before disappearing altogether in 1976.

Broach Marks

Broach marks refer to the ridges or "grain" appearance to the deck of the block where the machining operation leaves lines as the cutter moves across the deck. The factory broach marks are along the axis of the block centerline while most automotive machine shops cut and leave broach marks perpendicular to the centerline of the block, which are readily detected when suspecting a **restamp**. Some expensive and sophisticated shops, however, cut the blocks like the factory so they can restamp the block undetected. See also *Matching Numbers*.

Brock, Peter (1936–)

Peter Brock was a GM designer who worked under **William "Bill" Mitchell**, GM's Styling Chief. Following the American Manufacturers Association (AMA) ban on auto racing by the big three automakers in 1957, the **Corvette SS** project was halted. Mitchell had purchased the left over Corvette SS mule chassis and enlisted the help of Brock and **Chuck Poehlmann** to design a new body for his personal sports racer. The car was essentially complete when **Larry Shinoda** was brought in to do all the final detailing under Mitchell's direct guidance (Shinoda stayed on the project to help crew the car in **SCCA** competition for Mitchell and his driver, **Dr. Dick Thompson**). The resulting final design was based upon a concept by Brock for the **Q Car** styling exercise. Peter Brock is also credited with designing the body for the **Shelby Cobra** Daytona Coupe racer in 1965. Currently, Brock works as a motorsports photojournalist.

Designer **Peter Brock**

Bubble-up Phase

The first of GM's five phases for new car development, the bubble-up phase was implemented in the early development of the **C5 Corvette**. In this phase, the Design and Engineering teams began letting creative juices flow (or "bubble-up") with the goal of reaching Concept Initiation (CI), which was a formal review of those ideas by GM executives. Once past CI, the project moved into **Phase Zero**. See also *Phase One, Phase Two, Phase Three*.

Bucket

Depending on context, this can mean the headlight container for 1953, 1954 and 1955 models, 1963 to 2004 models, or the bucket seat for any model year.

Build Sheet

The build sheet is the factory document used on the assembly line that details all of the specific sub assemblies that must be brought together to produce a Corvette. The information on the build sheet includes its **Vehicle Identification Number** (VIN), color, engine, transmission, rear axle ratio, options, etc.

Bumpstick

Bumpstick is a slang term for a **camshaft**, since it is a "stick" (machined steel shaft) with "bumps" (lobes) that push the pushrods up which then push the lifters up and open the valves.

Bundle Of Snakes

Bundle of snakes refers to a type of high-performance **exhaust header** that wraps the individual exhaust pipes from each cylinder around each other so that equal length for all of the pipes

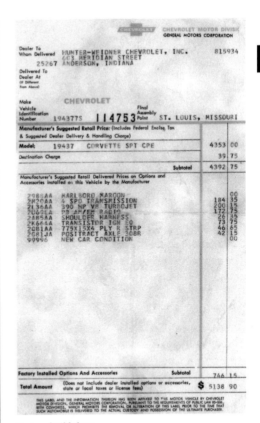

Factory **build sheet**

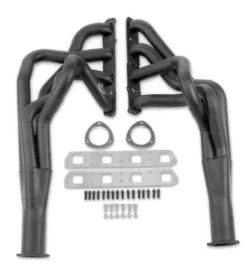

Bundle of Snakes exhaust headers

is achieved when they join together in the collector. Another advantage of this header configuration is that the equal length of the individual tubes helps in the scavenging of exhaust gases, thus reducing back pressure and increasing **horsepower**.

Burn Out

A burn out is usually done prior to a **drag strip** run. At a standstill, high engine revs and rapid clutch release cause the tires to spin, quickly overheating the tread rubber, making it hot and sticky. The subsequent acceleration run takes advantage of the sticky condition of the tires. A burn out can also be inadvertent. In this case, excessive tire spin generates lots of tire smoke but no motion. Several other slang terms for this include burning rubber, lighting them up, peeling out, peeling rubber and laying down rubber.

Burton, Jerry (1950–)

Jerry Burton is the founding editor and current Editorial Director of *Corvette Quarterly* magazine and four other publications. He holds a journalism degree as well as Master of Arts in telecommunications and film, and has been a practicing journalist for over 15 years, including working as motorsports editor for *AutoWeek* magazine and managing editor of *Racecar* magazine. Jerry has been long associated with Chevrolet and Corvette. He is the author of the award-winning "Heartbeat of America" slogan for Chevrolet, and is a founding member of the board of directors of the **National Corvette Museum** with full access to museum archives. A trusted personal friend of **Zora Arkus-Duntov**, Burton wrote the

Jerry Burton, author

exclusive authorized biography, *Zora Arkus-Duntov: The Legend Behind Corvette* (Bentley Publishers, 2002, ISBN: 0-8376-0858-9).

Busch Enterprises

Busch Enterprises manufactures and distributes a comprehensive line of aluminum and chrome washes and other polishing products for Corvettes and other marques. See the *Suppliers and Services Appendix.*

Buttonwillow

Buttonwillow is a relatively new race track in Southern California that opened in late 1995. It is the site where some performance driving schools are held along with **SCCA** road racing.

Buzzer

Buzzer refers to a **tachometer rpm** limit warning device used briefly in 1963, or the similar **speedometer** warning device that was optional in 1967–1969.

C is for...

Corvette Challenge Series

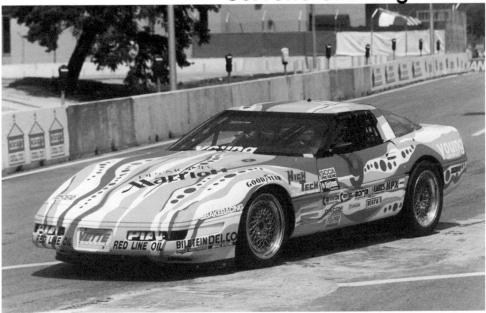

After Corvettes were expelled from
SCCA Showroom Stock in the 1980s,
Corvette marketing convinced the
SCCA to permit a Corvette-only series
of identical showroom-stock Corvettes.
From 1987 the **Corvette Challenge Series**
cars were a special order requiring an
SCCA license to purchase them. See the
full entry on page 46.

27

C1

C1 refers to 1953–1962 (first generation) Corvettes. See also *Solid Axles*.

C2

C2 refers to 1963–1967 (second generation) Corvettes. See also *Mid-Years*.

C3

C3 refers to 1968–1982 (third generation) Corvettes. See also *Sharks*.

C4

C4 refers to 1984–1996 (fourth generation) Corvettes.

C5

C5 refers to 1997–2004 (fifth generation) Corvettes.

C5R

The success of the Team Corvette C5Rs has put America's premier sports car at the pinnacle of international endurance racing with victories at **Daytona**, **Sebring** and **Le Mans**. In 2001 Corvette Racing captured six victories in the eight-race American Le Mans Series season and added the 2001 ALMS Manufacturer's Championship to Corvette's burgeoning trophy collection.

Corvette Racing completed a banner year in 2002 by finishing one-two in the GTS class at The 24 Hours of Le Mans and sweeping the Manufacturers', Drivers' and Team championships in the ALMS with nine victories in ten races.

The Corvette C5R relies on production hydroformed frame rails. This rigid structure allows engineers to tune the suspension for maximum grip. The race car's aerodynamic shape is based on production car CAD data, and a race-prepared LS1 engine provides championship-winning performance.

The Corvette C5R race program continues Chevrolet's tradition of racing

2003 Chevy Corvette **C5R** number 53 at Le Mans

2003 Chevrolet Corvette **C5R** Le Mans drivers (left to right) Franck Freon, Johnny O'Connell, Ron Fellows, Oliver Gavin, Kelly Collins and Andy Pilgrim

production-based vehicles to improve the breed. It is a commitment that has taken Chevy's two-seater from the runways of Sebring to the Mulsanne Straight at Le Mans. The exchange of information and the transfer of technology between the racing and production programs ensure that lessons learned on the track ultimately benefit Corvette drivers on the highway.

C5 Registry

The C5 Registry, which has changed its name to the Corvette Registry, is one of the most successful of the new Corvette club organizations. It hosts and maintains its own website at www.c5registry.com.

C6

C6 refers to the sixth generation of Corvettes that starts with the 2005 model year.

The **C6** 2005 Corvette

Cafaro, John (1955–)

GM designer John Cafaro was responsible for the shapes of Pontiac Fiero and Bonneville and the Chevy Camaro before joining the Corvette design team. He was the chief exterior designer and design team leader for the 1997 Corvette, and he stated that the GTP racecar, the **Corvette Indy** concept car and fighter jets all influenced his design decisions.

He was also responsible for all production Corvette design from 1991 to the present. Cafaro worked on the **C5R** Corvette race program, managing all bodywork design and graphic design packages for the Chevrolet Raceshop and GM Motorsports from 1992 to 1999. His creativity and work has received kudos that include: *Motor Trend* Car of the Year for the 1984 Corvette, *AutoWeek* Magazine Award for the 1997 Corvette coupe, North American International Auto Show Car of the Year for the 1998 Corvette convertible and *Motor Trend* Car of the Year for the 1998 Corvette convertible. Cafaro was inducted into the **National Corvette Museum**'s Hall of Fame in 2002.

Designer **John Cafaro**

Caliper

On a disc brake system, the caliper clamps the brake pads to the disc and takes their reaction force. The caliper straddles the disc and contains the hydraulic cylinders, pistons and brake pads. When the brakes are applied, brake fluid pushes against the caliper pistons, forcing the pads against the disc. Corvettes have used both fixed and sliding calipers. The **C2** and **C3** both used the four piston fixed caliper. Since the introduction of the **C4**, the Corvette has used a sliding caliper—with one or two pistons.

Callaway Engineering

Callaway Engineering is a company that produces high performance automobiles and engines. Starting in 1987, Callaway produced a Corvette dealer option twin-turbo Corvette. Chevrolet supported the program by assigning the build option B2K to the program. The most outrageous of these cars was the **Callaway Sledgehammer**, a joint program with **John Lingenfelter**. The Sledgehammer was driven from Callaway's shop in Old Lyme, Connecticut, to the TRC track in Ohio where it was clocked at over 250 mph. It was then driven home.

The Callaway companies consist of three operating entities:

- Callaway Cars produces and markets high performance automobiles and marine engines.

- Callaway Advanced Technology designs high performance engines and components for Callaway Cars and automotive, industrial, and research clients worldwide.

- Callaway Competition, GmbH, builds sportscars and endurance racing cars such as the Callaway Corvette LM, the Callaway C7— the company's first complete in-house designed and manufactured automobile— and the Callaway C12, a luxury high performance sportscar for both road and track.

The Callaway Cars and Callaway Advanced Technology entities are located in a two-building, 18,000-square-foot facility in Old Lyme, Connecticut; Callaway Competition, based in Leingarten, Germany, is the competition affiliate of The Callaway Companies. See also *Lingenfelter Performance Engineering*.

Callaway, Reeves (1947–)
Ely Reeves Callaway III is the founder of Callaway Engineering and oversees operations at Callaway Cars in Connecticut and at Callaway

Ely Reeves Callaway III

Competition in Germany. Reeves guides the projects and products of the Callaway Companies.

Callaway Sledgehammer
The Callaway Sledgehammer is a highly modified 1988 Corvette. Callaway added twin turbos, a six-speed **manual transmission** and other modifications to produce an 880 hp car with a top speed of

1988 Callaway Corvette **Sledgehammer**

254 mph and a 0–60 time of 3.9 seconds. The $400,000 Sledgehammer was 50-state street legal and very "civilized" in normal traffic driving.

Callaway Speedster

The Callaway Speedster is a limited edition of twelve cars, each built to order. The Speedsters are based on the **Callaway SuperNaturals** introduced in 1992 and are powered by the SuperNatural LT5 (490 hp/421 foot pounds) built to racing specification by Callaway's engine development company, Callaway Advanced Technology. They are 50-state emission compliant automobiles, meeting all requirements of the Federal Clean Air Act and the California Air Resources Board. For off-road use and exhibition, Callaway builds the unequaled SuperSpeedster with 750+ Twin Turbo LT5 horsepower.

Callaway SuperNatural

The Callaway SuperNatural Corvette was conceived and developed as a complete car, incorporating coordinated improvements in power, handling, braking, appearance and comfort. Performance of the SuperNatural is optimized without sacrificing drivability or durability, resulting in an outstanding performer, equal to or better than European exotics at a fraction of their cost. The SuperNatural 383 Corvette delivers consistent 0–60 times of 4.4 seconds and runs the quarter mile in 12.7 seconds at 114 mph on street tires with factory gearing.

Callaway Twin Turbo

The Callaway Twin Turbo option was first offered in 1987. Although it was not factory-installed, it could be ordered in advance through Chevrolet dealers. Fully assembled Corvettes were shipped from the **Bowling Green** factory to Callaway Engineering in Connecticut for engine conversion and other modifications. The special engine was rated at 345 hp and could take the car to a top speed of 177.9 mph with **overdrive** gearing.

Callaway Speedster

C

Callaway C7R **SuperNatural** Corvette

All Callaway Twin Turbos had **manual transmissions** and none were certified for sale in California. In 1987, 184 Twin Turbos were built and the Callaway option cost approximately $20,000. In 1988, 124 Twin Turbos were built, the option cost almost $26,000 and the horsepower rating was 382. In 1989, 69 were produced at a cost of almost $27,000. In 1990, 58 were produced and the cost of the option stayed the same as the previous year. In 1991, the final year, 62 were produced at a cost of $33,000 for the option.

1991 **Callaway Twin Turbo**

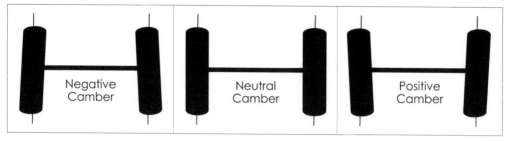

Illustration of **camber**

Camber

Camber refers to a wheel's inward or outward tilt from the vertical; camber is measured in degrees. A negative camber is present when the wheels are closer at the top than at the bottom (viewed from either the front or the rear); positive camber is present when the wheels are further apart at the top.

Camber Rod

More commonly called the **strut rod**, this rod is part of the 1963 to 1982 independent rear suspension (**IRS**) and controls the **camber** of the rear wheel. It is located directly below the **half shaft**. This same arrangement was used on the C4—in fact the camber adjustment bolt even carries the same part number.

Campbell-Ewald Advertising

Based in Detroit, Michigan, Campbell-Ewald has been Chevrolet's only advertising agency throughout its entire history. Campbell-Ewald was incorporated February 2, 1911, and between 1922 and 1933, it was the agency of record for all GM divisions including Chevrolet, Buick, Cadillac, GM Truck and Oakland Motor Car. Campbell-Ewald is currently a division of the Interpublic Group based in New York, which includes McCann Erickson Worldwide; Lowe and Partners; Carmichael Lynch, Foot, Cone and Belding and Jack Morton Worldwide.

Camshaft

A camshaft is a shaft with lobes on it that turns at one-half of the engine speed. In the case of a cam-in-block engine such as the Chevrolet V-8, as it turns, the camshaft pushes the valve lifters up, which then move the pushrods that work on the rocker arms on top of the head. The action of the rocker arms depresses the valve stems and opens the valves to either let fuel and air in or exhaust out. A slang term for a camshaft is a "**bump stick**".

Can Am

The Can Am was an **SCCA** pro racing series of the mid-1960s through the

Camshaft

early 1980s featuring unrestricted rules until 1974. The series resumed in 1978 with a 5.0-liter engine limit. Initially, some Corvettes entered the series and many Corvette drivers made the jump into specialty built race cars like Lola, McLaren and others. Many Can Am cars used Chevrolet V-8 engines.

Carbon Fiber

Carbon fiber is created from polymer strands which are stretched and then heated slowly while under tension to very high temperatures to create parallel carbon strands. The resulting fibers are 92–99 percent pure carbon, exceptionally strong and weigh significantly less than metals. A graphite fiber—which is 99-percent carbon—has the stiffness and strength of steel at ¼ its weight. Carbon fiber and graphite fiber are so similar that the two names are interchangeable.

Carburetor

A carburetor is a device that meters vaporized fuel and engine intake air, maintaining an approximately constant air-fuel ratio. The carburetor increases the ratio of fuel to air in response to varying engine operating conditions such as starting, idling, transient acceleration and maximum power.

Three single-barrel carburetors were used on the 1953, 1954 and 1955 Corvettes with the **Blue Flame Special** six-cylinder engine. From 1955 through 1981 four-barrel carburetors were used on Corvette V-8 engines (in 1956–1962

1967 Holley four-barrel **carburetor**—650 cfm

dual four-barrel-optioned engines were available). Starting with the 1982 model year, carburetors were replaced with electronic **fuel injection**, first as the unit injector **Cross-Fire Injection** (CFI); then in 1985 as the multi-injector **Tuned Port Injection** (TPI), and in 1992 as **Multi-Port Tuned Injection** (MTI).

Carlisle Events, Inc.
Carlisle, Pennsylvania, is the site of a series of car swap meets produced by Carlisle Events, Inc., during the year at its 80-acre fairgrounds. **Chip Miller** and **Bill Miller** are the co-owners of both Carlisle Events, Inc., and the Carlisle Fairgrounds. The all-Corvette show, Corvettes at Carlisle, is held every year on the third weekend of August. There is also a large show in the spring and fall for general car parts and several specialty car events throughout the year. See *Suppliers and Services Appendix.*

Carter AFB
The Carter AFB was a high performance four-barrel **carburetor** built by Carter in the early 1960s. It was used on the 327 cid/300 hp and the 327 cid/340 hp engines. Typically, the Carter AFB was rated at 600 cfm.

Carter WCFB
The Carter WCFB was a four-barrel **carburetor** used on Corvette engines both in single- and dual-quad configurations from 1955 to 1963. Typically, they were rated at 450 cfm.

Casting Number
When a part is cast the mold has a part number and a date code set so that the part is forever identified. Most older Corvette parts such as heads, blocks and manifolds, usually have a seven-digit casting number beginning with 3 to identify the part. On most Corvette blocks the casting number is located on the bellhousing flange behind the driver's-side head. See also *Matching Numbers.*

Castle Nut
This is a type of nut with notches cut across its face to accommodate a cotter pin driven through the notches and through a hole in the bolt which locks the nut in place. Castle nuts are typically used on mission-critical components such as the rear shock hangers on Corvettes. They get their name from the fact that they look like turrets on a castle.

Catalytic Converters
Catalytic converters are exhaust emission control devices that by virtue of their very large surface area in contact with the exhaust gas help drive partially oxidized products of combustion to their completely oxidized state. A coating of trace amounts of platinum, palladium or other rare earth metals is used to extend

Castle nuts are used to secure the shock hangers on Mid-Years and Sharks.

the effectiveness of the catalytic converter to lower temperatures, thus making the converter effective during starting and warmup where most of the regulated emissions occur. Corvettes were first fitted with catalytic converters in 1975. As a result of the catalytic converters, the use of unleaded gasoline was mandated. Early catalytic converters were of a high backpressure, single-stream design and required the dual exhaust merge via a **Y-pipe** into the converter and then split back to dual mufflers. Starting in 1982, horsepower was increased by the use of a single, low-backpressure, monolith converter. On 1992–1996 Corvettes, individual converters were used close to each exhaust manifold, and an "H" pipe containing a resonator was positioned between the converters and the exhaust pipes. Starting with the **C5** Corvette in 1997, (the first year of OBD II) discrete catalytic converters were used for each exhaust manifold and the exhaust pipes ran straight back from the converters to the mufflers.

CE Block

CE is often defined as Chevrolet Engine, and it designates the motor as a warranty replacement engine installed by the Chevrolet dealer's service department as an alternative to rebuilding a badly damaged original-equipment engine that failed under warranty. The engine pad carries a CE code instead of the traditional codes on production engines. The first number indicates the year and the next five digits are a sequential numbering for the unit that year: 20,000 to 49,999 is for Flint-built V-8s; 50,000 to 79,999 is for Tonowanda-built V-8s. The VIN is usually not stamped in

the pad, but is often misaligned and of irregular depth, due to it being hand-stamped by the dealer, if at all. These are relatively rare in Corvettes, as they indicate that Chevrolet warranty work was performed and the original engine was destroyed. These are the only cases of Chevrolet intervening in the life of a Corvette once it left the factory, since engine replacement required Chevrolet management authorization and most warranty work was simply handled by the dealer.

Central Office Production Order (COPO)

During the late 1960s and 1970s Chevrolet dealers would contact the Central Office in Michigan to request deviations from regular production options that were available for the model year. For instance, special color paint could be requested for an additional charge in the case of a fleet order. Generally, options that were requested had to be in current production for other models. Chevrolet engineering then had to grant approval for these vehicle parts combinations. These types of orders eventually became the groundwork to build factory race cars, and it was a convenient way to order competition-ready Corvettes directly from the assembly line.

Centrifugal Advance

This is a mechanism within the **distributor** that consists of two weights that rotate with the distributor shaft. As the rotational speed increases centrifugal force causes these weights to move outward against spring tension. The movement of the weights is transmitted

to the **breaker points** or breaker plate, advancing the **timing** and causing the **spark plugs** to fire earlier.

CERV I

CERV stands for Chevrolet Engineering Research Vehicle. **Zora Arkus-Duntov** designed a single-seat, open-wheel racer dubbed CERV I. It was used to test suspension and powertrain components as well as for demonstrating the performance and engineering capabilities of GM to the public. Its rear suspension

was the basis for the 1963 Corvette rear suspension. The CERV I is now owned by **Mike Yager**.

CERV II

The CERV II was **Zora Arkus-Duntov**'s most exotic experimental car. Like the **CERV I**, this car was built to do research on suspension and drivetrain components. For many years the CERV II held the Milford Proving Ground track record with an average speed of 206 mph. With short gearing the CERV II would

The **CERV I**

The **CERV II**

run 0–60 mph in 2.8 seconds. Some of the car's advanced features included four-wheel drive using a **Powerglide** type **torque converter** automatic transmission at each end of the car, side-mounted fuel cells, a monocoque frame, low-profile Firestone racing tires and a 377 cid all aluminum V-8 using Hillborn **fuel injection** and single overhead cams to produce 500 horsepower.

CERV III

The CERV III was a mid-engined, fully functional Corvette showcar that debuted at the Detroit International Auto Show in 1990.

CERV IV

During the development process of the fifth-generation 1997 Corvette, a fourth CERV was created for use as a development mule. CERV IV was the proof-of-concept vehicle for the C5 program. Of the four, CERV IV was the only one designed with a front-mounted engine.

CFI

See *Cross-Fire Injection*.

Chaparral

The Chaparral series consisted of race-only cars built by **Jim Hall** of Texas for

The **CERV III** showcar

The **Chapparal** 2J, nicknamed the "vacuum cleaner," was the first ground effects race car that allowed the car to sail at incredible speeds through the corners thanks to auxiliary motors that created a vacuum under the car to increase traction.

sports car racing in the unlimited and **Can Am** series with heavy support from GM's Chevrolet R&D. The bodies were inspired by **Larry Shinoda**'s Corvair Monza and powered by Chevrolet engines. Chaparrals used many visual cues that would later be incorporated into the **Mako Shark** and the 1968 Corvette. See also *Ground Effects*.

Cheetah

The Cheetah was a race car built in 1963 by **Bill Thomas** based on the 1963 Corvette fuel-injected engine and rear

suspension. The front-engined Cheetah weighed less than 2,000 pounds and had a 40/60 weight ratio front to rear. Thomas wanted to build a car to beat the Cobras and he had hoped to get support from Chevrolet. Chevy did not officially support him and, after a factory fire, Cheetah production ended. By all accounts, between 16 and 26 cars were built. Most Cheetahs ran C-Modified in SCCA races and some actually entered the first year **Can Am** races.

Chicago Corvette Supply

Chicago Corvette Supply is a major source of Corvette restoration parts and accessories. See the *Suppliers and Services Appendix.*

Chip

See *Microchip.*

Clamshell

A hood design that incorporates the front fender and is hinged at the front is sometimes called a "clamshell hood." When it opens it exposes the entire top of the engine, suspension and tires. The C4 (1984–1996) Corvette uses a clamshell hood.

Clift, Bob (1920–)

Clift was one of the Corvette engineers of the 1950s and 1960s who drove many of the Corvettes in testing. He was an avid **SCCA** racer in the 1950s, racing a modified 1954 Corvette. Clift was also heavily involved in the development and testing of the **Bricklin**. He currently resides in Hollywood, Florida.

Clutch

In an automobile with a manual transmission the clutch connects the engine's **flywheel** to the gearbox. Smooth coupling and uncoupling of the engine to the **drivetrain** is made possible by the gradual slipping of the clutch's friction discs and the cushioning effect of springs incorporated in the clutch disc facing.

The **Cheetah**

Clutch Pressure Plate

A clutch pressure plate assembly bolts to the **flywheel** and contains the springs, levers and **throw-out bearing** that disengage the clutch.

Cobra, Shelby Cobra

The Cobra came about when Carroll Shelby mated a Ford 260 cid V-8 (later a 289 cid Ford V-8) with an English A.C. Ace body and chassis. Weighing around 2,200 pounds, the somewhat crude Cobras ate Corvettes alive due to light weight and superior acceleration. Later Cobras had various versions of the Ford 427 cid motor in a re-designed chassis and were only tamed when **SCCA** began to equalize the weights on the cars. Ford saw a good thing and used the Cobra as

a means to give its cars a performance image while only having to mildly support Shelby.

Coil

See *Ignition Coil.*

Coil Bind

Coil bind occurs when a coil spring is compressed so tightly that one winding touches another winding and cannot close any more. In valve springs, this usually results in a broken spring.

Coil-over Shocks

When a coil suspension spring surrounds the **shock absorber** and is mounted to it, it is referred to as a "coil-over." Typically the mounting is threaded

Carroll Shelby with his **Shelby Cobra**

making the spring height adjustable. The 1957 **Corvette SS** used a coil-over shock front suspension. Coil-over shocks are a popular performance modification for C4 and C5 Corvettes, since they allow easy adjustment of ride height.

Cole, Edward (1909–1977)

Ed Cole was president of GM and former Chief Engineer of Chevrolet. The Corvette was already a clay model when he first saw it. But he recognized it instantly as the ideal symbol of a soon-to-be-reborn Chevrolet marque. What really excited Ed Cole was the bizarre notion that such a car—two seats, plastic body, six months from drawing board to driveway—could come from GM's most conservative car division. He also saw it as a great way to launch his Chevrolet renaissance.

Of his 47 years at General Motors, only ten were spent at Chevrolet, but they were Chevy's postwar growth years and they cemented the foundation for the division's long dominance of the American automotive market. His stated task when he became Chief Engineer in May 1952, was to bring a lightweight, low-cost V-8 into the Chevrolet engine lineup. He did and it was called the Chevy **small block**. For the next 50 years it would reign supreme as America's most significant automotive engine design.

As Chief Engineer and later as General Manager, Cole tripled the size of the engineering staff in 15 months. He also permitted **Zora Arkus-Duntov** to install the V-8 in the 1955 Corvette and, to promote the car, he cleared Chevy to go racing. Competition began with the February 1956 **Daytona Beach** trials. Subsequent competition forays included

the **Sebring** 12-hour, Jerry Earl's SR-2, and a factory-prepared car for **Dr. Dick Thompson**, the flying dentist.

Duntov developed the test mule for the **Corvette SS** race car at Sebring during the weeks leading up to the 1957 race. Though it was not raced, the test mule set the track record and convinced Juan Manuel Fangio and Stirling Moss to drive the SS. Chevrolet was embarrassed when the beautifully executed SS Corvette proved vastly unready. Cole would later allow GM styling boss **Bill Mitchell** to wrap a smooth body around the SS test "mule," call it the **Corvette Stingray Race Car**, and turn it into what-in retrospect-is the most important racing Corvette of them all. With Dick Thompson doing most of the driving, the Mitchell Stingray kept the high performance flame alive at Chevy in 1959 and 1960 and set the stage for the production **Sting Ray** era.

Cole was also the architect of Chevy's backdoor stock car racing escapades of the late 1950s. The 348 cid and the 409 cid (the first **big-block** engines)

Edward N. Cole

were designed during Cole's tenure at Chevrolet. He coached the small-car Chevy program into existence as well as the vehicle of which he was most proud and for which he may be best remembered—the Corvair. Low, light, rear-engined and air-cooled, the Corvair was in keeping with much of Cole's philosophy about cars. Like the Corvette, the Corvair "kicked the hell out of the status quo." Cole left Chevy to become GM group vice-president in 1961.

Promoted to Executive Vice President in 1965 and to the presidency in 1967, Cole found himself at the helm of GM where high performance had to take on a different meaning—tuning engines for fuel economy, not power. Under Cole's leadership, GM became the world leader in safety research. His 1972 declaration that all GM cars would be equipped with catalytic converters in 1975 spelled—at long last—the end of lead in gasoline. He retired in 1974 and died in a light plane crash in May 1977. Ed Cole was inducted into the **National Corvette Museum**'s Hall of Fame in 1998.

Collector Edition

To mark the end of the **Shark** series (**C3**) in 1982, a special "Collector Edition" was offered. Of the year's total production of 25,407 units, 6,759 were Collector Editions. In addition to a higher level of available options the limited series had a lifting rear hatchback window, special wheels similar to the 1967 bolt-ons, unique silver-beige paint, a silver-beige leather interior and special emblems. It was also the first Corvette with a sticker price in excess of $20,000—$22,537.59 to be exact.

Collector Edition

Compression Ratio

The compression ratio is the ratio of the total cylinder volume when the piston is at the bottom of its stroke to the volume when it is at the top of its stroke.

Contemporary Corvette

Contemporary Corvette is a Corvette recycler specializing in 1968 through present Corvette parts, both new and used. See the *Suppliers and Services Appendix.*

COPO

See *Central Office Production Order.*

Correct Engine

A "correct engine" describes a Corvette motor that has the correct **date codes,** plant and **casting numbers** for that model year, but does not have a serial number that matches the chassis, transmission or differential numbers of the Corvette in which it is installed. Aside from the matching serial number, it is otherwise correct, hence the origin of the term. See also *Matching Numbers.*

Corsa Performance Company

Corsa manufactures high-performance aftermarket exhaust systems for Corvette C4s and C5s as well as for a variety of other automobiles. See the *Suppliers and Services Appendix.*

Corvette

The *American Heritage Dictionary* defines it as "a fast, lightly armed warship, smaller than a destroyer, often equipped for antisubmarine operations." **Myron Scott** is credited with coming up with this name for Chevrolet's sports car.

Corvette Ads CD-ROM

A CD-ROM published by **Hi-Tech Software,** this disc contains advertisements used in the marketing of America's sports car. See the *Suppliers and Services Appendix.*

Corvette America

A major supplier of Corvette restoration parts and accessories, Corvette America is a division of Auto Accessories of America. See the *Suppliers and Services Appendix.*

Corvette Anthology CD-ROM

A CD-ROM updated and published annually by **Hi-Tech Software,** this disc contains a wealth of photos, facts, production figures, options, clip art and more. See the *Suppliers and Services Appendix.*

Corvette Black Book

The *Corvette Black Book* was first published in 1978 by Michael Bruce Associates, which updates and publishes it yearly. Written and compiled by **Michael Antonik,** this book is considered a definitive source of Corvette information and specifications, including options, colors, facts, statistics, charts, history, prices, codes, serial numbers and more for Corvettes from 1953 through the current model year. See the *Suppliers and Services Appendix.*

Corvette Central

Corvette Central is a major supplier of Corvette restoration parts and accessories. See the *Suppliers and Services Appendix.*

Corvette Challenge Series

After Corvettes were expelled from **SCCA** Showroom Stock in the 1980s, Corvette marketing (actually, John Powell) convinced the SCCA to permit this Corvette-only series of identical showroom-stock Corvettes. From 1987 the Corvette Challenge cars were a special order requiring an SCCA license to purchase them. They included options such as a fire suppression system, an exhaust system without **catalytic converters** and a full **roll cage** for the series. The Corvette Challenge ran for two years as a series of sprint races run in conjunction with other main events. After two seasons, the series was shut down when Powell couldn't come up with sponsorship money. See *photo on page 27.*

Corvette Clocks by Roger

Corvette Clocks by Roger is a Tennessee-based firm that restores and supplies clocks, clusters, gauges, radios, glove box doors and other interior items used in Corvette restoration. See the *Suppliers and Services Appendix.*

Corvette Club Of America

The Corvette Club of America is one of the largest and fastest-growing Corvette clubs in the nation. Based in **Bowling Green**, Kentucky, CCA is able to keep its members informed and aware of all the latest breaking news in the Corvette hobby. See the *Suppliers and Services Appendix.*

Corvette Enthusiast Magazine

A monthly magazine devoted to Corvettes, *Corvette Enthusiast* is published by Amos Automotive Publishing. See the *Magazine Appendix.*

Corvette Fever Magazine

This is a monthly magazine devoted to Corvettes published by Primedia Specialty Group. See the *Magazine Appendix.*

Corvette Hall Of Fame & Americana Museum

This private museum was the brainchild of Dr. Allen Schery, an anthropologist who was also the owner, creator and manager of the now-defunct institution. The concept of the museum was to establish a "time capsule" experience through 50 years of Americana History using Corvette sports cars as the continuous centerpiece. Located in Cooperstown, New York, it showcased 35 Corvettes in period dioramas along with nostalgia and memorabilia from the 1950s, 1960s and 1970s.

Corvette Indy

Built in 1985, the Corvette Indy was first shown at the Detroit Auto Show in 1986. Dubbed a research vehicle, the Corvette Indy showcased Chevrolet's advanced technology. The car, built by Lotus in England, really represented Lotus technology. For a brief period, Lotus was owned by GM. The "centerpiece" of the car was a mid-ship-mounted twin-turbo intercooled 5.7-liter 32-valve **DOHC** Lotus-designed V-8 Indy engine based on the LT5 production engine. The engine was nicknamed for its cousin, the Chevy Indy V-8 racing engine. **Horsepower** has never been published, but is estimated at approximately 600. Four-wheel drive, four-wheel steering and active suspension were a few of the advanced technologies showcased on the car. A CRT screen mounted on the dash provided rearward

C

Dave Hill, Zora Arkus-Duntov and Dave McLellan with the **Corvette Indy**, the concept car built in conjunction with Lotus Engineering in the late 1980s

vision via a remote camera. Indy incorporated technologies that later became standard on the **C5** Corvette, including electronic throttle control.

Corvette Magazine

This is a monthly magazine dedicated to Corvettes and the Corvette "lifestyle." See the *Magazine Appendix.*

Corvette Mike

Corvette Mike is an Anaheim, California-based dealership and facility that buys, sells, trades and services used and vintage Corvettes. See also *Vietro, "Corvette Mike"* and the *Suppliers and Services Index.*

Corvette Museum Delivery

Listed as option R8C, the **National Corvette Museum**'s in-house delivery program is a popular feature that lets buyers of new Corvettes pick up their cars under the golden 140-foot-diameter, 100-foot-tall Skydome in the midst of Corvette's history. The option is available through any Chevrolet dealer at a cost of $490. It must be specified at the time the order is finalized and a special ship code of "184590" must also be used to identify the Corvette for Museum Delivery.

Corvette News Magazine

In the 1950s, amazed at the growth of Corvette clubs, **Joe Pike** became the editor of a free magazine produced by Chevrolet that was given to every Corvette owner. Due to Chevrolet's lack of organization, the number of subscriptions became too large to manage, often due to mailing *Corvette News* to people who had not owned a Corvette in years. Chevrolet canceled the subscriptions in the early 1980s and made the publication available only

through general paid subscription. Since the exclusivity was lost, many readers did not bother to subscribe. Within a few years the magazine folded. Later, *Corvette Quarterly* would be an attempt to bring back *CN* on a subscription basis.

Corvette Postage Stamps

Several countries have recognized the Corvette on their postage stamps over the years. Among these are the Marshall Islands, Republique du Niger, Tatarstan, Liberia, Nanumaga-Tuvalo, Republique Federale Islamique des Comores, Kalmykia, Nevis, Dagestan, Guyana, Ajman, St. Vincent, Redonda, Netherlands Antilles and others.

Corvette Q Car

See *Q Car, Q Corvette*.

Corvette Quarterly Magazine

Dubbed "the official journal of America's world-class sports car," *Corvette Quarterly* is published four times a year by Campbell-Ewald Publishing, a division of **Campbell-Ewald**. See the *Magazine Appendix*.

Corvette Rubber Company

The Corvette Rubber Company is a major supplier of Corvette weatherstripping, pedals, pads, clutch parts, heater hoses and other restoration parts and accessories. See the *Supplier and Service Appendix*.

Corvette SS (Super Sport)

The Corvette SS was a race-only Corvette designed to run endurance races at **Sebring** and **Le Mans** in 1957. The light magnesium body covered a tubular space frame featuring a **deDion** rear axle. It had the looks and the potential to be a

Foreign countries don't always get it right, as illustrated in this Liberian **Corvette postage stamp**. The stamp says the car is a 1965 Corvette Stingray when, in actuality, it is a 1963 Sting Ray split window coupe.

winner but, due to a bushing failure at Sebring, it retired early. GM's decision to stop active factory participation in motorsports brought the car's career to an end before it could accomplish anything. The fiberglass "mule" built to test the chassis showed that there was enormous potential in the design. The mule body was scrapped and the car later resurfaced as the **Corvette Stingray Race Car**.

Corvette Stingray Race Car

Built on the chassis of a **Corvette SS** race car, the Stingray race car was created under the direction of GM design chief **Bill Mitchell**. Never an official Corvette race car, the Stingray was successfully campaigned at numerous events nationally during 1959 and 1960, driven by **Dr. Dick Thompson**. It became the basis for the new 1963 **Sting Ray** production car.

Corvette Summer (The Movie)

Released in 1978 and directed by Matthew Robbins, *Corvette Summer* starred Mark Hamil, Annie Potts and Danny Bonaduce. Ken (played by Mark Hamil) has built a customized **Stingray**

C

Zora Arkus-Duntov behind the wheel of the **Corvette SS**

1959 **Corvette Stingray Race Car**

in shop class to be used for cruising for girls. When the car is stolen by a ring of car thieves, his relentless search takes him from Los Angeles to Las Vegas. There he meets an aspiring hooker (Annie Potts) who helps him track the hot wheels down.

Corvette! The Sensuous American

The first product offering from Michael Bruce Associates, *Corvette! The Sensuous American* was a series of nine hardbound Corvette books. These were published at the rate of three per year during the years of 1976, 1977 and 1978 and sold directly to customers by subscription only. A second series of nine similar books was published in 1983, 1984 and 1985. The 18 *Corvette! The Sensuous American* books were sold to subscribers with a no-reprint guarantee to improve the likelihood of value appreciation. The books are bought and sold today primarily between private individuals. See also *Antonik, Michael* and *Corvette Black Book*.

Cowl Induction

Cowl induction is the process of obtaining air for the **carburetor** from the high pressure area at the base of the windshield, usually from a hood scoop that opens to the rear. The L88 hoods from 1967 to 1969 used cowl induction. Later in 1973 cowl

Corvette 427 cid **crankshaft**

induction was again used to obtain cooler air as underhood temperatures climbed due to **emission** control equipment. In 1975 it was discontinued and replaced with forward facing scoops which ran over the top of the radiator.

Cowl Vents

These are vents on **C1** and **C2** Corvettes located just below the windshield at the top of the cowl. Controls inside the passenger compartment open and close the vents via cables to allow or prevent fresh outside air from entering the car.

Crankshaft

The crankshaft is the main shaft of the engine. The pistons connect to it via the rods. The crankshaft converts the downward force of the pistons into the rotating motion required to propel the car.

Cross-Fire Injection (CFI)

Cross-Fire Injection is an early electronic fuel injection system used on the 1982

Cross-Fire Injection system

and 1984 Corvettes that utilized two **throttle-body** injectors on a cross ram manifold.

Cruise Control

Cruise control or "speed control" was first available on 1977 Corvettes as option K30. The option became K35 in 1981 and K34 in 1984. It permitted setting the car to cruise and maintain a desired speed automatically, instantaneously disengaging with the slightest pressure on the brake pedal. Cruise control became standard equipment starting with the 1988 Corvette.

Cuisinart Wheels

In 1988 Corvettes were fitted with lower profile Goodyear Z-rated P255/ 50ZR-16 tires on 16-inch "Cuisinart" wheels, nicknamed so because they looked like the food processor blades. An optional **Z51** (for coupes only) and Z52 **Performance Handling Package** offered 12-slot Cuisinart 17 x 9.5-inch wheels with Goodyear 275/40ZR-17 tires.

The Corvette **Cuisinart** wheel

Cunningham, Briggs Swift (1907-2003)

Briggs S. Cunningham II was an American yachtsman and racer who built a series of sports cars and racers in the early 1950s for international and SCCA racing. In 1960, he took a team of three Corvettes to **Le Mans**; one of them won the GT class. This win was a tremendous boost to Corvette and was used to justify many other racing projects.

Currin, Phil ("Phast Phil") (1946–)

Phil Currin is a Corvette racer of the 1970s who won the first IMSA GTO championship with a 327-powered 1963 Corvette in 1972, beating out all of the **big-block** cars. Not completely out of racing, he still runs a shop in Gainesville, Florida, and in 1995 captured the Solo II National Championship in the BSP class (two-seat coupes and select sedans, street prepared).

Custom Autosound Manufacturing, Inc.

Custom Autosound is a manufacturer of high-quality Corvette audio systems that have a retro look and fit directly without modification to the console, as well as "stealth" audio systems that can be hidden. See the *Supplier and Service Appendix*.

Customs, Customizing

Some owners do not like having a car that looks like everyone else's so they modify their cars to reflect personal tastes. Customs are cars that have been modified from stock to a configuration that the owner desires to enhance the appearance or performance or both. Popular customizations to Corvettes include flaring the fenders, adding

spoilers to the front and/or rear, adding a third tail light, louvers and so forth. Custom paint jobs have taken many forms including different colors, special hues (pearl white), "ghost" designs, striping and flames.

Cylinder Head

The cylinder head is the detachable upper-most portion of an engine that attaches to the cylinder engine block and seals the cylinders. It contains all or part of the combustion chamber, as well as the **valves** and **spark plugs**. It also contains water passages for cooling and oil passages for lubrication. In most engines a **gasket** is used between the cylinder head and the engine block to form a seal that is both air- and liquid-tight.

Cypress, Cypress Gardens

Cypress refers to the **NCRS** Corvette show that was held each January on the third weekend at the Cypress Gardens Park in Winter Haven, Florida. Held from 1979 through 1999, this event drew a very good turnout for both the show and the swap meet through 1999; the show moved to Orlando (Kissimmee) in 2000 and is held at various Florida locations yearly. Cypress Gardens Park closed in 2003.

This highly **customized** 1976 Shark owned by the author has flared fenders, front and rear spoilers, "Monza" headlights, Daytona louvers on the fenders, a tilt-nose and blue and silver pearl paint.

D  is for...

Drag Race

A **drag race** is an all-out, straight-line, acceleration run between two cars, typically over a distance of 1/4 mile. Here, the "Christmas Tree" has just turned green at Maple Grove Raceway outside of Reading, Pensylvania. See the full entry on page 58.

Dashboard

The panel at the base of the windshield that spans the width of the interior and contains gauges, switches, instruments and controls for the operation of the car and its accessories is called the dashboard or dash.

Date Code

Almost every mechanical part made for a Corvette has a date code either cast or stamped into it. Date codes are used to check if the part is correct for that Corvette. For example, an engine with a date code of E134 (May 13, 1964) would not be correct for a 1963. The date code for a **small block** Corvette engine is on the bellhousing flange behind the **distributor**. On early **big blocks** it was on the passenger side near the pan rail, but later (1970) moved up to the same location as on the small blocks. See also *Matching Numbers*.

Davies Corvette Parts

Davies is a Florida-based supplier of Corvette parts and accessories. See the *Suppliers and Services Appendix*.

Daytime Running Lights

Daytime running lights are a safety feature intended to increase the visibility of oncoming vehicles to lessen the risk of head-on collisions. They can either be headlights that automatically come on at lower intensity when the car is started with the headlight switch in the off position or, as in the case of the Corvette C5, they can be auxiliary amber lights located within the recessed dual grilles.

Daytime running lights became standard with the 1998 C5 Corvette.

Daytona, Daytona Beach

Daytona usually refers to the Daytona International Speedway, which is the site for NASCAR racing's Daytona 500 and Firecracker 400 (now the Pepsi 400), IMSA racing's 24 Hours of Daytona, Speed Weeks in February and Bike Week in March. At the 1956 Daytona Speed week held on the beach, **Zora Arkus-Duntov** set a new record by achieving a 150.583 mph two-way average in a Corvette.

deDion Axle

This is a final drive system that consists of a tube connecting the two wheels located by either **leaf springs** or **trailing arms** and a differential mounted on the chassis that drives the wheels through u-jointed **half shafts**. Essentially, it is a cross between **independent rear suspension** (IRS) and a live axle that keeps the wheels upright. Another advantage is that it reduces **unsprung weight** due to the fact that the differential is separate from the axle. This feature also eliminates the torque reaction that tends to lift the right

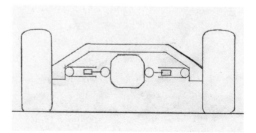

A **deDion** rear axle layout

wheel of a live axle off the ground leading to premature wheel spin. **Zora Arkus-Duntov**'s 1957 **Corvette SS** race car was equipped with a deDion axle.

Delco

Delco is a division of GM which builds many parts for GM cars including Corvettes.

Delco-Bilstein Shocks

Delco-Bilstein **shock absorbers** were more highly damped gas-charged shock absorbers developed as a collaborative effort between GM's Delco division and Bilstein and offered as a $189 option (FG3) on 1984–1989 Corvettes. Pressurizing the damper fluid reduced the possibility of fluid cavitation and subsequent loss of effectiveness.

Delco-Bose Stereo System

These stereo systems were specifically designed for the Corvette as a collaborative effort between Delco and Bose, available in numerous configurations (with eight-track tape player, cassette, CB-radio, etc.) as options from 1984 through 1996.

DeLorenzo, Tony Jr. (1943–)

Tony DeLorenzo, Jr., was a Corvette racer who raced an Owens Corning Fiberglass 1968 Corvette L88 and won an **SCCA** A-Production championship. He also raced other Corvettes.

Design Specialties Custom Products

A major supplier of custom-manufactured Corvette parts and accessories. See the *Suppliers and Services Appendix*.

DeWitts Reproductions

DeWitts is a Michigan-based manufacturer of Corvette high performance "direct fit" aluminum radiators for all 1955–2004 models and restoration **radiators** and **surge tanks** for 1960–1972 models. All DeWitts restoration models are reproduced from original tooling and are licensed by General Motors. The company is also the only American manufacturer of C3 assembled rear storage compartment units and rear storage components. See the *Suppliers and Services Appendix*.

Die Cast Models

Die cast models are scale models that are formed by introducing molten metal into a reusable mold by pressure, by gravity or by centrifugal force. Corvette die cast models are very popular among Corvette owners and are available in $1/64$, $1/43$, $1/24$ and $1/18$ scales by various manufacturers. See also *Ertl, Franklin Mint, Johnny Lightning, Mattel Hot Wheels*.

Digital Instrumentation

Digital gauges electronically display numerals to indicate information such as miles per hour, engine **rpm** and oil pressure instead of using sweep

Custom-made blue fluorescent **digital instrumentation** in the author's highly customized 1976 Shark

needles as on analog gauges. Digital instrumentation was first used on **Bill Mitchell's Mako Shark II** showcar and then on production Corvettes beginning with the 1984 model year.

Dipstick

The dipstick is a steel rod with markings on it to measure the fluid levels of the engine oil and/or transmission fluid.

Direct Bolt-ons (DBO)

See *Bolt-ons, Bolt-on Wheels*

Direct Current (DC)

Direct current refers to electrical current that flows continuously in one direction (as opposed to alternating current which alternates flow direction). Automotive electrical systems use direct current stored in their batteries.

Disc Brake

In this type of brake a **caliper** squeezes a pad against each side of a rotor (disc) to stop the vehicle. Disc brakes were first installed on Corvettes in 1963 on the five **Grand Sport** Corvettes. These special Girling systems were never used on any production Corvettes. In 1965

a four-piston, fixed-caliper design was introduced as a no-cost option, but were actually fitted to all cars unless the drum brake (credit) option was marked. Disc brakes became standard equipment for 1966. In 1967 the design changed internally, eliminating the more complicated (expensive) machining and the piston insulators. In 1984, a new single piston floating caliper design was introduced.

Displacement

Displacement is the total empty volume of the cylinders in an engine with the **pistons** at their lowest point in the cycle. Displacement is reported in cubic inches for older Corvettes and in liters for modern Corvettes. Displacement units for Corvettes are frequently abbreviated as cid (cubic inch displacement) or l (liters).

Distributor

As the name implies, a distributor distributes the spark to each cylinder to initiate combustion. The distributor typically contains the **breaker points** and cam, **centrifugal** and **vacuum advance** mechanisms and a shaft driven by the **camshaft** at one half engine speed. The high voltage needed to initiate combustion is generated by the collapsing magnetic field in the **coil** as the distributor points are opened. The LT1 engine was the last Corvette engine to use a distributor.

Doane, Dick (N/A)

Dick Doane was a Chevrolet dealer and racer in the Chicago area who received one of the first **Grand Sports** in 1963. He took the Grand Sports to some of

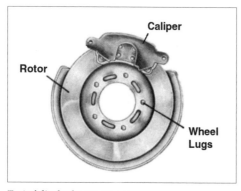

Typical **disc brake** components

their first races at Meadowdale, near Carpentersville, Illinois, and Rantoul AFB for their first competition.

Documentation

Documentation is any material that gives information about a particular vehicle and provides provenance on its origin, history, previous owners and so forth. See also *Build Sheet, Protect-o-Plate, Tank Sticker, Window Sticker*.

DOHC (Dual Overhead Cam)

DOHC is an abbreviation for Dual Overhead Cam, in which two **camshafts** are positioned above the **valve train** of the **cylinder head**. The cam either opens valves directly by the use of tappets (cam followers) or a rocker arm that rides on the cam lobes. The rocker method is least common. Typically, one cam operates the exhaust valves while the other actuates the intake valves. By utilizing direct valve opening there is often room to operate two valves for the intake and two for the exhaust, resulting in a four-valve-per-cylinder engine. A DOHC layout is usually combined with a crossflow head that permits intake gases to enter from one side and exhaust gases to exit from the other. The lower mass and increased stiffness of the direct acting cam system allows more extreme valve opening and closing rates. The result is increased air/gas flow in and more exhaust out, producing more power for a given displacement than a standard pushrod **OHV** engine. This type of valve train can operate at higher rpm than a pushrod style valve train. The LT5 engine introduced in the 1990 Corvette **ZR-1** was the first Corvette to use the DOHC configuration.

Dolza, John (1902–1986)

The original Corvette fuel injection manufactured by GM's Products division was conceived by a GM research engineer, John Dolza. **Zora Arkus-Duntov** contributed to the production development of the system. The 283 cid engine combined with fuel injection had an actual output of 290 hp, not the often quoted 283 hp.

Doug Rippie Motorsports (DRM)

Founded by Corvette racer **Doug Rippie**, DRM is a Minnesota-based provider of high performance components for **C4** and **C5** Corvettes in addition to performing competition-quality conversions on C5s. See the *Suppliers and Services Appendix*.

Downforce

A car body moving through the air generates drag and lift forces that increase with the square of speed. If the body and its aerodynamic appendages are very carefully designed it can generate a downforce that actually pushes the car onto the road. This can be very useful in cornering, braking and accelerating. Aerodynamic devices such as spoilers and wings can increase downforce, and many Corvette aftermarket parts suppliers offer such items. The only problem is that few, if any, of them have been tested in a wind tunnel, and may in fact slow the car down without having much downforce-increasing effect.

Dr. Rebuild

Dr. Rebuild is a Connecticut-based manufacturer and supplier of restoration parts for 1953–1982 Corvettes. See the *Suppliers and Services Appendix*.

Dr. Vette Brake Products

Based in Florida, Corvette Stainless Steel Brakes, Inc. (aka Dr. Vette Brake Products) is a major supplier of Corvette brake, suspension and steering components. See the *Suppliers and Services Appendix*.

Drag Race

A drag race is an all-out, straight-line, acceleration run between two cars, typically, over a distance of ¼ mile. An electric starting device (called a "Christmas Tree") consists of several amber lights that flash downward in sequence culminating in a green light used to start the race. If the driver starts before the green light is lit, a red light goes off and the car is automatically disqualified from the race. Many **drag strips** are equipped with timing lights at 60 feet and at the finish line (called traps) to record the speeds of the vehicles. The driver's initial reaction times are also measured. There is a long braking distance after the ¼-mile mark so the drivers can get their cars stopped. Corvettes have historically been favorites for drag racing. See *photo on page 53*. See also *ET, Snyder, Charles*.

Drag Strip

A drag strip is a measured ¼-mile (1,320 feet) straight-line course on which two cars race side-by-side with the goal of achieving the fastest elapsed time (**ET**) from start to finish.

The following components are essential to a dragstrip:

- Pre-stage beam: A light beam-to-photocell connection in each lane that triggers the small yellow pre-stage lights atop the Christmas Tree. The pre-stage lights signal to drivers that they are close to staging, approximately seven inches behind the starting line.

- Stage beam (starting line): This light beam-to-photocell connection controls the starting and timing of each race. It triggers an independent lane timer for elapsed time and will trigger the red foul light if a driver leaves too soon. A race cannot be started until both drivers are fully staged.

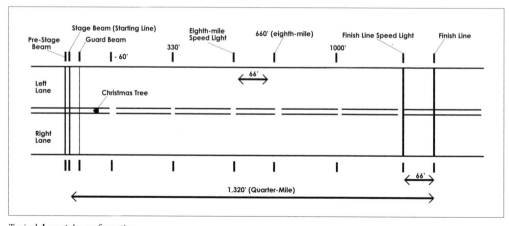

Typical **drag strip** configuration

- Guard beam: A light beam-to-photocell connection located 16 inches past the stage beam that is used to prevent a competitor from gaining an unfair starting line advantage by blocking the stage beam with a low-installed object such as an oil pan or header collector pipe. If the guard beam is activated while the stage beam is still blocked, the red foul light is triggered on the Christmas Tree and the offender is automatically disqualified.

- Christmas Tree: The electronic starting device between lanes on the starting line. It displays a calibrated-light countdown for each driver.

- Interval timers: Interval timers are part of a secondary timing system that records elapsed times, primarily for the racers' benefit, at 60, 330, 660 and 1,000 feet. The ⅛-mile speed light, located 66 feet before the 660-foot mark, is used to start the ⅛-mile speed clocks in each lane; those timers record speed for the first half of the run.

- Speed-trap and elapsed-time beams: The first of these light beam-to-photocell connections is located 66 feet before the finish line and is used to start the speed clocks in each lane. The second beam, located at the finish line, shuts off both the elapsed-time and speed clocks in each lane and triggers the win-indicator light. The 66-foot speed trap is where speed is recorded.

Drivetrain
This is a term that collectively includes the power-transmitting components of any automobile including the **clutch** and gearbox or **automatic transmission**, driveshaft, **u-joints**, differential, **half shafts**, wheels and tires.

Driving School

Depending on the context, a driving school can be a formal high performance driving school such as those run by Skip Barber, **Bob Bondurant**, Jim Russell and others, an **SCCA** racing clinic needed for a racing license or a state mandated school to prevent points from showing on your driving license record for moving violations.

Drum Brakes
Prior to 1965 all Corvettes had duo-servo drum brakes. A hydraulic wheel cylinder pushes the front shoe into the rotating drum. The resulting friction force then pushes the rear shoe against the inside of the cast-iron drum, which stops the car. Most of the braking effect comes from the rear shoe that is loaded by the front shoe. This servo effect coming from the front shoe makes the brake very sensitive to small changes in braking surface coefficient of friction. Since air does not circulate well inside the drum, drum brakes can get very hot and fade, losing their braking effectiveness. Some heavy duty brakes on Corvettes used vented drums and backing plates and either semi-metallic or metallic linings on the shoes to resist heat fading. The lower coefficient of friction of these materials, particularly when the brake was cold, led to quirky braking performance.

Dual Quad
The dual quad option consisted of a pair of four-barrel **carburetors** on the 265 and 283 cid engines used in 1956–1961

Corvettes. The dual quad setup used two **Carter WCFB** carbs on an aluminum intake manifold.

Duntov Award

Frequently called the Duntov Award, the **NCRS** Duntov Mark of Excellence Award was created by the National Corvette Restorers Society in 1985 in honor of **Zora Arkus-Duntov**, and it is the highest award that the NCRS bestows. The award recognizes excellence in the restoration and preservation of 1953–1974 Corvettes. To achieve it a Corvette must first attain a judging score of at least 97 percent out of 100 percent based on an original "as manufactured" standard at a National or Regional NCRS event. The owner must also present the car for a rigorous performance verification (PV) test of all vehicle mechanical components and functions, all of which must operate as those of a new car, without a single failure. Finally, the car must again score at least 97 percent at a National NCRS Convention to receive the Duntov Award. The process of achieving the Duntov Award requires attendance at a minimum of three events, and must be completed within a three year period.

Duntov Cam

The Duntov cam is a high-performance **camshaft** for **small block** Chevrolet engines designed by **Zora Arkus-Duntov** in 1956. This cam became the standard for high-performance solid lifter cams for many years.

Durant, Dick (N/A)

Dick Durant was a racer of the 1960s and 1970s who started in **SCCA** C-Modified Specials and took B-Production Corvettes to some championships until he switched to **Can Am** in the early 1970s. Later he raced Corvettes in SCCA Production and GT again, along with just about anything else on wheels. He currently lives in Irvine, California.

Dynamometer (DYNO)

A dynamometer is a machine that artificially loads the engine or power train and measures the engine's **horsepower** and torque. Basically there are two types of dynamometer: an engine dynamometer measures power delivered to the **flywheel**; a chassis dynamometer measures power delivered to the drive wheels. Portable chassis dynamometers are often available at major Corvette shows and events (e.g., Corvettes at Carlisle) where, for a fee, owners can learn their Corvette's actual horsepower delivered to the rear wheels.

E is for...

Expansion Tank

An **expansion tank** is a reservoir in a sealed cooling system that is connected to the radiator cap or radiator neck and keeps the cooling system filled at all times. The arrow shows the expansion tank on this 1996 LT4 Corvette. See the full entry on page 66.

Earl, Harley (1893–1969)

The Corvette was Harley Earl's idea and he is rightly called the father of the Corvette. The Corvette most certainly would never have gone from the **Motorama** dream car to a production reality without Earl's backing. After World War II, he was impressed watching Jaguars and MGs run at road-racing venues like Watkins Glen. He believed America needed its own sports car and he convinced GM to develop its own two-seater. Earl kept the Corvette program secret, code naming it **Project Opel**. He was close to **Ed Cole** at Chevrolet and decided to give the "Bowtie Division" the first shot at the car. Cole was sold the first time he saw the prototype and he knew it was just what the stodgy Chevrolet division needed.

In January 1953 the Corvette debuted at Motorama in New York; six months later the Corvette went into production. Earl's main accomplishment was making automotive design an institution. Harley Earl put the sizzle back into the American car business after World War II and his expressive designs defined an entire era. He was the first man to design a car with a wraparound windshield and cars without running boards. He also tantalized the motoring public with dream cars like the 1938 Y Job and the 1951 Le Sabre.

He grew up in Hollywood in the early 1900s and quickly developed designs with a flare for the dramatic. His father ran a custom coach building company, and young Harley was put to work—as Chief Designer. He would often produce clay models for customers, showing them what their future vehicles would look like. Earl later became close friends with Lawrence Fisher, who became president of the Cadillac Division of General Motors in 1925. Fisher asked Earl for some design help on the new LaSalle. His successful design caught the attention of GM Chairman **Alfred B. Sloan**.

Earl moved to Detroit in 1927 and quickly set about making GM one of the world leaders in design. In 1937 his Art and Colour Department (he used the English spelling of color to denote prestige) was renamed General Motors Styling. Among Earl's most memorable designs are the Chevy Nomad, the Cadillac Eldorado Brougham, all of he early 1950s Buicks and of course, the Corvette. Harley Earl died on April 10, 1969. He was inducted into the **National Corvette Museum**'s hall of fame in 1998.

Harley Earl

Eastwood Company, The

The Eastwood Company is a major supplier of restoration tools and supplies for Corvettes and other marques. See the *Suppliers and Services Appendix.*

Eckler's Corvettes

Eckler's is a major supplier of Corvette restoration parts and accessories. This company was founded by Ralph Eckler. It has been sold several times since his tenure. See the *Suppliers and Services Appendix.*

Edelbrock Performance Parts

Edelbrock is a major manufacturer and supplier of high-performance parts for Corvettes and other marques. See the *Suppliers and Services Appendix.*

Electrical System

The electrical system consists of various components and sub-systems of an automobile, including the **ignition system**, **starter** motor, battery, **alternator**, **voltage regulator**, lights, **ignition coil**, electrical accessories and all wiring, switches and relays.

Electronic AC Control

Also frequently called electronic climate control, this is the system that maintains the environment inside a Corvette. It consists of many components, including the air conditioner, heater, fans, vents, ducts and a control panel to set and adjust the temperature, fan speed and direction of airflow within the vehicle for heating, cooling and defrosting.

Electronic Climate Control

See *Electronic AC Control.*

Electronic Control Module (ECM)

This electronic component contains the computerized controls for the engine and transmission, as well as for the interaction between the two. It also houses the controls for the **ABS**, traction control and air bags. The first version of an ECM used on a Corvette was Chevrolet's "computer command control," which became standard equipment with the 1981 model year. The system automatically adjusted engine **timing** and air-fuel mixture by making ten adjustments per second. An improved version was added in 1982 with the introduction of **Cross-Fire Injection** that made 80 adjustments per second.

Electronic Engine Management (EEM)

With EEM the engine's ignition and fuel systems are integrated and controlled by a **microprocessor**-based system.

Electronic Fuel Injection (EFI)

See *Fuel Injection.*

Electronic Traction Control (ETC)

This is an enhanced form of traction control whereby a **microprocessor**-based system senses slippage at either of the drive wheels and compensates by directing additional torque to the wheel that is not slipping to maintain optimal traction.

Emissions

Emissions is a collective term for exhaust emissions that contain the unburned hydrocarbons, carbon monoxide, oxides of nitrogen and other noxious gases that result when gasoline is burned as fuel in

E

an engine. **Catalytic converters**, which convert the raw combusted emissions into a more environmentally friendly form, first appeared on Corvettes in 1975.

Engine Mounts

See *Motor Mounts*.

Engine Oil Cooler

An oil cooler is a small heat-exchange unit similar to radiators used to cool engine oil and/or **automatic transmission** fluid. This was used on the L98 **C4**. It was dropped on the LT1 when Mobil 1 became the factory fill oil. Mobile 1 could deal with higher temperatures and Chevrolet was able to save money by eliminating the oil cooler.

Engine Pad

The engine pad is a flat raised surface in front of the right cylinder head where the assembly identifier and a partial **VIN** is stamped into each engine. This information was once the most important part, as it indicated whether the Corvette had its original engine or not. Engines are now frequently counterfeited by restamping non-original blocks. See also *Restamp*.

Ertl/Racing Champions

Ertl is a manufacturer of **die cast models** of Corvettes and other vehicles. See the *Suppliers and Services Appendix*.

The limited edition **Ertl** Corvette 50th Anniversary Commemorative Collection in 1/43 scale

ET (Elapsed Time)

ET is an abbreviation for Elapsed Time and denotes the time it takes for a car to start and cross the finish line in a drag race usually ¼ mile long. ET is usually expressed with a speed, such as 14.301 @ 102 mph, meaning the car took 14.301 seconds to start and finish the ¼ mile and it was traveling at 102 mph as it crossed the finish line.

ET Brackets

In **bracket racing**, drivers are often grouped into classes by ET, so that there are slow cars in one group, medium-speed cars in another and very fast cars in the last.

EX-122

EX-122 was the official factory designation for the prototype Corvette show car that debuted at the 1953 **Motorama**. The EX stood for Experimental vehicle. EX-122 is currently owned by **Kerbeck Corvettes** in Atlantic City, New Jersey, where it has been restored to its pristine Motorama condition.

Exhaust Header

An exhaust header is an exhaust manifold made of tubular steel rather than cast iron. The header is less restrictive than a manifold, which results in less back pressure and increased power.

E

EX-122 made its debut on the turntable of the 1953 GM Motorama held at the Waldorf Astoria Hotel in New York City.

It should be noted, however, that the LT1 cast manifolds are more efficient than a welded exhaust manifold since there is no turbulence over the welds. This is only true of the "shorty" headers though. Long headers are more efficient than the cast manifolds. See also *Bundle of Snakes*.

Exhaust header

Expansion Tank

An expansion tank is a reservoir in a sealed cooling system that is connected to the radiator cap or radiator neck and keeps the cooling system filled at all times. The coolant expands as the engine heats up and some of it flows into the expansion tank; when the engine cools down, the coolant flows back into the cooling system from the expansion tank. 1963 was the first year to use an expansion tank. Expansion tanks are also frequently called surge tanks or overflow tanks. See *photo on page 61*.

F
is for...

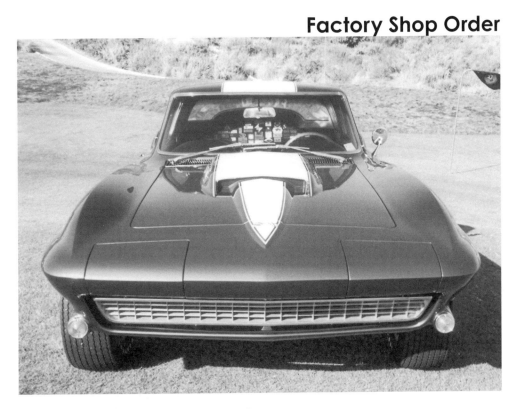

A **factory shop order** was a mechanism to special order a car with non-standard equipment. The FSO was applied to Corvette just once, when this special '67 was built for top-selling Corvette salesman Bob Wingate. See the full entry on page 68.

F41

The optional heavy duty suspension package available on 1960s and 1970s Corvettes was known as F41. It lowered the car by one inch and was stiff enough for racing. It consisted of special heavy duty coil springs on the front end, with heavy duty shocks both front and rear and a heavy duty seven-leaf rear spring.

Factory Shop Order (FSO)

The FSO was a means of getting special non-standard options made available on a production-line Corvette. There is only one documented example of a Factory Shop Order Corvette known to exist. In 1967 a car was built for Bob Wingate as a special favor. Wingate led the nation for a number of years in a row for single-handedly selling the most Corvettes for an individual—over 160 in 1967 alone. This car was built in St. Louis, and has been restored by current owner Bob Radke. See *additional photo on page 67.*

Fan Shroud

The fan shroud is the **fiberglass** or plastic covering between the fan and the radiator that channels the air pulled by the fan through the radiator. The fan shroud also serves to protect the fan and is often merely called the shroud.

Fehan, Doug (1948–)

Doug Fehan is the program manager for Corvette Racing and was responsible for creating the program in the late 1990s. Under his leadership the Corvette C5R has captured 25 victories in 45 starts, including wins at the 24 Hours of Daytona, 24 Hours of **Le Mans**, 12 Hours of **Sebring** and virtually every other road racing circuit in North America.

Fellows, Ron (1959–)

One of the most versatile drivers in racing today, and arguably one of the best road racers in the world, Canadian Ron Fellows has logged laps in **SCCA**,

Bob Radke's **Factory Shop Order** 1967 Coupe—the only documented FSO known to exist

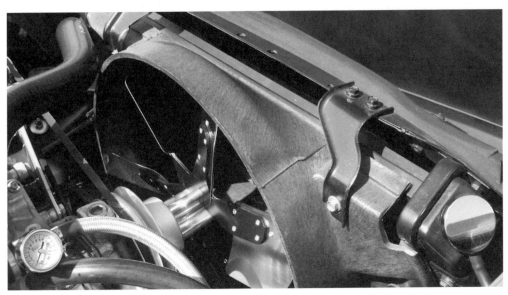

The fiberglass **fan shroud** of a 1976 Corvette

NASCAR, American Le Mans Series racing and more. His expertise has helped make the **C5R**, Corvette's current racecar, a credible contender in sports car racing and a regular winner at some of racing's most important events. He helped drive the Corvette racecar to two class wins at **Le Mans**, and wins at **Sebring**, **Road Atlanta**, Laguna Seca and the **Daytona** 24 hour race.

2003 Corvette Racing program manager **Doug Fehan**

2003 Le Mans Chevrolet Corvette racing driver **Ron Fellows**

Fender Flares

Fender flares are a custom bodywork feature often fitted to Corvettes—and other vehicles—to provide clearance for bigger tires. See also *Flared Fenders, Flares.*

Fiber Optics

Fiber optics describes a method of directing light from its source to its destination using transparent glass fibers as the conduit. In 1968–1971 Corvettes fiber optic light monitors mounted on the center console let the driver know which external lights were operative. They were discontinued with the 1972 model year.

Fiberglass

Derived from the trade name Fiberglas, fiberglass is now a generic term for flexible filament glass. In the manufacturing process to produce Corvette parts like fenders, doors, hoods and underbodies, the glass fiber is chopped, impregnated with plastic resin and fillers and then molded with heat and pressure. Bodies made of fiberglass plastic will not rust. Since 1953 Corvette bodies have been made of fiberglass. Along the way the manufacturing process has been improved so that with today's version, SMC (sheet molding compound), parts finish as well as steel. SMC parts are still more expensive than their stamped steel equivalent, but their much-lower tooling cost makes them cost effective at low volume. SMC parts are competitive with aluminum for weight, however, they are much more dent resistant.

Fiberglass Reinforced Plastic

See *Fiberglass.*

Final Drive Ratio

The final drive ratio is the relationship between the rotational speed of the driveshaft and the drive wheel's axle shaft. As an example, let's say the driveshaft rotates 3.56 turns for every 1 turn of the drive axle shaft; the final drive ratio is 3.56:1. The final drive ratio can be changed by increasing or decreasing the number of teeth on the gears within the differential.

Firing Order

This denotes the sequence in which the cylinders fire in an engine. The Chevrolet **small block** firing order is; 1-8-4-3-6-5-7-2 with the left bank, front to rear, being odd-numbered and the right bank being even-numbered.

Fitch, John (1917-)

A pioneer in Corvette racing, John Fitch is considered a racer extraordinaire. He was the Sports Car Club of America's

Corvette racer **John Fitch**

(SCCA) first national champion; he won the second **Sebring** 12-hour race in 1953 and in the same year was named "Driver of the Year" by *Speed Age* magazine. Fitch was the only American ever to drive for the Mercedes-Benz factory team and he also raced the **Corvette SS** and the test mule, which later became the **Corvette Stingray Race Car**. He was the first manager of Connecticut's Lime Rock Park Raceway, as well as one of the prime movers behind the project.

After retiring from racing Fitch became a successful specialty car builder and safety engineer. He developed the familiar yellow crash barrels seen on highways and racetracks called "Fitch Barriers" that have saved the lives of many motorists. Fitch was also responsible for conducting the world's first Advanced Driving School. John Fitch was inducted into the **National Corvette Museum**'s Hall of Fame in 2000.

Fixed Roof Coupe (FRC)
The FRC was the low-end, entry level Corvette introduced in 1999. It was a fixed roof hardtop version of the convertible. The internal code name for the stripped, fixed hardtop was the **Billy Bob** Corvette, suggesting that it was less than a true Corvette. Chevrolet ultimately found a new use for the Billy Bob, turning it into the most expensive Corvette in the lineup, the **Z06** high performance Corvette.

Flared Fenders, Flares
As tires became wider, stock Corvette fenders could not contain them. In racing the fender was often cut and reshaped so that a larger tire could be housed within

The fenders on the author's 1976 Corvette were **flared** to accommodate oversized tires on custom wheels.

it. In the late 1960s and 1970s flaring Corvette fenders was quite common. Many Sting Rays had flared fenders since they were originally designed to hold 6.70x15 and 7.25x15 tires; the F60-15, G60-15, and L60-15 tires were much too wide without flares. The most common flaring styles were a small flare that extended only slightly outward from the body but radiused the wheel opening and the "ZL1 Flare" which was much larger, extending outward about three inches and flowing down the fender both in front of and behind the tire opening.

Flared fenders were allowed on some race cars in the 1960s, depending on the series, and later became very common in the 1970s in order to cover the huge slicks that most used. Customizers often flared the fenders on their street Corvettes to give them that race car look. The ultrawide P315/35ZR17 rear tires of the **ZR-1** demanded fender flares. Here, the entire body starting in the doors was flared out to cover the tires.

Flint

Flint, Michigan, was the location of the original Corvette assembly plant. The 300 1953 Corvettes were hand-built on a short assembly line built quickly for the rushed production. Flint was also an engine assembly plant and all early Corvette **small blocks** came from this plant. The engine stamp pad typically has an F or V at the beginning to note that it is built in Flint, i.e., F0I23RF, VI024HC.

Float Bowl

The float bowl is a fuel storage chamber within the **carburetor** that receives and holds fuel until it is needed by the engine.

Flywheel

With a manual transmission, the flywheel is a heavy metal disk mounted to the rear of the **crankshaft** that smoothes the power surges resulting from each cylinder's firing. With an **automatic transmission**, a thin disc or flex plate is attached to the end of the crankshaft and connects to the rotating case of the **torque converter**. The torque converter case serves as the flywheel. The flywheel has a gear toothed ring pressed onto its outer edge that is engaged by the **starter** motor when the engine is cranked. The flex plate has a similar toothed ring welded to its outer perimeter. In **manual transmission** cars the flywheel is also part of the **clutch** assembly.

Street cars use relatively heavy flywheels made of cast iron since they must isolate the **drivetrain** and the driver from engine vibration. Racers sacrifice vibration isolation for performance and thus are willing to use much lighter flywheels. They may even be made of aluminum although the **clutch** facings are generally still of cast iron because they must be compatible with the slippage and heat of repeated brutal clutch use. Production flywheels are always tested for their burst speed, which must be well above the highest conceivable rpm the engine can possibly reach.

Forrester, Dana (1947–)

Dana Forrester is a watercolor artist who began painting Corvettes in 1989 and has won many awards in regional and national exhibitions and art festivals. He also designed a 2003 package for Corvettes called the Milestone Edition (www.milestoneseditions.com) that

"Like An Old Song On The Radio," a watercolor painting by **Dana Forrester**

benefits the **National Corvette Museum** A book has been published about his art career entitled *Against The Wall: The Architectural and Automotive Art of Dana Forrester* (Neighbors and Quaid Publishers, Oklahoma City, ISBN 0-9632-8829-6). See the *Suppliers and Services Appendix*.

49 States
A "49 states" Corvette is fitted with **emissions** equipment mandated by federal law, rather than with the mandatory federal equipment plus special additional emissions equipment required by California for cars registered in that state. 1981 was the first year the Corvette was emissions-legal in all 50 states.

4+3
The 4+3 was the optional four-speed **manual transmission** with the addition of a hydraulically controlled planetary **overdrive**. The transmission was set up to engage second, third and fourth overdrive until the driver went full throttle. This setup gave a fuel economy improvement of one–two miles per gallon. It was available for 1984–1988 Corvettes.

427
See *Big Block*

Franklin Mint, The
The Franklin Mint is a high-quality manufacturer of collectibles and precision **die cast models**, including an

The 1/24-scale **Franklin Mint** model of the 1969 Corvette Big Block Coupe

extensive line of Corvette models in both ¹⁄₄₃ scale and ¹⁄₂₄ scale. See the *Suppliers and Services Appendix.*

FRC
See *Fixed Roof Coupe.*

FSO
See *Factory Shop Order.*

FTD (Fastest Time of Day)
This is an abbreviation for Fastest Time of Day. In autocrossing and hill-climbing, class winners and most classes also have a trophy for the person who does the Fastest Time of Day, which is the quickest time to run the course.

Fuel Injecton
Fuel injection is a method of fuel delivery to the engine that utilizes a pump and injectors instead of a **carburetor** to meter fuel. Early Corvettes used the mechanical **Rochester Ram Jet** fuel injection system used on their high performance Corvette engines from 1957 to 1965. **Cross-Fire Injection** (CFI), an electronic unit fuel injection system, was used on the 1982 and 1984 Corvettes. The first Corvette application of electronic controlled port fuel injection, **Tuned-Port Injection** (TPI), based on the Bosch L-Jetronic system was fitted to 1985 models. As fuel injection technology continued to evolve, more sophisticated versions of the original multipoint system were used: **Multi-Port Fuel Injection** (MFI) and then Sequential Fuel Injection (SFI).

A Rochester **fuel injection** unit on a 1962 Corvette

Fuel Pump

A fuel pump is a mechanical or electric motor pump that pulls gasoline from the fuel tank and delivers it to the **carburetor** or injector pump or fuel rail. From 1953 through 1984, Corvettes used mechanical fuel pumps that were actuated via a cam and lever off the **crankshaft**. In 1985, with the advent of true **Tuned-Port Injection**, an electric in-tank fuel pump was utilized which did double duty as both a fuel pump and sending unit to provide data for the **Electronic Control Module** (ECM). Both the mechanical and electric units were manufactured by GM's AC-Delco division.

Fuelie

Fuelie is a slang nickname for fuel-injected 1957–1965 Corvettes.

Fuse

A fuse is a piece of wire that "blows" (melts) when excessive electrical current is passed through it. When the fuse blows it causes an interruption in the circuit it is connected to, thus protecting the circuit from overload and the car from the potential risk of fire.

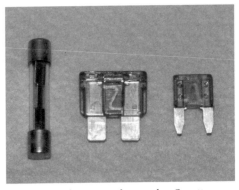

Various types of automotive **fuses** used on Corvettes

G

is for...

Gullwing Doors

Gullwing doors are vehicle doors that are hinged to open vertically rather than horizontally. The Corvette Aerovette (shown here) and Reynolds Aluminum Corvette (XP-895) showcars were equipped with gullwing doors. See the full entry on page 84.

Gale, Dan (1943–2000)

The man who made the **National Corvette Museum** a reality, Dan Gale was a charter member of the National Corvette Restorers Society Library, Archives and Museum Committee dating back to 1986. He was also a charter member of the Board of Directors of The National Corvette Restorers Society Foundation (the name was later changed to The National Corvette Museum Foundation). In 1990 he was elected president of the NCM Foundation Board of Directors and oversaw the opening of the National Corvette Museum Annex and held a national leadership role in the Capital Campaign that started in the fall of 1991.

In 1993 Gale oversaw construction of the building and displays that began that year and he coordinated the grand opening of the museum in 1994. He served as Executive Director of the Museum in 1994 and 1995 and continued as a member of the board of the NCM Foundation to 1997. Dan Gale died on October 4, 2000, from complications

Dan Gale was Executive Director of the National Corvette Museum.

resulting from a stroke. In September 2004 Gale was inducted into the National Corvette Museum Corvette Hall of Fame.

Gap

When referring to **spark plugs**, the gap is the distance between the center and side electrodes. In reference to contact points, it is the spacing between the points in the contact breaker of the **distributor**. It can also denote the distance between adjacent body panels such as the hood and fender.

Garner, James (1928–)

Garner is a well-known television and film actor who established a team to race L88 Corvettes under the **American International Racing** (AIR) banner in 1968.

Gasket

A gasket is a thin and relatively soft material installed between two metal surfaces to ensure a good seal. Common gasket materials include cardboard, rubber, silicon, copper and cork.

Gauge

A gauge is an instrument that monitors and registers a quantity. This quantity can be the amount of fuel left in the tank, the speed in miles per hour, engine temperature and so forth.

Gauge Cluster

See *Instrument Cluster*.

Gear Ratio

A gear ratio is the ratio of the number of revolutions of a driving gear relative to

Gearshift Lever

The lever on the center console or floor of a Corvette that the driver uses to select various gears available in the transmission is known as the gearshift. Gearshifts are used for both standard and automatic transmissions.

Gelcoat

Gelcoat is a quick-setting resin used in **fiberglass** molding processes to provide an improved first surface finish for the composite. Gelcoat is the first resin layer applied to the mold after the mold-release agent, which becomes an integral part of the finished laminate.

Generator

The generator is a device in an automobile electrical system that converts mechanical energy from a drive belt into electrical energy to operate the ignition and accessories and keep the battery charged. Corvettes were equipped with six-volt generators in 1953 and 1954. Corvettes from 1955–1962 had twelve-volt generators. In 1963 the generator was replaced by the **alternator** for Corvette electrical systems. In a generator the current generating conductors are part of the rotating armature so that the full current output of the generator must be commutated to DC current through the brushes. Once solid state diodes were economically available, turning the device inside out and making the current generating

the number of revolutions of the driven gear; e.g., if the driving gear makes four revolutions and the driven gear makes only one, the ratio is 4:1.

conductors part of the non-rotating case made the alternator practical.

Get On It, Getting On It

Slang expressions for hard acceleration include "get on the gas," i.e., full throttle, wide-open throttle, floor it.

Glass Packs

Glass packs are straight-through mufflers that use fiberglass packing in their expansion chambers to muffle the noise somewhat. Louder than stock mufflers, they improved performance slightly due to lower back pressure. They were very popular in the 1960s and 1970s on Corvettes but, with the introduction of **catalytic converters** in 1975, and noise laws by 1980, their popularity dwindled. Glass packs tended to have a short useful life because the high velocity of exhaust gas roaring through the muffler tended to erode the fiberglass packing.

Glove Box, Glove Compartment

The glove box is a small compartment for stowing driving gloves, sunglasses, registration and insurance papers, etc. On 1953–1962 Corvettes the glove box is located beneath the "waterfall" between the seats. For 1963–1967 Corvettes the

The **glove box** was between the seats on C1 Corvettes.

The **glove box** was moved in front of the passenger seat on C2s. A map pocket replaced the glove box on C3s.

glove box was relocated directly in front of the passenger seat. In 1968–1977 map pockets occupied the area in front of the passenger seat and the glove box was moved to a center compartment behind the seats. In 1978–1982 the glove box was enlarged behind the passenger seat. A padded structure nicknamed the "**breadloaf**" because of its shape was located in front of the passenger seat where the glove compartment should have been in 1984–1989 Corvettes. In 1990 a fully functional glove box returned.

GPH (Gallons per Hour)

This is an abbreviation for Gallons Per Hour. A fuel pump is typically rated according to how many gallons of gasoline it will supply per hour working against a defined backpressure.

Grand Sport

In 1962 **Zora Arkus-Duntov** began building a lightweight Sting Ray designed strictly for competition and to beat the **Cobra**. The target weight was 2,000 pounds. It used a hand-laid-up plastic body similar to the 1963 body design, although the rear **split window** was replaced with a single window. The body was also made of paper-thin **fiberglass** to save weight and it had several functional air scoops and a working trunk, while the headlights were exposed under Plexiglas covers. The tube frame chassis made use of many aluminum parts and thin stamped steel. Some Grand Sports included an air jack system for pit stops. The first Grand Sports were equipped with the standard 360 hp **Ram Jet** fuel injected 327cid engine. Five Grand Sports were built as coupes. Later, two were modified to be convertibles.

One of the original five **Grand Sports** built by
Zora Arkus-Duntov

G

The limited edition 1996 **Grand Sport**—only
1,000 were made

There has been some recent
speculation that a total of six Grand
Sports were actually made, and GM is
looking for the sixth one that is rumored
to be in storage somewhere.

In 1996 Chevrolet released a
commemorative Grand Sport production
model in Admiral Blue with an Arctic
White stripe down the hood. It had the
LT4 engine and six-speed transmission.
Unlike the race-only versions in 1963,
these were street cars with lots of luxury
options. Only 1,000 1996 Grand Sports
were built and sold (746 coupes and 254
convertibles).

This car never would have been created
without **John Heinricy**. According to
the person who was John Heinricy's

and **Dave Hill**'s supervisor at GM, he basically turned the **C4** work over to Heinricy and told Hill to concentrate on the **C5**. The last few years of the C4 were John Heinricy's ballgame.

Green Fade

In the manufacturing process of new brake pads, gases of the bonding agents are trapped in the pad. When the pads are heated these gases can escape and force the pad off the rotor or coat the pad with material that does not grip as well. Brakes are **bedded in** for this reason by heating the green pads to fade temperatures to permit these gases to escape. See also *Brake Fade*.

Greenwood, John (1945–)

John Greenwood was a Corvette racer of the late 1960s and 1970s, most famous for his Stars and Stripes Corvettes running on BF Goodrich Street Radials. He won the **SCCA** National Championship in 1970 for A-Production. Later, his cars became more and more radical in looks and design, taking every possible advantage of the rules.

In the mid-1970s Greenwood started some custom Corvette designs such as the Sport Wagon and GT bodies that were marketed mainly through **Eckler's**. John still has a Corvette operation outside Orlando at Sanford, Florida.

Ground Effects

A car running just inches off the ground is running in the "ground effect." The ground effect has been extensively studied in recent years. Race cars try to create a vacuum under the car that sucks the car onto the road (negative lift). Front and rear wings, venturi underbodies and side skirts are their stock in trade. At high speeds these effects can create as much as four times the weight of the car in **downforce**. This negative lift is used to dramatically increase the cornering and braking acceleration that is possible but it comes at the price of greatly increased drag.

There are a considerable number of aftermarket air dams, spoilers, rocker panel extensions and wings purported to create downforce. They probably have some effect but unless they are optimized in a wind tunnel they are not achieving their potential. However, we can say, definitely, that they increase drag.

Ground Straps

A ground strap is a wire cable (usually braided and often flat) that is used to ground various components such as the radio antenna, **motor mounts**, sill plate, exhaust and accelerator to the chassis. Since Corvette bodies are made of **fiberglass** or plastic, they do not offer the inherent grounding capability of metal car bodies. By grounding, or connecting, the negative battery terminal to the Corvettes chassis, only one insulated wire is required to carry current to the device because the frame serves as a return wire to complete the circuit.

Gross Horsepower (GHP)

Gross horsepower, or ghp, refers to an engine's maximum power output as measured by a **dynamometer** under ideal conditions without power-robbing accessories such as the **alternator** or full exhaust system. See *Brake Horsepower*.

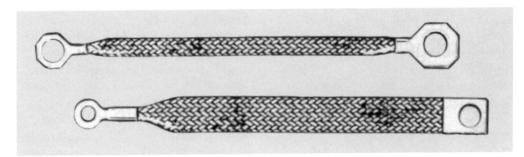

Typical Mid-Year radio **ground straps**

GRP (Glass Reinforced Plastic)
This is an abbreviation for Glass Reinforced Plastic. See *Fiberglass*.

GS II
See *CERV II*.

Guldstrand, Dick (1927–)
Dick Guldstrand was a Corvette racer from Southern California who pioneered several new ideas in Corvette racing in the late 1950s and 1960s. From 1963 to 1965, he won three consecutive **SCCA** Pacific Coast Championships. In 1966 Guldstrand won the GT class at the **Daytona** 24-hour race, and finished ninth overall. The following year, he raced at **Le Mans** and set a track record in the GT class while leading the race for 13 hours. In both 1966 and 1967, Guldstrand drove a **Grand Sport** Corvette at the 12 hours of **Sebring** for Roger Penske.

In 1968, Guldstrand opened Guldstrand Engineering Inc., in Culver City, California. Soon, he was designing and building high performance cars for competition throughout North America, South America and Western Europe. His company prepared the L88 Corvettes owned by actor **James Garner**'s **American International Racing** team for competition.

Dick Guldstrand played a major role in the development and testing of the 1985 Corvette. He set new track records at the Mid-Ohio 24 hours, finishing both first and second overall. He also set new track records at the 12 hours at Willow Springs for enduro cars, once again finishing first and second overall. His personal involvement, along with his GSS race team, set the stage for the future racing series, as well as Corvette's domination of the Showroom Stock class running against Porsche.

In the mid-1980s Guldstrand produced the GS80, a special Corvette with performance and handling equipment created by Guldstrand Engineering. It was widely acclaimed by the press and enthusiasts for its superior handling and overall performance. The GS80 had the biggest production run of all the Guldstrand cars and has virtually received cult status.

In 1990 Guldstrand announced that he was developing the Guldstrand Grand Sport 90. A world-class exotic supercar based on the Corvette **ZR-1** chassis, the GS90 sported an entirely new body along with major upgrades to its engine, suspension, wheels, tires and rear end. The finished product debuted on the Chevrolet stand at the 1994 Los Angeles Auto Show, and was produced on a build-

G

Corvette racer and supertuner **Dick Guldstrand**

to-order basis. More recently, Guldstrand has released his custom-built 427 cid **C5s** for sale. Guldstrand was inducted into the **National Corvette Museum** Hall of Fame in 1999.

Guldstrand Engineering & Motorsports

Guldstrand Engineering & Motorsports is a Corvette and Camaro performance facility that offers supertuning services, custom fabrication and performance parts and accessories. See the *Suppliers and Services Appendix.*

Gullwing Doors

Gullwing doors are vehicle doors that are hinged to open vertically rather than horizontally. The name came about because the doors, when open, resemble a seagull in flight with wings spread. The Corvette **Aerovette** and **Reynolds Aluminum Corvette (XP-895)** showcars were equipped with gullwing doors. See *photo on page 77.*

Gymkhana Suspension

The gymkhana suspension was an optional package available on 1974–1982 Corvettes. The option (FE7) consisted of stiffer front springs, a thicker front **sway bar** and re-valved shocks.

H is for...

Jim Hall

Jim Hall was an early proponent of the all-composite monocoque design. He pioneered the high-mounted rear wing (seen here on the Chaparral 2E), the racing automatic transmission and active ground effects. He also enjoyed a very close working relationship with Chevy R&D and Frank Winchell. In addition to his Chaparral race cars, Hall also raced a Grand Sport in the early 1960s. See the full entry on page 86.

Half Shafts

The 1963–1996 Corvette **independent rear suspension** used a pair of mini-driveshafts equipped with **u-joints** on each end where they attach to the differential in the center and the stub axles on the outside. These mini-driveshafts are known as "half shafts." They serve the dual function of transmitting torque and acting as the upper lateral control suspension member. The **C5-6** uses half shafts with pot joints very similar to front drive axle shafts. They can change length and do not act as the lateral suspension control member.

Hall, Jim (1935–)

Jim Hall was born July 23,1935, in Abilene, Texas, and was reared in Colorado and New Mexico. In 1954 when he was a student at CalTech, he began driving his brother's Austin Healey sports car at weekend road races.

In 1960, Jim fitted a Formula 2 Lotus with a 2.5-liter Climax and drove in his first Formula 1 race at **Riverside**. In 1961, he won main events at Palm Springs in a Cooper Monaco and at Las Vegas in a Birdcage Maserati.

Jim won the Elkhart Lake 500 in 1962, co-driving with Hap Sharp. He then won the Hoosier Grand Prix at Indianapolis Raceway Park, beating Hap Sharp, Dan Gurney and **Roger Penske**. He drove for Stirling Moss' BRP Formula 1 team in 1963, finishing twelfth in World Championship points.

In 1963 Jim built his Chevrolet-powered **Chaparral** 2. Laguna Seca, Watkins Glen, **Road America** and the

Typical C2–C3 **half shafts**

Daytona 200 were just a few of the races he won. The Chaparral 2 won 16 of the 21 races entered in 1965. From 1963 to 1970 his engineering genius turned out a series of dramatic race car innovations. He was an early proponent of the all-composite monocoque design, he pioneered the high-mounted rear wing, the racing **automatic transmission** and active **ground effects**. He also enjoyed a very close-working relationship with Chevy R&D and Frank Winchell. Many of the concepts developed on Chaparral race cars had their genesis in this relationship. See *photo on page 85*.

Halogen
See *Quartz Halogen Bulb*.

Hardtop, Auxiliary
Auxiliary hardtops have been factory options available for Corvette convertibles since 1956:

- 1956–1962   RPO #419
- 1963–1975   RPO #C07
- 1989–1996   RPO #CC2

There were no factory auxiliary hardtops available for 1953–1955 Corvettes; however, some aftermarket companies manufactured removable hardtops in 1955 and they were available through some Chevrolet dealers. These aftermarket hardtops also fit 1953 and 1954 Corvettes. There were no factory hardtops for the C5.

Harmonic Balancer
As part of the **crankshaft** pulley, the function of the harmonic balancer is to dampen the torsional vibrations coming from the crankshaft and the **camshaft**

Arrow points out the **harmonic balancer**.

and to keep those vibrations from damaging the engine and from spreading through the rest of the car. "Vibration Damper" would be a more accurate name for it.

Harrison Radiator
From 1960 through 1972, Corvettes were factory-equipped with aluminum radiators manufactured by the Harrison Radiator Company of Lockport, New York. Harrison, at that time, was a subsidiary company of General Motors (they have long since become independent). Aluminum has a much higher thermal coefficient (ability to transfer heat) than traditional copper/brass automotive radiators; this resulted in high-performance Corvette engines that ran cooler. Aluminum is easily corroded and demands the use of coolant additives that prevent this from occurring.

Hatchback
A hatchback is a vehicle configuration in which the slanted rear window or

The 1982 Collector's Edition Corvette featured a **hatchback**.

surrounding deck surface lifts, acting as a hatch. The 1982 **Collector Edition** Corvette was the first Corvette to incorporate a hatchback. The total 1982 production run of 25,407 Corvettes included 6,759 Collector Editions.

Head Gasket
The gasket used to seal the engine's **cylinder heads** against the block is known as the head gasket. It performs the very difficult task of sealing combustion gases, coolant and oil under the strain of a wide range of working temperatures.

Headers
See *Exhaust Header*.

Headliner
The headliner is the covering for the inside of a car's roof. In the case of the Corvette, the headliner has usually consisted of a vinyl-covered **fiberglass** tray. Headliners were first used with 1963 Corvette Sting Ray coupes, since that was the first year of a coupe. Before the 1986 **C4** convertible, Corvette convertibles never used headliners, and their auxiliary hardtops were never equipped with them either. Starting with the 1986 C4 all Corvette convertibles have had insulated tops with a headliner.

Headrest
The headrest is a head-restraining device that extends the back of the seat to prevent whiplash in the event of a crash. Headrests were first offered as an option (A82) on 1966 Corvettes at a cost of $42.15 and were discontinued in 1970 when a new seat design with a higher back made them obsolete.

Heads-Up Display (HUD)
A heads-up display is an electronic display that projects a lighted virtual image of the **tachometer**, **speedometer** and other **gauges** in the plane of the front bumper just below driver's line of sight. This enables the driver to see this vital information without taking his eyes off the road and with only modest refocusing. It is also sometimes called a head-up display. It was first offered as an option (UV6) on the 1999 Corvette C5 at a price of $375. The HUD became standard on the **Z06** model in 2002 and it remains an option for other C5 models.

Heat Shield
A heat shield is a device that reduces the heat radiating from a hot body like an exhaust pipe to the body of the car. Corvettes usually have heat shields on their exhaust pipes and secondary shields under the carpeting against the lower part of the firewall as well as around the

C5 **heads-up** display

transmission and **catalytic converters** to minimize engine and exhaust heat from entering the passenger compartment. Primary heat shields are made of corrosion resistant metal. The secondary heat shields are made of puffy glass fiber covered with a reflective foil similar to home insulation.

Heater Delete, Heater/Defroster Delete

When a 1963–1967 Corvette was ordered without the heater/defroster unit (C48), a credit of $100 was applied to the purchase price. This deletion was popular with Corvette owners living in areas where the weather was warm all year long and for Corvettes that would be used primarily for racing. Federal Motor Vehicle Safety Standard (MVSS) requirements include defroster performance so it is no longer possible to delete the heater.

HEI (High Energy Ignition)

This is an abbreviation for High Energy Ignition system. GM abandoned **breaker point distributors** in 1975 and began using the HEI distributor, which features a higher-voltage coil and a magnetic breakerless system. It isn't available in a mechanical **tach drive** version, so owners of 1963 to 1974 Corvettes who wish to upgrade to HEI will need to get a customized tach drive HEI distributor or convert their mechanical (cable-driven) tach to an electronic unit. Corvettes built from 1956 to 1962 can use the generator drive on the distributor for the tach.

Heinricy, John (1947–)

John Heinricy joined GM in 1970, shortly after receiving his bachelor's degree in engineering from South Dakota School of Mines and Technology. He was named Experimental Engineer with Chevrolet in 1972, and in 1976 was promoted to Senior Experimental Engineer.

In 1979 Heinricy was named Development Engineer with Chevrolet at the Milford Proving Grounds, and became Assistant Staff Engineer at Milford in 1981, responsible for Citation X11, 1983 Monte Carlo SS and the 1984 and 1985 Corvette development. In 1985 he was promoted to Product Engineering Manager for the former Chevrolet-Pontiac-GM of Canada Engineering Group at Chevrolet Motor Division, responsible for Corvette and Camaro, and became Vehicle Development Manager for the Corvette platform in 1989.

In May 1993 Heinricy was appointed Assistant Chief Engineer for the Corvette. He became Chief Engineer for the Camaro and Firebird in 1997, and in 2001 became Director of Vehicle Dynamics for GM cars and trucks. As of early 2004, Heinricy was Director of

John Heinricy

High Performance Vehicle Operations, responsible for low-volume, high-performance cars and trucks, including the Cadillac V series, Redline ION, Cobalt SS Supercharged and Trailblazer SS.

Active racing Corvettes, Camaros, and Pontiac Firebirds professionally since 1984, Heinricy has won nine driving championships and several team championships, including winning the SCCA National Championship in a Z06 in 2001, 2002 and 2003. He was a member of the driving team that broke three world speed records in 1990 driving a Corvette ZR-1, and drove one of the C5R Corvettes in GT2 competition.

High Gear

High gear refers to the top or cruising gear in a transmission. For example, in a six-speed gearbox, sixth gear or high gear is an overdrive ratio.

High Speed Events

In NCCC, high speed events are typically run on race tracks at speeds far above those possible on public highways. They are equivalent to SCCA Solo I events. Cars competing are required to meet minimum safety requirements and include basic safety equipment such as roll bars and safety harnesses.

Hill, David (1943–)

Dave Hill is the current Chief Engineer of Corvette. Hill was with GM's Cadillac division before he replaced Dave McLellan, who retired in 1992. Although McLellan's team did much of the work on the C5 concept, Hill continued its development into actual production. Hill's production based C5s have raced successfully all over the United States.

Dave Hill, Corvette's third chief engineer, addressing the media at the Corvette 50th Anniversary Celebration in Nashville

The **C5R** is a purpose built race car loosely based on the production car. It has performed competitively as far away as **Le Mans**. The **C6** promises to be even more of an expression of Hill's engineering direction than the C5, which was already in progress when he joined the Corvette program.

Hill, Tom (1957–)

Corvette engineer Tom Hill frequents **Bloomington** and many **NCRS** meets, where he often speaks. He began work at **St. Louis**, moved with Corvette to **Bowling Green** and worked on the 1983 Corvette, the only remaining example of which is on permanent display at the **National Corvette Museum**.

Holley

A 100-year-old carburetor company located in **Bowling Green**, Kentucky, that manufactures high performance **carburetors**. The Holley four-barrel 4150 and 4160 series were used as standard equipment on some Corvettes during the 1960s. The two-barrel 2300 series was used for the **tri-power** setups on **big block** 1967–1969 Corvettes. In the 1970s Holley engaged **Zora Arkus-Duntov** to help develop its stillborn electronic **fuel injection** system.

H

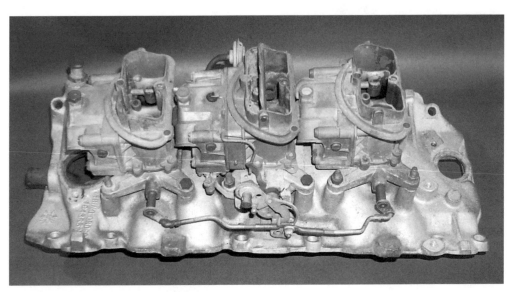

A Corvette 427 "tri-power" setup—three **Holley** two-barrel carburetors mounted on an aluminum tri-power intake manifold

Homologated

This refers to a production car that has met all the requirements of a motor sports governing body and certified as eligible for one or more classes of automobile racing.

Hood

The hood is the hinged portion of the car body that covers the engine. Corvettes have always had front-hinged, rear-opening hoods. The **C4** (1984–1996) Corvettes had a **clamshell** hood that included the upper portions of the fenders, headlights and nose of the car as well.

Hood Scoop

A scoop is an opening in the **hood** of the car that permits cooler ambient air to flow more directly into the engine's intake system. Corvettes have traditionally had faux hood scoops over the years.

Horsepower (HP)

Horsepower is the unit used to measure and express the rate at which work is done, generally expressed in foot pounds. One horsepower is equal to 550 foot pounds per second, or 33,000 foot pounds per minute.

HotRod Hardware, Inc.

HotRod Hardware is a supplier of clocks, décor, furniture and collectible accessories for Corvettes and other marques. See the *Suppliers and Services Appendix.*

Hufstader, Gibson (1930–)

Gibson (Gib) Hufstader had a career with Corvette that spanned over 45 years. He was involved with the **Grand Sport**, **Aerovette**/Four-Rotor Corvette, Twin Turbo LT5 and many other Corvette projects. Now retired, he started at

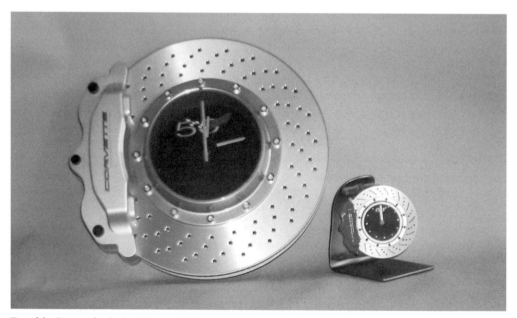

Two of the Corvette disc brake clocks available from **HotRod Hardware**

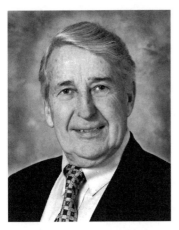

Corvette engineer **Gibson Hufstader**

Chevrolet in the early 1950s and began working as a development engineer for Chevrolet R&D. In 1960 Hufstader worked to help make the **clutch** for the 427 mystery engine (Daytona race engine). Hufstader is also responsible for seven United States patents that include the electric air pump, cog wheel belt disc drive and the arrangement of the two-rotor **Wankel** engines with transaxle and accessory drive.

Hufstader worked with **Zora Arkus-Duntov** as a design release engineer for chassis which included brake development for the racing brake package. His other accomplishments also include designing the initial engine package for the twin turbo and the packaging of the **ZR-1** engine. He was inducted into the **National Corvette Museum**'s Hall of Fame in 2001.

Hydraulic Cam

A **camshaft** that is designed to work with **hydraulic lifters** is known as a "hydraulic cam." Each cam is cut to work with a type of lifter and cannot be mixed without causing serious damage to both the cam lobes and the lifters. See *Roller Cam, Solid Cam*.

Hydraulic Lifter

A hydraulic lifter is a type of **valve** lifter that uses hydraulic oil pressure to maintain zero valve clearance (no clearance between metal parts) to reduce valve noise.

I is for...

Instrument Cluster

The **instrument cluster** is a grouping of various gauges in the dashboard. Over the years, Corvette has had a variety of different instrument cluster designs. This instrument cluster is from a 1996 LT4 Corvette. See the entry on page 98.

IBIZ, Inc.

IBIZ is a leading manufacturer and distributor of detailing products for Corvette interiors and exteriors. Based in Florida, the company's fossilized carnauba car wax is the official wax of the **Corvette Club of America** and the **C5 Registry**. See the *Suppliers and Services Appendix*.

Identification Numbers

See *Vehicle Identification Numbers (VIN)*.

Idiot Lights

Idiot light is a common term for warning lights that indicate a problematic condition (e.g., "GEN" or "OIL"), rather than **gauges** which give detailed information.

Ignition Coil

An ignition coil is a type of pulse transformer that multiplies the low voltage received from the battery or **alternator** to many thousands of volts when the **breaker points** open and close. The coil contains a primary winding, a slot iron core, and a secondary winding. The high voltage output of the coil is directed to the appropriate **spark plug** by the **distributor**.

Ignition Points

See *Breaker Points*.

Ignition Shielding

Since Corvette bodies are not made of metal, electrical interference from the **ignition system** is not isolated from the passenger compartment and,

The chrome-plated **ignition shielding** is visible behind the triangular air cleaner on this Shark.

consequently, may be heard when the radio is turned on. To combat this problem, metal shielding was used, prior to the **C4**, to surround the **distributor** and coil. In some earlier models, the spark plug wires were covered as well. With **C4** and beyond the shielding is taken care of in the radio and antenna system.

Ignition Switch

The ignition switch, found on the dashboard of 1953–1968 Corvettes and on the steering column from 1969 on, connects and disconnects the **ignition system** from the battery and starter motor so the engine can be started and stopped as desired. **C5** brought the switch back to the dashboard. Since 1968, turning the ignition key switch on also unlocks the steering column, an anti-theft feature.

Ignition System

The ignition system consists of the battery, coil, **distributor**, condenser, **ignition switch**, plugs and related wiring that provides the spark to ignite the air-fuel mixture in the combustion chamber.

Corvette ignition systems have continued to evolve. The **C5** ignition system has no distributor but has multiple coils mounted with the **spark plugs**. In this configuration the crank sensor is part of the ignition system as well.

Impeller

An impeller is a rotating wheel with vanes used in pumps to circulate fluids. Impellers are found in engine **water pumps**; the **torque converter** of an **automatic transmission** is also an impeller.

Independent Rear Suspension (IRS)

IRS is a suspension system that permits each rear wheel to react to the road surface independently of anything that affects the other wheel. The **limited slip differential** is mounted on the chassis and two **half shafts** deliver power

Typical Mid-Year/Shark **independent rear suspension**

from the differential to the wheels. The transverse **leaf spring** independent rear suspension introduced on the 1963 Corvette remained basically unchanged until the 1984 model year when the **trailing arm** was replaced with a pair links to introduce anti squat. With the **C3** and **C4** designs, **camber** was controlled by a lateral **camber rod** (also called a **strut rod**) under the half shaft that connected the bottom of the differential to the bottom of the wheel hub. The trailing arm (C3) or trailing rods (C4) attached with rubber bushings to the frame and defined fore and aft control of the wheel.

The 1984–1996 IRS still used the **U-jointed** half-shafts as suspension lateral link members. The **C5** used an IRS with distinct upper and lower control arms and steer links much like an independent front suspension. In this configuration

Inspection marks on the rear suspension of a 1978 Corvette Pace Car

the final drive shafts had to change length with the ride, so a plunging pot-jointed shaft was used.

Injection
See F*uel Injection*.

Inspection Marks
The quality assurance marks placed on various Corvette components while the car is being built as it moves down the assembly line are known as inspection marks. In the early days of Corvette construction these inspection marks were stamped, while now they are usually made with crayon or grease pencil.

Instrument Cluster
The instrument cluster is a grouping of various gauges in the **dashboard**. See *additional photo on page 95*.

Intake Manifold
The intake manifold is a casting with tubular chambers that the air-fuel mixture flows through to reach the **intake ports**. Corvette intake manifolds are made of cast iron, aluminum or now, high temperature plastic.

Intake Ports
The intake ports are the passages in the **cylinder head** through which the air-

The **instrument cluster** of a Mid-Year Corvette

fuel mixture flows from the **carburetor** or **fuel injection**, through the **intake manifold** to the **intake valves**.

Intake Valves
The **valves** in the **cylinder head** that are activated by the **camshaft** to open allowing the air-fuel charge into the

cylinders are called intake valves. The valves then close to seal and become part of the combustion chamber during the compression and power strokes.

IRS
See *Independent Rear Suspension*.

A big block Corvette tri-power aluminum **intake manifold**

The four large rectangular holes are the **intake ports**; the smaller holes are passages for cooling fluid.

J is for...

Jim Jeffords

Jim Jeffords began the 1957 season at Sebring as a driver on the Chevrolet Corvette Racing Team. He was invited to help form a Corvette race team for Chicago-based Nickey Chevrolet in 1958. Jeffords was virtually unbeatable as he easily took the titles in 1958 and 1959 in the Nickey Chevrolet "Purple People Eater" Corvette. See the full entry on page 102.

Jack

The device used to lift a car, primarily for changing a tire, is known as a jack. From 1953 through 1996 Corvettes always came equipped with scissor jacks. Since 1997 when Extended Mobility Tires (EMT) became standard equipment on **C5**s, no spare tires or jacks have been included with the cars, with the exception of the **Z06** which does not use EMT tires. The Z06 comes equipped with a jack, a compressor and a can of aerosol tire sealant.

Scissor **jacks** like this one were standard equipment with all C1–C4 Corvettes.

Jack Stands

Jack stands are adjustable pyramid-shaped supports used in pairs or groups of four to support a car that has been raised for maintenance, repair or storage. Though usually made of steel, aluminum and **magnesium** can also be used for jack stands.

Jeffords, James "Jim" (1926–)

James "Jim" Jeffords was a two-time National Driving Champion, recognized for his performance in Nickey Chevrolet's "Purple People Eater", and Chevrolet powered specials like Jerry Earl's **SR-2**, the Scarab, and the Chevrolet-engined Maserati Birdcage. Jeffords began racing in the early 1950s and he drove in the first **Road America** race at Elkhart Lake in September 1955. His spectacular early success earned him his first ride in a Corvette in May of 1956 at Road America. Jim maintained his close association with Corvette over the next

Typical **jack stand**

five years, competing first in the World Championship race in Caracas, Venezuela and then ending the season at Nassau Speed Week in December of 1956.

He began the 1957 season at **Sebring**, Florida, as a driver on the Chevrolet Corvette Racing Team. Jim was invited to help form a Corvette race team for Chicago-based Nickey Chevrolet in 1958. Jeffords was virtually unbeatable as he easily took the titles in 1958 and 1959 in the Nickey Chevrolet "Purple People Eater" Corvette.

In February of 1960 Jefford's driving skill and reputation landed him behind the wheel of Lucky Casner's Camoradi Corvette. Jeffords drove it to a first place in the Grand Premio de la Habana in February of 1960 and followed it with an eighth overall (first GT) in the Grand Premio de la Cuba on February 27. Jeffords pioneered the use of the fuel-injection and **RPO 684** (heavy duty racing suspension) to create bulletproof racing machines. Jeffords has served on the

Board of Directors at Road America since 1958 and in 2002 he was inducted into the **National Corvette Museum**'s Hall of Fame. See *additional photo on page 101*.

Jet

A jet is a calibrated nozzle in a **carburetor** through which fuel is drawn through and mixed with air. Carburetors contain several jets including the idle, main and power jets. These various jets insure the proper combustible mixture is available for all conditions of engine load and speed. Carburetor jets can be changed to increase the engine's performance or enhance fuel economy.

Johnny Lightning

Manufactured by Playing Mantis, the Johnny Lightning series of **die cast models** features several Corvettes as well as other vehicles. See the *Suppliers and Services Appendix*.

Corvette racer and inventor **Jim Jeffords**

One of the 50 **Johnny Lightning** Limited Edition die cast models commemorating the Corvette's 50th anniversary

J-Stroke

A street racer's slang term, a J-stroke is produced by first starting in reverse and accelerating hard to make the tires spin; while the tires are still spinning in reverse you engage a forward gear (much easier with an automatic transmission where you shift from R to D) and continue burning rubber in a forward direction. The car's rear tires typically will move sideways somewhat resulting in burned rubber marks on the road in the shape of a J. Corvettes equipped with Positraction produced two J-strokes side-by-side, whereas non-posi cars produce a single J-stroke. This childish and irresponsible practice was primarily engaged in during the late 1960s and early 1970s when manufacturers warranted their cars for five years/50,000 miles. Since "laying J-strokes" quickly destroys tires, rear axles, differentials, **u-joints** and transmissions, few individuals in their right minds do this if they have to pay for the damage. Corvettes are designed and tested to tolerate this kind of abuse. See also *Burn Out*.

Jump Start

This term describes using heavy duty cables with spring-loaded clamps at each end to connect the battery of one car to the dead or weak battery of another. The connections of the cables are positive-to-positive and negative-to-negative from the source and recipient batteries. The source car is usually running to prevent depletion of its own battery power.

Junkyard

See *Boneyard*.

K is for...

Knock-Off Wheels

Knock-off wheels were optional aluminum wheels manufactured by Kelsey-Hayes and offered for the Corvette from 1963 to 1966. These wheels featured a special hub with a single large winged nut that held the wheels on. Faster to change than bolt-on wheels, knock-off wheels were favored for racing. See the full entry on page 107.

Kelsey-Hayes

Kelsey-Hayes has been a major supplier of wheels for the Corvette over the last 50 years, including steel rally wheels, the aluminum **knock-off wheels**, aluminum **bolt-on wheels** and a wide assortment of aftermarket wheels for the Corvette and other marques.

The Hayes Wheel Company was founded by C. B. Hayes in 1908 and was originally located in Albion, Michigan. In 1927 Hayes merged with the Kelsey Wheel Company, and in 1930 moved to Jackson, Michigan. Kelsey-Hayes is now based in Romulus, Michigan. At one time, the firm manufactured 50 percent of all automotive wheel hubs in the United States. See also *Rally Wheels*.

Kerbeck Corvettes

Located in Atlantic City, New Jersey, Kerbeck has been the world's largest Corvette dealer since 1994, selling more Corvettes than any other dealership. Kerbeck also owns the original 1953 **Motorama** Corvette, **EX-122**. See the *Suppliers and Services Appendix*.

Kickdown

A kickdown is a device linked to the accelerator on a car equipped with an **automatic transmission** that permits the driver to select a lower gear for increased acceleration or hill climbing by depressing the throttle pedal. By "kicking down" the accelerator pedal, the automatic transmission switches to a lower gear, which is the equivalent of downshifting a manual transmission.

King Of The Hill

King of the Hill is a nickname for the **ZR-1** Corvette.

King of the Hill was a popular nickname for the potent ZR-1. This was the only view most people ever saw of an accelerating ZR-1.

Knoch, Al
See *Al Knoch Interiors*.

Knock-Off Wheels, K.O. Wheels
Knock-off wheels were optional aluminum wheels manufactured by **Kelsey-Hayes** and offered for the Corvette from 1963 to 1966. These wheels featured a special hub with a single large winged nut that held the wheels on. Knock-off wheels had been used in racing because they were much faster to change than traditional bolted-on wheels. The winged nuts were beaten on and off with a copper or lead hammer. Knock-off wheels are very attractive and genuine original Kelsey-Hayes knock-offs increase the value of **mid-year** Corvettes significantly because they are so rare. As nice as they look, however, serious safety problems are a very real concern. The center lock nut must be kept tight or the wheels can come off the car while it is in motion, resulting in disaster. Many reproduction knock-off wheels offered today use a safety pin to prevent the knock-off spinner from loosening and coming off. See *photo on page 105*.

Ko-Motion
Ko-Motion was a specially-prepared 1967 Marlboro Maroon Corvette Roadster owned by **Charlie "Astoria Chas" Snyder** in Astoria, New York. The car was purchased from **Baldwin Chevrolet** and modified by **Joel Rosen**, who owned **Motion Performance**. An L88 crate engine, ordered through Baldwin's parts manager, John Mahler, was installed in the car and the frame was gusset-welded by Baldwin to prevent twisting from the additional torque. Snyder raced at the local drag strip frequently, turning 11.5-second times at 124 mph, and won repeatedly in the car he named "Ko-Motion." He was killed in Vietnam in August, 1968. The car, raced posthumously by Mahler and Rosen, set the A/Corvette World Record with an **ET** of 11.04 seconds at 129

A limited edition Ertl Racing Champions model of **Ko-Motion** in 1/18 scale

mph. Further modifications to the car resulted in a 10.74 second elapsed time at National Speedway in New York, with the accomplishment registered in Snyder's name. See also *Ertl/Racing Champions.*

Konner, Malcolm (1941–1983)

Malcolm Konner was the founder of Malcolm Konner Chevrolet located in Paramus, New Jersey. The dealership was an early supporter of the Corvette and consistently sold them in high volume. See also *Malcolm Konner Special Edition Corvettes.*

L is for...

L

Ever since 1963 all Corvette engines
have been known as **L series engines**,
using the first letter of their RPO codes.
This 454 cid LS6 engine offered in 1971
Corvettes generated a massive 425 bhp.
See the full entry on page 110.

L

L Series Engines

Since 1963 Corvette engines have been designated by their **RPO** codes, all of which start with the letter L. See also *Big Block, Small Block*. See *drawing on page 109*.

1963

L75	300hp	AFB
L76	340hp	AFB, Hi-Lift cam
L84	360hp	FI, Hi-Lift cam

1964

L75	300hp	AFB
L76	365hp	Holley, Hi-Lift cam
L84	375hp	FI, Hi-Lift cam

1965

L75	327/300hp	
L79	327/350hp	AFB, hydraulic lifters, Hi-Lift cam
L76	327/365hp	Hi-Lift cam
L84	375hp	FI, Hi-Lift cam
L78	396/425hp	

1966

L79	327/350hp
L36	427/390hp
L72	427/425hp

1967

L79	327/350hp	
L36	427/390hp	
L68	427/400hp	
L71	427/435hp	
L88	427/430hp	
L89	435hp	Aluminum heads

1968

L79	327/350hp	
L36	427/390hp	
L68	427/400hp	
L88	427/430hp	
L71	427/435hp	
L89	435hp	Aluminum heads

1969

L46	350/350hp	
L36	427/390hp	
L68	427/400hp	
L88	427/430hp	
L71	427/435hp	
L89	435hp	Aluminum heads

1970

L46	350/350hp
LT1	350/370hp
LS5	454/390hp

1971

LT1	350/370hp
LS5	454/390hp
LS6	454/425hp

1972

LT1	350/255hp
LS5	454/270hp

1973

L82	350/250hp
LS4	454/275hp

1974

L82	350/250hp
LS4	454/270hp

1975
  L48   350/165hp
  L82   350/205hp

1976
  L48   350/180hp
  L82   350/210hp

1977
  L48   350/185hp
  L82   350/210hp

1978
  L48   350/185hp
  L82   350/220hp

1979
  L48   350/195hp
  L82   350/225hp

1980
  LG4   305/180hp   California legal
  L48   350/190hp
  L82   350/230hp

1981
  L81   350/190hp   Legal for 50 states.
                    No optional engines
                    offered.

1982
  L83   350/200hp   Legal for 50 states.
                    No optional engines
                    offered.

1984
  L83   350/205hp   Legal for 50 states.
                    No optional engines
                    offered.

1985
  L98   350/230hp   No optional engines
                    offered.

1986
  L98   350/230hp   Iron heads
  L98   350/235hp   Aluminum heads

1987
  L98   350/240hp   No optional engines
                    offered.

1988
  L98   350/240hp   Convertible & coupes
                    with 2.59:1 axle ratio
  L98   350/245hp   Coupes with 3.07:1
                    axle ratio

1989
  L98   350/240hp   Convertible & coupes
                    with 2.59:1 axle ratio
  L98   350/245hp   Coupes with 3.07:1
                    axle ratio

1990
  L98   350/245hp   Convertible & coupes
                    with 2.59:1 axle ratio
  L98   350/250hp   Coupes with 3.07:1
                    and 3.33:1 axle ratios
  LT5   350/375hp   Avail. on ZR-1 only

1991
  L98   350/240hp   Convertible & coupes
                    with 2.59:1 axle ratio
  L98   350/245hp   Coupes with 3.07:1
                    and 3.33:1 axle ratios
  LT5   350/375hp   Avail. on ZR-1 only

1992
  LT1   350/300hp
  LT5   350/375hp   Avail. on ZR-1 only

1993
  LT1   350/300hp
  LT5   350/405hp   Avail. on ZR-1 only

L

1994

LT1	350/300hp	
LT5	350/405hp	Avail. on ZR-1 only

1995

LT1	350/300hp	
LT5	350/405hp	Avail. on ZR-1 only

1996

LT1	350/300hp	
LT4	350/330hp	Only available with manual transmission

1997

LS1	350/345hp

1998

LS1	350/345hp

1999

LS1	350/345hp

2000

LS1	350/345hp

2001

LS1	350/345hp	
LS6	350/385hp	Avail. on Z06 only

2002

LS1	350/345hp	
LS6	350/405hp	Avail. on Z06 only

2003

LS1	350/345hp	
LS6	350/405hp	Avail. on Z06 only

2004

LS1	350/345hp	
LS6	350/405hp	Avail. on Z06 only

Lace

Lace describes a type of custom paint in which patterns that looked like lace were painted on the car. Often the technique involved using actual lace cloth through which paint was sprayed. This was a popular customizing fad during the late 1960s through the mid 1970s.

Lacquer

Lacquer, specifically nitro-cellulose lacquer, is a type of paint that was used on early Corvettes from 1953 through late 1981. With the opening of the **Bowling Green**, Kentucky, Corvette assembly plant in June of 1981, a **urethane** enamel, base coat/clear coat paint system was introduced. Nitro-cellulose lacquer paint was subject to cracking and fading over time and, due to EPA restrictions, is not legally available in the United States due to its high toxicity. Acrylic automotive lacquers are legally available, but they are not as popular as the base coat/clear coat finishes which yield a better overall finish and much higher gloss.

Lake Pipes

Lake pipes were performance exhaust pipes that usually ran along the outside rocker panel of the car. Due to the fact that they had no mufflers, they were ticket magnets for cruisers equipped with them.

Lake pipes should not be confused with Corvette **side exhausts**. Lake pipes tend to get very hot due to the exhaust gases flowing through them, whereas Corvette side exhausts have an outside covering that remains relatively cool. Drivers of cars with lake pipes generally have burn

marks on the backs of their legs from exiting over the hot exhaust pipe.

Laminated Glass

Laminated glass, also called safety glass, consists of a thin layer of rubbery plastic sandwiched between two sheets of annealed glass. Like any annealed glass, the windshield is easily broken. It is the plastic interlayer that keeps it together. Laminated windshields are required on all cars sold in the United States. Laminated glass tends to crack so as to not seriously impair vision as opposed to tempered glass that breaks into many small pieces..

Large Journal

Large journal refers to the journal size of the **crankshaft** of the **small block** Chevrolet engine. The main journals were 2.450 inches diameter and the rod journals were 2.100 inches diameter. See also *Small Journal*.

Lateral Acceleration

The term lateral acceleration refers to the sideways acceleration which is measured in g's. As a car moves through a curve, centrifugal force acts on it and tries to pull it outward; to counteract this, the tires develop an equal and opposite force acting against the road. Lateral acceleration is usually measured on a skid pad.

Lauve, Henry (1910–1998)

Henry deSégur Lauve designed the original **EX-122 Motorama** Corvette. Lauve, born in 1910, studied art at the Sorbonne in Paris and later did post-graduate work at art schools in Vienna and Rotterdam. He proved to be an incredibly talented illustrator and worked in the Paris fashion industry in the 1930s. Lauve joined GM in 1939 and he became the chief designer at Buick during the 1940s. In 1950 he was named GM's interior design chief and he also worked on advanced vehicles. His talent was keenly observed by **Harley Earl,** who recruited him for his private design studio. As was Earl's prerogative, he set the agenda and tone for his department and relied on his talented team of hands-on designers to execute his theme.

Working under Earl's directive, Lauve penned the sweeping lines of the prototype Corvette. Lauve was originally slated to become Earl's successor as the head of GM's Art and Colour Department when Earl retired in 1958. When **Bill Mitchell** learned of Earl's plan, he influenced Earl to give him the job instead. Once Mitchell became the top man, Lauve's fate was sealed: Mitchell cleaned house of Earl's top designers, and Lauve was among the first to go.

LCD

See *Liquid Crystal Display.*

Le Mans

Le Mans, France, is the home of the 24 Hours of Le Mans, a 24-hour endurance race traditionally held in June of every year. Corvette **C5Rs,** the official Chevrolet-sponsored race-prepared Corvettes, have had a very respectable showing since they started entering the event in 1997. Corvettes first raced at Le Mans in 1960.

A typical Corvette steel **leaf spring** on a Shark

Lead-Free Gasoline

Gasoline without any tetraethyl lead or other lead compounds added to increase its octane rating and reduce its knock or detonation tendencies is know as lead-free. **Catalytic converters** are chemically poisoned by the lead additives in gasoline. The Corvette first required unleaded gas in 1975, the year it was equipped with a catalytic converter.

Leaf Spring

A leaf spring is composed of one or more long, slightly curved and flexible steel (or composite **fiberglass**) plates. Plates (or leaves) of diminishing lengths are mounted on top of each other and clamped together. The material, length, thickness and number of leaves determines the flexibility and load capacity of the spring. The Corvette has always used leaf springs in the rear and they have used them in the front of the car since 1984. The Corvette has used fiberglass/epoxy composite springs since 1981. See also *Monoleaf Spring*.

LED

See *Light Emitting Diode*.

Lifters

Also called "cam followers" or "tappets," lifters are small cylindrical objects that ride on the lobes of the **camshaft** and push the **pushrods** up to open the **valves**. There are two basic types of lifters: hydraulic and solid. There are also two kinds of surface contact with the cam lobe, sliding and rolling. Hydraulic lifters are a cylinder and piston that fills with engine oil under pressure to take up the slack in the upper **valve train**. Low oil pressure, loss of pressure from the lifters or plugged oil holes in the lifters can result in a "clattering" sound that's referred to as "noisy lifters." Hydraulic lifters do not require periodic adjustment. As the name implies, solid lifters are solid cylinders that make full mechanical contact with the cam lobes and pushrods. Preferred for racing and other high-performance applications because of their lighter weight, solid lifters require periodic adjustment to

maintain the correct amount of valve lash. Roller lifters have a small roller on the camshaft side that actually rolls on the lobes of the cam reducing friction; roller lifters can be either hydraulic or mechanical (solid). Each type of lifter, because of the different curvatures of the cam contact surface requires different cam lobe profiles to achieve the same opening/closing result.

Light-Emitting Diode (LED)

A light-emitting diode is a semiconductor diode that emits light when a current flows through it. LEDs can emit infrared, red, orange, yellow, green or blue light. They are used in brake/tail light and CHMSLs (Center, high-mounted stop lamps) among their many automotive applications.

Limited Slip Differential

A differential is required so that the inside and outside drive wheels can run at different speeds when negotiating a tight curve. Without a differential the axle will "crow-hop" as the tires are forced to skid on the road. The simple open differential, however, can only transmit as much torque as is available to the tire carrying the lowest weight and experiencing the lowest coefficient of friction. With a solid axle (C1 and C2 Corvettes) this can mean that virtually no torque can be transmitted in a right hand turn as load transfer and axle torque reaction conspire to unload the right tire. The limited slip differential recouples the two wheels so that maximum torque can be transmitted while allowing the car to negotiate turns without "crow-hopping." Limited slip differentials use cone or disc **clutches**, viscous fluid,

or gears or cams to torque-couple the otherwise independent axle shafts together, forcing both wheels to transmit drive torque regardless of the traction available to either one. The limited slip differential used in Corvettes is known as a **positraction**. In this design, a disc clutch in the differential couples the two wheel shafts together. The clutch is preloaded with springs so it always transmits some torque. This is called the bias. The clutch pack is also squeezed by the reaction force of the differential's bevel side gears. This reaction force is directly proportional to the torque being transmitted by the differential. Thus as the input torque to the differential is increased, the side thrust load on the bevel side gears compresses the clutch pack adding to the torque that can be transmitted through the differential.

Line Lock

Useful at the **drag strip**, a line lock is a scheme for locking the brakes on the front wheels without having the brakes applied to the rear wheels. By locking the front wheels, the rear wheels can be spun to heat up the tires, thus enabling a better launch on a drag strip.

Lingenfelter, John (1945–2003)

John Lingenfelter was a well-known NHRA driver, engineer and super-tuner of **small block** Chevrolet engines. His twin turbo and supercharged Corvettes are among his most innovative creations. Lingenfelter was critically injured during a NHRA Summit Sports Compact drag racing event at Pomona, California, on October 27, 2002, when he hit a retaining wall at approximately 190 mph in an attempt to set a world record. After

L

John Lingenfelter is best known for his performance engines.

approximately a year in a semi-comatose state following surgery, Lingenfelter died on December 25, 2003.

Lingenfelter Performance Engineering

Founded and run by the late **John Lingenfelter**, Lingenfelter Performance Engineering is a well-known and highly regarded source of performance components for Corvettes in addition to performing modifications that include twin turbos and superchargers to increase the speed and performance of Corvettes and other marques. Lingenfelter Engineering sells a street-legal Twin Turbo **C5** rated at 750 hp. They have continued to develop this package which now produces 930 hp. See the *Suppliers and Services Appendix.*

Linkage

Linkage refers to any series or combination of rods and levers used to transmit motion from one component to another, such as the linkage from the accelerator pedal to the **carburetor** or the **gearshift** lever to the transmission.

Liquid Crystal Display (LCD)

An LCD is a thin, sealed sandwich of filament liquid crystal material between two glass plates. The glass plates are cross polarized on their first and fourth surfaces so that light is not transmitted through the sandwich. The second and third glass surfaces are coated with an almost invisible conducting layer formed in the pattern of the display. The conducting layers are connected back to a computer and power supply. The liquid crystal material has the unique property of being able to rotate polarized light. In the off state the material is randomly oriented. When charged between the conducting layers, the material takes on an orientation that twists the polarized light output of the first and aligns it with the second polarizer, lighting the display element. A colored mask can add a full spectrum of color to the display. LCDs were first used for **digital instrumentation** readouts on the 1984 Corvette.

Lobe

Lobes are the egg-shaped protrusions on a **camshaft** that, during rotation, activate the **pushrods** which cause the **intake** and exhaust **valves** to open and close. Lobes are also used on other devices, such as mechanical distributors. See also *Valve Train.*

Logic Module

The logic module is an electronic control unit that contains a small computer

that performs control functions such as metering the **fuel injection** and controlling the ignition, among other tasks. The logic module debuted as standard equipment on the 1981 Corvette.

Long Block

Called a "Targetmaster" engine by GM, a long block refers to a replacement engine assembly that includes the block, crank, cam, **pistons**, rods, heads, **valve train** components, **timing gears** and chain all assembled and ready to install. The **oil pump** is also usually installed as well; it may be carbureted or fuel injected, and can be ordered configured for either a **manual** or **automatic transmission**. Long blocks are ordered through Chevrolet or other marque dealerships for various vehicles.

Long Island Corvette Supply

Long Island Corvette Supply is a major source of restoration and accessory parts for **Mid-Year** (1963–1967) Corvettes only. See the *Suppliers and Services Index*.

Loud Pedal

Loud pedal is a slang term for the accelerator pedal.

Low Beam

The low beam is the primary filament in a two-headlight system or the main (dual-filament) headlights of a four-light system. The low beams are used for most urban night driving situations and against oncoming traffic.

Low Gear

Low gear is first gear in a **manual transmission**, and it is used to start the vehicle in motion from a standing stop. In **automatic transmissions** it is usually designated "L" (low) or "1" (first).

Low Tire Pressure Warning Indicator

The low tire pressure warning indicator was first offered as an option (UJ6) on the 1989 Corvette. Tire pressure is constantly monitored and when the pressure falls below a preset threshold, the indicator light on the dash panel becomes illuminated to warn the driver of the condition. With the **C5** the driver can read individual tire pressures as well.

Ludvigsen, Karl (1934–)

Considered one of the world's foremost automotive journalists and historians, Karl Ludvigsen has served on the staffs of *Auto Age*, *Sports Car Illustrated* and *Motor Trend*, and is a former editor of *Car and Driver*. He has also held management positions within General Motors, Fiat and Ford. Several of his most

L

Author **Karl Ludvigsen**

notable books include *Porsche: Excellence Was Expected* (Bentley Publishers, 2003), and what many consider to be the premier book about Corvette, *Corvette: America's Star Spangled Sports Car* (Princeton Publishing, 1978).

Lug Nuts
The nuts that fasten the wheels to the wheel spindle studs are known as the lug nuts. They usually have a 45-degree conical seat to enhance their clamping performance.

Lumbar Support
The lumbar support is a feature of the seat back and can be adjusted to provide support to the lower lumbar region of the driver's back. Lumbar support was included in the Sport Seat Option (AQ9) that became available with the 1984 Corvette.

M is for...

Dave McLellan

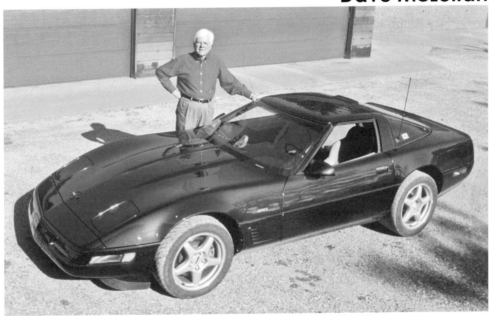

In 1975 **Dave McLellan** succeeded
Zora Arkus-Duntov as Corvette chief
engineer. McLellan's low-key style
hid an intense bulldog determination
to find a path to greater glory for the
Corvette, which resulted in the all-new
1984 Corvette. Both the C4 and the
mighty ZR-1 (shown) were products
of McLellan's watch as Corvette chief
engineer. See the full entry on page 125.

M

M20, M21

Muncie four-speed transmissions designated M20 and M21 were used in C2 and C3 Corvettes. The M20 was the four-speed option code for 1963–1965 with the wide ratio (2.54:1 first gear) or close ratio (2.20) being determined by the engine option. In 1963, the M20 was a Borg Warner T10D transmission until January when a switch to the Muncie was made. In 1966, the M20 code referred only to the wide ratio four-speed and M21 referred to the close ratio four-speed. During the 1970s M20 also stood for the new Borg Warner four-speed, the Saginaw four-speed in 1977 and again the Borg Warner (2.64).

M22

The M22 was the heavy duty version of the **M21**, Muncie four-speed transmission, also known as the "rock crusher" due to the excessive noise it produced. The gears were cut at a much lower angle to yield a higher torque rating; this cut angle made it very noisy but permitted it to handle much more powerful motors than standard-cut gears. The M22 was only available with certain engines, such as the L88, **ZL1** and the ZR1 packages of the 1970s.

M40

M40 was the option code for the three-speed **torque converter automatic transmission** used from 1968 to 1981. (The M35 was the designation for the **Powerglide** used from 1953 thru 1967.) In 1976 the L82 used the TurboHydramatic 400 while the base L48 had the TurboHydramatic 350.

MAF (Mass Air Flow Sensor)

MAF is an abbreviation for the mass air flow sensor used with the **tuned-port injection** to determine the demands on the engine and adjust fuel delivery accordingly.

Bosch originated the MAF and this was the first one used in Corvettes. It was succeeded by the Speed Density system which was ultimately replaced by the AC-Delco system. See *Corvette Fuel Injection* by Charles Probst (Bentley Publishers, ISBN 0-8376-0861-9) for a comprehensive discussion of Corvette fuel injection.

Magnaflux® Crack Detection Process

Magnaflux® is a registered trademark of the Magnaflux Corporation for its magnetic dye penetrant testing which is a particle inspection process for detecting cracks in steel or iron parts such as engine blocks, connecting rods, **crankshafts** and heads. The metal is magnetized, submerged in magnetic dye and examined under black light; any cracks appear as red lines on the surface. It is not the only such process but is the most well-known, and usually performed as part of a total engine overhaul or **restoration**, as well as during race preparation.

Magnesium

Magnesium is a light, ductile silver-white metal that is often used to replace aluminum to save weight. More expensive than aluminum, magnesium is approximately 35 percent lighter. Perhaps the most common automotive

use of magnesium is in cast transmission cases, some engine parts and occasionally wheels. Production alloy wheels, often called "mag wheels" are usually made of aluminum. The 1981 Corvette used magnesium valve covers to save weight to meet EPA mileage requirements. In addition, Showroom Stock Corvette race cars used magnesium wheels.

Main Bearings
The main bearings are the bearings that locate and support the **crankshaft**. The caps for these bearings are secured by two bolts (two bolt mains) or sometimes four bolts (four bolt mains) each.

Mako Shark I (XP-755)
The Mako Shark was originally built on a 1961 chassis and debuted in 1962 as one of **Bill Mitchell**'s styling exercises. It was dubbed The **Shark,** but was renamed the Mako Shark I when Mitchell's design

team produced the 1965 Mako Shark, the styling model for the 1968 Corvette.

Mako Shark II
The Mako Shark II was **Bill Mitchell**'s 1965 Corvette design exercise. While the 1965 showcar was only a styling model, Mitchell's studio produced a fully running, functional styling car for 1966. This car was the basic styling model for the 1968 Corvette. It was later redesigned and called the Manta Ray showcar.

The **Mako Shark II** showcar was the basic design for the 1968 Corvette.

M

The original Shark showcar was rechristened the **Mako Shark I**.

Malcolm Konner Special Edition Corvettes

The Malcolm Konner Special Edition Corvettes were built by special arrangement with the Malcolm Konner Chevrolet Dealership in Paramus, New Jersey, in order to commemorate the dealership's founder, **Malcolm Konner**, and his contribution to the success of early Corvettes. All coupes, 50 of these Corvettes were built and twenty had **manual transmissions**, with the remainder equipped with **automatics**. The option (**RPO 4001ZA**) consisted of a special silver-beige on black two-tone paint scheme and graphite leather interior and cost $500. Ten manuals and ten automatics) were built with RPO **Z51** heavy-duty suspensions. One of the Malcolm Konner Special Edition Corvettes became the first **Callaway Twin Turbo** engine conversion.

Mallet Cars, Ltd.

A leading supplier of Corvette performance parts and conversions and a GM contractor that works with the GM Powertrain division. See the *Supplier and Service Appendix.*

Manifold Vacuum

This refers to the vacuum that is created inside the **intake manifold** between the throttle butterfly and the **piston** as it moves downward in the cylinder, sucking in charge during the intake stroke.

Manta Ray

By the time the **C3** Corvette debuted in 1968, the **Mako Shark II** was already old news, so it was decided to do a major restyling of the Mako Shark II and unveil it as the Manta Ray for the showcar circuit in 1969. The biggest styling change was the long, graceful tail reminiscent of the **Astro-Vette** showcar, although other changes were significant as well, including the new all-aluminum **ZL1** engine, and **Bill Mitchell**'s signature side pipes.

Manual Transmission

A manual transmission, also called a stick-shift transmission, is a **drivetrain** component that has various gearsets

The Mako Shark II show car was restyled for 1969 and dubbed the **Manta Ray**.

contained within it which multiply the torque and reduce the rotation speed of the engine, delivering power to the drive wheels of the vehicle. Although these gearsets could be selected by either column-mounted or floor-mounted levers, on Corvettes the shift levers have always been floor-mounted. A friction **clutch** actuated by a pedal is used in conjunction with the shift lever to decouple the engine from the transmission during shifting. This effects smooth gear selection by gradually introducing friction to the **flywheel** as the pedal is released to engage the transmission with the engine's rotation.

Map Pocket
In 1968, with the debut of the **C3 Shark** Corvettes, conventional **glove boxes** were eliminated and replaced with a map pocket on the passenger side of the **dashboard**. The map pockets lasted through 1977 and glove boxes again returned to Corvettes in 1978.

Marlboro Motor Raceway
Marlboro Motor Raceway was a 1.7-mile, counterclockwise road course

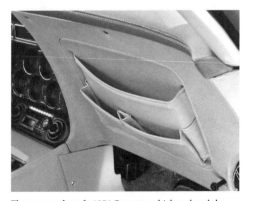

The **map pocket** of a 1976 Corvette, which replaced the conventional glove box from 1968 through1977

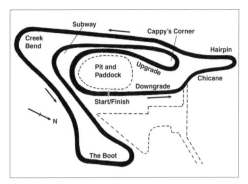

The track layout of the **Marlboro Motor Raceway** in Maryland

built around a short oval near Marlboro, Maryland. It opened in 1955, and was still in use in the 1960s, hosting, among other things, early **Trans Am** races and other **SCCA** events.

Martin, John (1939–)
John Martin was a St. Louis area Corvette racer in the mid 1960s who was the only Corvette racer to place in the **SCCA** Divisional Championships in 1965 when Cobras were reigning supreme. He later raced Indy cars at Indianapolis and then became the owner of Indy cars and teams.

Matching Numbers
Matching numbers in the most correct sense means that the car's **Vehicle Identification Number** (VIN) matches with the partial VIN on the engine and the one on the transmission. To be a true "matching numbers car," the engine identifier and the transmission identifier also match the options on the **build sheet**. The codes for the other major components such as the rear end, radiator and **alternator** should also match. Many other items plus individual components (i.e., heads, block, **intake manifold**, etc.) also have **date codes**

M

either cast or stamped into them and these should match as well. All too often a seller claims his Corvette has matching numbers when all that matches is the engine casting code and maybe the casting date; frequently the partial VIN doesn't match, is not there, or has been **restamped**. In addition, often the transmission, rear end, alternator, and so on have been ignored or forgotten.

It should be noted, however, that the **NCRS** permits restamping the engine code and VIN and calls it "**restoration**" if it is correctly restamped for the actual engine.

Matching numbers is not the same as original numbers. While an original car will have matching numbers, a car can also be created with matching numbers, a distinction that is often missed.

Mattel Hot Wheels

Mattel's Hot Wheels is a line of **die cast model** Corvettes and other vehicles available in ¹⁄₄₃ scale. Some are available in larger scales as well. See the *Suppliers and Services Appendix*.

McLean, Robert (N/A)

Robert McLean was a young design engineer who worked for **Harley Earl** during the early development of the Corvette. McLean moved the Chevrolet stovebolt six-cylinder engine back seven inches and dropped it three inches lower into a shortened Chevrolet convertible frame. He also designed a lower-profile valve cover and specified using sidedraft carburetion to clear a low hoodline. Earl liked the lower profile and gave McLean and his staff the approval to proceed with

A pair of 50th Anniversary Corvette **Mattel Hot Wheels** models in a plastic display case

a fully trimmed and detailed mock-up. The mock-up was shown to Chevrolet Chief Engineer **Ed Cole** who pushed it to production over the delaying tactics of GM top management.

McLellan, David (1936–)

David R. McLellan was born in Munising, Michigan. After graduating from Wayne State University, he started at General Motors on July 1, 1959, and was assigned to the Milford Proving Grounds. After assignments in vehicle vibration and responsibility for the just-built Vehicle Dynamics Test Area, he moved to Chevrolet, first in Camaro development and then design. Chevrolet sponsored him as an MIT Sloan Fellow in 1973.

In 1975 he succeeded **Zora Arkus-Duntov** as the second chief engineer in Corvette history. He inherited a Corvette that was overweight and saddled with **emissions** hardware. In the late 1970s and early 1980s Corvette performance was an oxymoron. But McLellan's low-key style hid an intense bulldog determination to find a path to greater glory for the Corvette. As a result of his efforts, the all-new 1984 Corvette was state-of-the art in aerodynamics, emissions control, weight savings and electronics.

McLellan began helping Corvette road racers fashion winning programs. To him the race track was an extension of the proving grounds, a view also fostered by Duntov. With lieutenants like **Doug Robinson, John Heinricy, Jim Minneker** and Scott Allman, Dave directed a Corvette endurance racing juggernaut so powerful that it was finally dismissed from **SCCA** competition. In the hands of racing legends like **Kim Baker, Tommy Morrison, Dick Guldstrand, Doug Rippie** and John Powell, Corvettes won all 19 **SCCA** endurance races contested in 1985, 1986 and 1987.

Not to be deterred, McLellan and Chevy's Frank Ellis worked with Powell to launch the million-dollar **Corvette Challenge Series** in 1988. A fabulous showcase for Corvette performance,

M

Dave McClellan, the Corvette's second chief engineer

it was also a convenient venue for final development work on McLellan's penultimate C4 project, the ZR-1.

Featuring Corvette's first double-overhead cam engine and bodywork so subtly altered it could easily be confused with the standard Corvette, the ZR-1 was introduced to the automotive press at the 1989 Geneva Auto Show. It was a stunning debut. Almost 15 years after McLellan took over an orphan car line seemingly unsuited for the modern world, the Corvette was universally acknowledged once again as **King of the Hill**.

On July 2, 1992, McLellan stood by as the one-millionth Corvette was driven off the Bowling Green assembly line. Meanwhile, the next generation Corvette (the **C5**, for 1997 release) was being concepted in Chevrolet R&D and would pass concept initiation just after his retirement in 1992.

McLellan is the author of *Corvette From The Inside* (Bentley Publishers, ISBN 0-8376-0859-7). See *additional photo on page 119.*

Metalflake

Metalflake is a custom paint with a very heavy content of metallic particles that makes the paint sparkle in bright light. Popular with customizers of Corvettes and other cars in the late 1960s through the early 1970s, its poor durability and propensity for cracking relegated it to the "fad paint" category and is rarely used today.

Michaelis, Terry (N/A)

Terry Michaelis was the owner of Terry Michaelis Corvette Supplies, one of the first to offer quality interior parts for restoration of Corvettes in the mid-1970s. A flamboyant entrepreneur, he was known for his publicity stunts for attracting attention to his business. Michaelis also started *Corvette Fever Magazine*. He is said by many to have made and lost millions in Corvettes more times than everyone else put together. Highly controversial, Michaelis is also the founder of Pro-Team Corvette.

Microchip

Often simply called a chip, a microchip is a small silicon wafer with miniature electronic circuitry etched into it that functions as a complete circuit board.

Microprocessor

A microprocessor is a semiconductor-based processing unit and it is the principal component in a microcomputer. C4 and C5 Corvettes use several microprocessors for various engine, **emissions**, vehicle dynamics and body functions.

Mid America Motorworks

Formerly known as Mid America Direct, Mid America Motorworks is a major supplier of Corvette **restoration** parts and accessories. Mid America is also known for its Fun Fest party that attracts some 5,000 to 6,000 Corvettes every September. See the *Suppliers and Services Appendix.*

Mid America Raceway

Located west of St. Louis, Mid America Raceway is a 2.89-mile course with varying elevation changes, a very long straight and ten corners (seven right and three left turns). There are eleven flag

stations, number 11 being on the straight after the drive-over bridge near the end of the **drag strip**. MAR has a drag strip that is slightly short of being a full quarter-mile (1,320 feet) at only 1,200 feet. MAR was the site of the second **Trans Am** and numerous **SCCA** National races.

MAR was built in late 1965 and was the site of the second SCCA Trans Am race in the spring of 1966, following the series opener at **Sebring**. Over the years, MAR has hosted many drag races and road races. St. Louis Region ran its National and Regional races until 1984 when MAR closed its doors to road racing and St. Louis International Raceway (now Gateway International Raceway) opened its new road course in 1985. The drag strip is still in active use.

Mid-Year (Mid-Years)

A Mid-Year Corvette is a **Sting Ray** (C2) built between 1963 and 1967. Although these models are no longer in the middle of Corvette models, the name has stuck since they were made in the middle of the 1960–70 decade.

Miles Per Hour (MPH)

Miles per hour is a measure of speed or velocity that specifies the number of miles a vehicle will travel in one hour at any given speed.

Miller, Bill (1943–)

Bill Miller is the co-founder and co-owner of **Carlisle Events**, and co-owner of the Carlisle, Pennyslvania, Fairgrounds. **Chip Miller** (no relation) was his partner.

William M. Miller Jr. grew up in Central Pennsylvania, graduating from East Pennsboro High School in 1961. He attended college, but his love for automobiles sent him to work full time at a Chevrolet dealership. Bill began as a salesman and worked his way up to sales manager, general manager and eventually dealer. He owned two Chevrolet dealerships—in Downington, Pennsylvania, and Woodbine, New Jersey—a Volkswagen dealership in Carlisle with Chip Miller as partner and a Ford dealership in Elizabethtown, Pennsylvania. He didn't sell his last dealership until 1995, when the events at Carlisle were becoming too popular for Bill to keep both jobs. Over the years Miller has owned hundreds of cars, and he has 16 currently in his garage.

Miller has been in the automotive industry for more than 40 years,

M

Bill Miller, co-owner of Carlisle Events

including the 30 years he's been running the automotive events at the Carlisle Fairgrounds.

Miller, Chip (1942–2004)

Chip Miller was the co-founder and co-owner of **Carlisle Events** and co-owner of the Carlisle, Pennsylivania, Fairgrounds. Elliott S. "Chip" Miller was born in Abington, Pennsylvania, on October 27, 1942, and died March 25, 2004. He graduated from the State University of New York with a degree in mechanical power technology. His first job out of college was at an auto body shop, where he learned how to restore classic cars. He then designed conveyors until 1981, when he and **Bill Miller** (no relation) bought the Carlisle Fairgrounds, and he focused full time on Carlisle Events.

He became fascinated with Corvettes after seeing an ad for a new 1957 Corvette. Chip owned a total of 80 Corvettes in his life and at the time of his death he had more than 25 Corvettes and about 14 other vehicles. He was also interested in racing, especially vintage

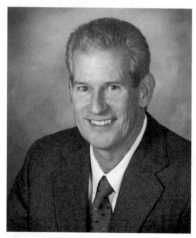

Chip Miller was co-owner of Carlisle Events.

Corvettes. His weekend event, Corvettes at Carlisle in late August each year, brings together as many as 12,000 Corvettes, a wide range of Corvette vendors and a major Corvette auction.

Minneker, Jim (1948–)

Jim Minneker is the Chief of Powertrain Engineering for Corvette and is informally known as the father of the LS1 engine. Additionally, he has successfully raced **ZR-1s** and C5s. Jim is now responsible for the powertrain interface for all GM performance vehicles.

Mitchell, Bill (1912–1988)

William T. Mitchell loved the Corvette more than he loathed the buttoned-down committee-oriented culture of mid-century General Motors. As a result, GM gained enormously from Mitchell's design genius, and Bill was able to indulge his passion for drawing—and driving—fast cars. Bill was hired by GM in December 1935. Less than a year later, he was Chief Designer at Cadillac. Mitchell succeeded **Harley Earl** as GM Design Chief and the Corvette became "his baby."

GM was officially out of racing, so Bill rented a garage near GM's Warren, Michigan, Tech Center and formed his own team. He bought and rebodied **Zora Arkus-Duntov**'s **Sebring** SS mule car, dubbed it the **Stingray**, and hired **Dr. Dick Thompson**—the Washington, D.C. dentist—to do the driving. The car was **SCCA** C-Production champion in 1960. It has since been celebrated as the missing link between the SS and the **Grand Sports** of 1963, and quite possibly the most successful factory racer in the history of the marque.

Mitchell battled against the notion of a four-seat Corvette and won. He took on divisional general managers, salespeople, engineers, bean counters and anyone else who attempted to tamper with his baby. He wrote in 1977 that "a good designer has to be creative, and to be creative you have to be dissatisfied and discontent. It makes for a terrible personality."

Mitchell and Zora Arkus-Duntov often had heated arguments about the Corvette which Mitchell, who was in the more powerful position, invariably won, at least in the short run. An example of Mitchell's overbearing behavior was the split rear window of the 1963 Corvette coupe, which Duntov vehemently opposed. Mitchell won that match and the split window went into production, albeit for just one year.

Mitchell hated committees almost as much as market research. "You can line up any group of cars from the past to the present and I'll bet I can tell you which ones were committee-designed and which

Corvette Design Chief **Bill Mitchell**

ones we left to the designer. The 1967 F cars—too many fingers in the pie; the 1970 F cars—they were never touched by a committee." Said he of market research: "Frank Lloyd Wright did not go around ringing doorbells asking people what kind of houses they wanted. There is not one good-looking car I designed that market research had anything to do with." Bill Mitchell died on September 12, 1988. He was inducted into the **National Corvette Museum**'s Hall of Fame in 1998.

MN6

MN6 was the option code for the six-speed manual transmission on Corvettes from 1989 through 2004.

Modulator

A modulator is a pressure-regulating device in **automatic transmissions** used to vary internal oil pressure to meet engine requirements.

Monoleaf Spring

A monoleaf spring is a spring made with a single leaf as opposed to the traditional multi-leaf spring. The single leaf is made variable in width and thickness to give it constant strain properties along its length. This is the most efficient use of the material in a spring application. These springs can be made of steel, **fiberglass** or a filament graphite/fiberglass matrix. Monoleaf rear springs were first used on 1981 Corvettes equipped with **automatic transmissions** (**manual transmission** and FE7 1981 Corvettes still used steel multi-leaf rear springs). The **C4** used fiberglass monoleaf springs front and rear. Monoleaf springs are used front and rear on the **C6**. See also *Leaf Spring*.

M

Monterey Historic Automobile Races

The Historic Automobile Races are the largest event held during the renowned classic car weekend in Monterey, California every August. More than 40,000 visitors annually attend the Historic Races, which greatly supports the local charitable contributions of the Sports Car Racing Association of the Monterey Peninsula (SCRAMP). The Rolex Monterey Historic Automobile Races celebrated its 30th year at Laguna Seca Raceway in 2003. The Monterey Historics, as they are popularly known, are a tribute to motor racing history, historic automobiles and the people who made them. Each year more than 375 of the finest historic race and sports cars are entered in 14 race groups that span nearly every era of motorsports history.

Corvette fiberglass body innovator **Robert Morrison**

Morrison, Robert (1910–2002)

Robert Morrison is recognized as the man who developed the molded **fiberglass** (MFG) process for Corvette's fiberglass body. In 1953 the Chevrolet Corvette became the first production automobile with a molded fiberglass reinforced plastic body after Morrison convinced General Motors that reinforced plastic had a place in automotive production.

When Chevrolet agreed to proceed with this material, Morrison initiated all of the necessary financing, production facilities, engineering support, tooling and production personnel to make it happen. He partnered with automotive engineers as well as raw material suppliers which resolved Chevrolet's concerns about a production site, equipment and scheduling.

As the cooperative process developed, the basement of Morrison's home in Ashtabula, Ohio, became an impromptu design center for the 1953 Corvette Convertible fiber glass parts. MFG employees and GM's engineers worked side by side on a ping-pong table until suitable business space was established.

Robert Morrison passed away on September 16, 2002, at the age of 92. He was inducted into the **National Corvette Museum**'s Hall of Fame in 2003.

Morrison, Tommy (1941–)

Kentucky native Tommy Morrison consistently raced Corvettes as a privateer during the 1970s and 1980. After a brief period with legendary Corvette tuner and racer **Dick Guldstrand**, he formed Morrison-Cook Motorsports in the early 1980s. In addition to running very competitively in the **SCCA** Showroom Stock endurance series and in the

subsequent **Corvette Challenge Series**, Morrison led the team that set numerous world speed and endurance records at Fort Stockton, Texas, with **ZR1** and L98 Corvettes in 1990. His likeness is on permanent display in the **National Corvette Museum** in **Bowling Green**.

Motion Performance

In the late 1960s and early 1970s, Motion Performance of Baldwin, Long Island (New York), produced some incredible performance cars using monster motors such as 450hp 350s and 550hp 427s. **Joel Rosen** produced Camaros, Corvettes, Vegas, Novas, and Maco Sharks with various engines, depending on the customer's pocketbook. The Maco Shark was a body kit that transformed the 1968–1976 Corvette into a **Mako Shark II** look-alike. Another car was the Corvette GT, which featured fixed headlights mounted in the upper fenders like the Datsun 240Z. Most came with a Motion Performance **stinger** painted across the tail and along the rear fenders forward. Today, these are rare cars since many were undoubtedly "restored" to their factory original condition. See also *Ko-Motion; Snyder, Charles; Baldwin Chevrolet.*

Motor Mounts

Motor mounts are the rubber and steel supports that elastically connect the engine and transmission to the vehicle frame. These supports absorb the twisting movements of the power train caused by engine torque and abrupt transmission shifts and they also help to isolate the passenger compartment from the noise and vibration produced by the power train.

Some race cars use solid motor mounts, and polyurethane mounts are also available.

Motorama

Motoramas were General Motors-only auto shows that showcased GM's vision for the future. They featured new models and future styling ideas. The shows ran from 1949 to 1961 visiting major cities around the country.

The **EX-122** Corvette was a 1953 Motorama showcar. The public acclaim convinced GM to produce the car for sale.

Mouse, Mouse Motor

"Mouse motor" is a slang nickname for the **small block** Chevrolet engine. Ostensibly, if the **big block** was called a "**rat**" then the small block must be a "mouse".

MPH

See *Miles Per Hour.*

Multi-Port Fuel Injection (MFI)

Multi-Port Fuel Injection uses individual fuel injectors to spray fuel into each **intake port**, downstream of the **intake manifold**. Corvette first received multi-port fuel injection for the 1995 model year.

Muscle Cars

The term "muscle car" was coined for the high horsepower cars built in the mid-1960s through the early 1970s. Examples include Chevelle SS, Plymouth Road Runner, GTX, Dodge Super Bee, Plymouth Baracuda, Dodge Challenger, Charger, Olds 442, GTO, Cyclone,

M

Torino, Pontiac GTO, and others. These cars usually had large engines (around 400 cid) and/or high horsepower that delivered extraordinary performance. Technically speaking, the Corvette has never been regarded as a true muscle car, since it is only a two-seater. The Corvette is a sports car, although it has always been a favorite quarry of street racers driving muscle cars.

Muskegon Brake and Distributing

Muskegon Brake is a worldwide supplier and distributor of Corvette brake, suspension and other underbody parts for early and **mid-year** model Corvettes. See the *Suppliers and Services Appendix*.

N is for...

National Corvette Museum

Located in Bowling Green, Kentucky, across the street from the Corvette assembly plant, the **National Corvette Museum** is a non-profit institution that opened in September 1994. See the full entry on page 134.

National Corvette Museum

Located in **Bowling Green**, Kentucky, across the street from the Corvette assembly plant, the National Corvette Museum is a non-profit institution that opened in September 1994. The National Corvette Restorers Society (**NCRS**) started a building drive in 1988 which eventually enabled construction of the museum to begin. Many supporters and donors, including members, helped to make it a reality. The NCM has a continually changing display so visitors will see something new on each visit. After **Zora Arkus-Duntov** died, his ashes were placed in the NCM and there is a tribute to the man most responsible for the character of Corvette. The only surviving 1983 Corvette is also housed there, on loan from Chevrolet, as are many special Chevrolets. The Museum also has a store that carries a wide variety of Corvette merchandise. See the *Suppliers and Services Appendix*. See *additional photo on page 133*.

Naturally Aspirated

This term, also sometimes called normally aspirated, describes an engine that relies on vacuum in the **intake manifold** and cylinders to induct air or the air-fuel mixture for combustion.

NCCC (National Council Of Corvette Clubs, Inc.)

The National Council of Corvette Clubs, Inc. (NCCC) was founded as an all volunteer, nonprofit organization in 1959 by a small group of Corvette owners/enthusiasts. The purpose of NCCC was (and still is) to promote interest in Corvette ownership and operation, to publish information on the use and operation of the Corvette and to establish

A display showing Bill Mitchell and his Corvette designs inside the **National Corvette Museum**

an organized effort to encourage others to participate in the enjoyment connected with the use of the Corvette.

In the early days, the number of clubs was small and they were all located east of the Mississippi. Today there are more than 280 clubs in 15 regions both east and west of the Mississippi. With more than 15,000 members, the NCCC is the largest nonprofit, all-volunteer Corvette organization in the United States. See the *Suppliers and Services Appendix*.

NCRS (National Corvette Restorers Society)

Formed in 1974, the National Corvette Restorers Society is a nonprofit hobby group of 15,000-plus families dedicated to the restoration, preservation, history and enjoyment of Corvettes made from the model years 1953 through 1986. See the *Suppliers and Services Appendix*.

Net Horsepower

Net horsepower is a measurement of an engine's maximum power output (**horsepower** and/or torque) measured on a **dynamometer** with standard intake and exhaust systems and all accessories (e.g., **alternator**, **power steering** pump) connected.

Neutral

Neutral is the gear position in both **automatic** and **manual transmissions** in which the engine is disengaged from the drive wheels.

Nitrous Oxide (N₂O)

Also simply called nitrous, nitrous oxide is commonly known as laughing gas. Nitrous is often used in drag racing to boost engine performance for short periods. Nitrous is an oxidizer and is stored as a liquid under high pressure. Released as a gas with an excess of gasoline and metered into the combustion chamber along with the normal air-fuel mixture considerable energy is added to the combustion process. During combustion, the N_2O releases its oxygen which combusts with the excess gasoline, thus boosting power often more than 25 percent.

NORS (New Old Replacement Stock)

NORS is an abbreviation for New Old Replacement Stock. These are original boxed parts made many years ago, and they are usually more desirable than reproduction parts, although they may not be correct. The reason for this is that many parts used for Corvettes on the assembly line were never sold as replacement parts. Ostensibly, the replacement parts could be configured differently than the parts that the car was delivered with.

NOS (New Old Stock)

This is an abbreviation for New Old Stock, referring to original parts in their original boxes (as opposed to reproduction parts) that have been stored for several years. The difference between NOS and NORS parts is that the NOS item is identical to the part used on the assembly line.

Numbers Matching

See *Matching Numbers*.

is for...

Maurice Olley

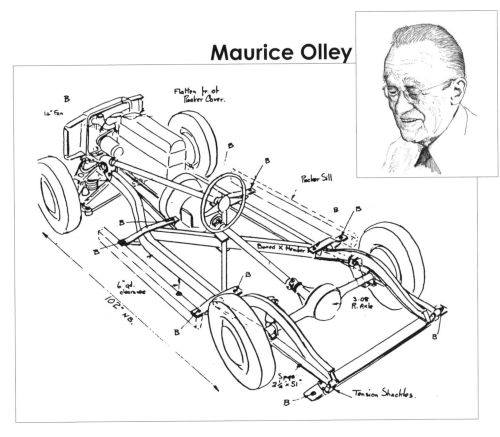

On June 12, 1952, **Maurice Olley** created a sketch for the new sports car frame, showing locations for the radiator, wheels and body mounting points. His engineering effort was the basis for all 1953–1962 Corvettes. See the full entry on page 139.

Octane Number

The octane number is a measure of a gasoline's anti-knock quality. It is the average of the octane ratings measured by the Motor Method and the Research Method. The scale from zero to 100 is based on specific reference fuels; however, by using exotic fuels the octane number can go above 100. The higher the octane rating, the less the tendency to knock during combustion. For example, a gasoline with an octane number of 93 has less tendency to knock than a gasoline with an octane number of 87. Prior to **electronic engine management systems**, Corvettes designed for high performance demanded high-octane diets.

Starting in 1971, in anticipation of **catalytic converters**, Corvettes were detuned to run on low lead fuel. By 1975, all Corvettes ran on 91 octane unleaded fuel. On these models, there is no increase in **horsepower** from using 93 octane fuel. On the other hand you can't do any damage with premium fuel.

If regular fuel causes detonation in a **C4** or **C5** Corvette, the computer retards the timing to stop even incipient detonation. Generally, detonation is most prevalent at part throttle and low **rpms** so that maximum performance is seldom affected.

Odometer

The odometer is an instrument for measuring and registering the miles and fractions (tenths) of miles or kilometers a vehicle has been driven. Most Corvettes have been equipped with an independent trip odometer that can be reset to zero for convenient measurement of the miles driven on a trip or between refuelings.

Off Road Exhaust

Commonly mistaken for and confused with the N14 **side exhaust** (side pipes) option, the optional off road exhaust (**RPO** 441 for 1962 and N11 for 1963–1968) was a low-restriction exhaust system intended for racing use.

OHC (Overhead Cam)

OHC is an abbreviation for overhead cam, which describes a camshaft located above the **cylinder heads** rather than inside the engine block.

OHV (Overhead-Valve Engine)

OHV is an abbreviation for overhead-valve engine. In this configuration, the **intake valve** and exhaust valve are located directly over the **pistons**.

Oil Filter

The oil filter is a device that removes suspended impurities or particles of foreign matter from the engine's lubricating system. **C1** and **C2** Corvettes used canister-style filters. The more convenient and less expensive spin-on oil filter became standard with the 1968 **C3** Corvette.

Oil Pan

The oil pan is a removable part of an engine that attaches to the bottom of the cylinder block and acts as the engine's oil reservoir. Oil pans are usually made of stamped steel or cast aluminum alloy and they are equipped with a screw-in plug for draining used oil. Corvette oil

pans are heavily baffled to minimize the possibility of oil starvation under extreme accelerating, braking or cornering.

Oil Pump

The oil pump is a pump that delivers oil to all the moving parts of an engine. The oil pump in Gen I and II engines is driven from the **camshaft** on the other end of the **distributor** shaft. The LT5 and the Gen III engines use a gerotor pump concentric with the front main bearing of the **crankshaft**.

Olley, Maurice (1889–1972)

Maurice Olley was an expert chassis engineer who was recruited by GM in 1932. Early in his career, Olley had worked for Rolls-Royce in England and in America before joining GM's Cadillac division. When **Harley Earl** originated and pursued his dream of a two-seat sports car, Olley, who was **Ed Cole**'s head of Chevrolet R&D, was assigned the task of designing a chassis for the functional car.

On June 12, 1952, Olley created a sketch for the new sports car frame, showing locations for the radiator, wheels and body mounting points. He laid out the Corvette chassis in traditional sports car style after studying several sports cars of the era. His body was based on a plastic-bodied Chevrolet convertible being developed in Chevrolet R&D. His engineering effort was the basis for all 1953 through 1962 Corvettes. Though it was refined by **Zora Arkus-Duntov**, it was Olley's engineering that created the Corvette. See *drawing on page 137.*

Original Equipment

Original equipment refers to the parts and components with which a vehicle was fitted when it came from the factory. This includes the standard and optional equipment installed at the factory, rather than dealer-installed accessories.

O-Ring

An O-ring is a circular sealing ring, usually made of rubber, silicone or a similar flexible material, that is shaped in crossection like the letter O. The O-ring is compressed into adjoining grooves to provide a seal. Common Corvette O-ring applications are in the fittings of the **air conditioning** system.

Typical **O-rings** in various sizes

Overdrive

Overdrive refers to a gear ratio of less than 1:1. Overdrive transmissions have one or more overdrive ratios which yield reduced fuel consumption, less engine noise and reduced engine wear. The 1984–1988 Corvette optional **4+3 manual transmission** (**RPO** MM4) was an overdrive transmission with three overdrive gears.

The ZF six-speed transmission that debuted as an option for the 1989 Corvette is an overdrive transmission as well. Fourth gear is 1:1. Both fifth and sixth gears are overdrive ratios.

Overflow Tank

See *Expansion Tank*.

Overhaul

This term generally refers to the rebuilding of an engine that includes a valve job, and replacing such items as the **pistons**, rings, rod bearings and head and intake/exhaust manifold **gaskets**.

Oversteer

Oversteer is a handling characteristic in which less **steering lock** is applied as the car's speed increases around a constant-radius turn. In this condition, the rear tires are the first to slide because they run at larger slip angles than the front. Race drivers describe an oversteering car as "loose" because the rear end tends to swing wide. **Active handling** makes the limit-handling terms "oversteer" and "understeer" meaningless; the car simply follows the path called for by the driver on the steering wheel until a directionally stable limit is reached. See also *Understeer*.

P is for...

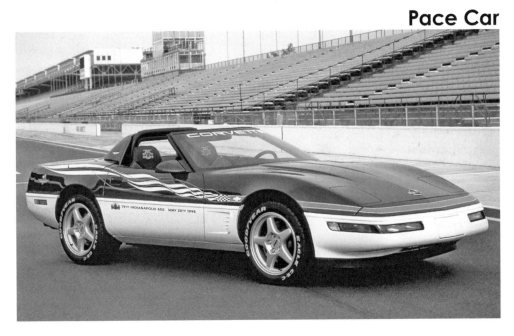

In 1995, Corvette was chosen as the **Pace Car** for the Indianapolis 500 for the third time. True to past practice, Chevrolet offered replicas of the pace car to the public. The 1995 pace car was finished in a striking maroon over white color scheme. See the full entry on page 142.

P

Pace Car

A pace car is a car used to start a race or control speeds during a yellow caution period. In the Corvette world, a pace car refers to the replicas of the Corvette used as the Indianapolis 500 Pace Car. There have been five Corvette pace cars thus far: 1978, 1986, 1995, 1998 and 2002. Each pace car had distinctive markings, badges and color schemes that distinguished it from regular production Corvettes. Chevrolet has always offered replicas of their pace cars for sale as an **RPO** or model. These cars are identical to the actual pace cars with the exception of the special strobe lights used to signal the race cars on the track. See *additional photo on page 141*.

Pad

The pad is the replaceable steel backing plate and friction material on a **disc brake** that contacts the rotating disc when the brakes are applied.

Paddock, The

The Paddock is a major supplier of Corvette restoration parts and accessories. See the *Supplier and Service Appendix*.

Palmer, Jerry (1942–)

Jerry Palmer, now retired, was Executive Director of Design for General Motors North American Operations. Palmer was largely responsible for the design of the Four-Rotor Corvette—later renamed the **Aerovette**—which he notes was the most challenging design of his career, and led to the inspiration for many design features for the **C4** Fourth Generation Corvette. He was appointed Chief Designer in the Chevrolet III Studio in 1974 and began working on the design and advanced aerodynamics that became the 1984 Corvette. Palmer also supervised the design and development of some of the division's most successful designs, notably the 1982 Camaro Z28

The 1978 Corvette **Pace Car** replica—the first of five Corvette pace cars

General Motors Executive Director of Design **Jerry Palmer**

and the 1987 Beretta. Palmer was named Executive Director of Advance Design in October 1986, and in April 1990 also assumed responsibility for the operations of the GM Advanced Concept Center in Thousand Oaks, California. He was inducted into the **National Corvette Museum**'s Hall of Fame in 2000.

Pantera

Ford imported the DeTomaso Pantera with a Ford 351 cid V-8 in the early 1970s to spark its sports car image once the **Cobra** and GT40 were gone. The Pantera was a mid-engined car designed by Tom Tjaarda of Ghia in Italy. Later it failed to meet DOT bumper and crash regulations and was no longer imported.

The De Tomaso **Pantera** was imported by Ford and sold through the company's dealers.

Paragon Reproductions

Paragon Reproductions is a major supplier of new, used, reconditioned and reproduction restoration parts for 1953–1982 Corvettes. See the *Suppliers and Services Appendix*.

Passive Keyless Entry (PKE)

The 1993 Corvette was equipped with a standard Passive Keyless Entry (PKE) system. Unlike other keyless entry systems that required the driver to push a button on a key fob transmitter, the Corvette PKE required no specific action—the system automatically unlocked the driver door (or both doors, depending on the setting) and turned on the interior light when the driver approached the vehicle. The system automatically locked both doors when the driver walked a few feet away. The system also offered a remote hatch release on the coupe only.

PAX Index

PAX Index is an abbreviation for Professional Autocross Index, which is a handicapping system to equalize the various performance levels of cars so that comparisons can be made directly of how well an A-Stock car did against an H-Stock car, for example, even though times are drastically different. The PAX Index is based on the performance levels of cars from the previous year.

PCV (Positive Crankcase Ventilation)

PCV is an abbreviation for Positive Crankcase Ventilation, which is an **emission** control system in which the crankcase vapors are discharged into the engine intake system and are burned

in the cylinders rather than being discharged directly into the atmosphere. It is also sometimes called closed crankcase ventilation.

Pearl Paint

Pearl is a type of paint similar to metallic paint, but instead of minute metal particles, it uses tiny mica flakes. Mica is a kind of semi-transparent, crystalline mineral that absorbs and reflects light prismatically. This gives a dramatic, multi-dimensional, iridescent effect to the paint. It is sometimes called "pearl coat."

Penske, Roger (1937–)

Although today Roger Penske is better known as a CEO and race team owner, at one time he was closely involved with Corvette. While attending Lehigh University, Penske raced a 1957 Corvette at local tracks. He continued his weekend racing pursuits after college, and in 1962 *Sports Illustrated* named him Driver of the Year. He drove one of the infamous Corvette **Grand Sports** in 1963, and started his own race team a year later. In his first year of competition in the Grand Sport, he beat the formidable

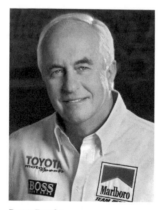

Roger Penske

Shelby **Cobra** at the Nassau Speed Weeks competition to win the Tourist Trophy.

Penske Racing is the most successful Indy car racing team in history with 120 race wins, 11 national championships, and 144 pole positions. In addition, Penske Racing has won the Indianapolis 500-mile race 13 times, including consecutive wins in each of the last three years. Penske-prepared, Toyota-powered chassis are driven by Helio Castroneves and Sam Hornish, Jr., in the Indy Racing League IndyCar Series under the Marlboro Team Penske banner.

Performance Handling Package

The Performance Handling Package (**RPO** Z51) was an option for Corvettes from 1984 through 1990. It consisted of heavy-duty front and rear springs, stabilizer bars, bushings, fast steering ratio, engine oil cooler, an extra (pusher) radiator fan and larger tires on directional alloy wheels.

Perkins, James (1935–)

Just out of Baylor University, Jim Perkins landed a job in 1960 sorting parts at a Chevrolet warehouse, and launched a career and an involvement with Chevrolet that would last through several decades. Along the way, his route up the ladder at Chevy led him all over the country. He was San Diego zone manager, Dallas zone manager, director of customer service for the Mideast region, director of marketing policy and dealer relations for all of General Motors, and assistant general sales manager at Buick.

In 1984 Jim left Chevrolet to join Toyota. As senior vice-president of its brand-new Lexus Division, he was instrumental in the design,

Jim Perkins

development, and introduction of Toyota's first luxury brand.

Four-and-a-half years after leaving GM, he was lured back. In May 1989 he succeeded the retiring Bob Burger as Chevy general manager. During the seven years he ran Chevy, he increased truck production, won the respect and admiration of dealers, drove three Indy 500 **pace cars** and supervised a Chevy racing program that produced five NASCAR manufacturer's championships and six Indy 500 victories.

His generosity with Chevy's time and treasure kept the **National Corvette Museum** viable through its early years. Perkins went to bat time and again for the Corvette as planners worried over budgets and resources. He was inducted into the National Corvette Museum's Hall of Fame in 1999.

Petcock

A petcock is a small valve that is used for draining liquids. Most automobile radiators have petcocks on their bottoms for draining coolant.

Peters, Tom (N/A)

Tom Peters designed the **C6** Corvette as well as being responsible for the final design of the Cadillac XLR.

Phase Zero

General Motors divides its car and truck programs into developmental phases numbered from 0 (zero) to 3. Once the **C5** design had passed Concept Initiation (CI), it entered Phase Zero where specifications were finalized, a budget established and a business plan was put into place. Detailed design and engineering began in earnest when the car entered Phase Zero.

Phase One

In the development of the **C5** Corvette, Phase One was the developmental stage in which parts were ordered and test cars were built and run. Assembly plant conversion plans were also made during this phase.

Phase Two

Phase Two consisted of final testing and the commencement of official production in the **C5** Corvette's development cycle.

Phase Three

Phase Three involved "continuous production and improvement."

Along the way, the new **C5** rolled through various reviews, or "gates" as they have come to be known, ending with continuous production and the opportunity to improve the product in manufacturing.

P

Pickett, Greg (1947–)

Greg Pickett was a Corvette racer in the late 1970s and 1980s who raced **SCCA** Production and IMSA GTO, winning several championships for Chevrolet.

Pike, Joseph (1912–1994)

Joe Pike was the National Sales Promotion Manager for Chevrolet. In that capacity, he personally set about the task of creating a market for the Corvette by promoting the message that the Corvette is more than just a car—it is a lifestyle.

Pike established a national organization of Corvette clubs to provide social outlets for Corvette people. He also promoted races and rallies for Corvette people to enjoy their cars and to experience their performance in safe, responsible ways. He founded the National Council of Corvette Clubs (**NCCC**). He even designed NCCC's distinctive steering wheel logo.

Pike was also the editor of *Corvette News*, the Corvette owners' publication now known as *Corvette Quarterly*. Corvette News was a pioneer in single-marque publications.

For many years, **Joe Pike** was Chevrolet's National Sales and Promotion Manager and a huge supporter of Corvette.

Pike's voice was respected by GM management. He was close to Chief Engineer **Ed Cole** and he played a key role in shooting down a proposal for a four-passenger Corvette. Pike also did little things to boost the image of the Corvette, like naming the colors of the car after famous racetracks-such as Sebring Silver or Nassau Blue. Pike was the one who suggested offering leather upholstery and wooden steering wheels in the early 1960s because they were found in leading European sports cars.

Joe suffered a stroke in 1990 and was confined to a wheelchair. He died in 1994, just before the opening of the **National Corvette Museum**. After Joe's death, former Chevrolet General Manager **Jim Perkins** said, "If you look at the people responsible over the last forty years for the enduring greatness of the car, you see Joe Pike front and center." He was inducted into the National Corvette Museum's Hall of Fame in 1998.

Pilgrim, Andy (1965–)

C5R driver Andy Pilgrim began his racing career in his native England, racing karts, and was an undefeated regional champion in 1977. He moved

Andy Pilgrim

to the United States in 1981 and started racing cars in 1984. Since joining the Corvette racing team several years ago, he has achieved back-to-back wins, three podium finishes at **Le Mans** and numerous wins in North American championships. In addition, Pilgrim's unbeaten world record of 116 consecutive race finishes in IMSA / PSCR events is unprecedented. Off track, Pilgrim drives a fifth-generation production Corvette.

Pilot Bearing

The pilot bearing is the bearing at the output end of the **crankshaft** supporting the transmission input shaft.

Pininfarina Corvette Sting Ray Rondine

In 1964, while at Pininfarina, American-born Tom Tjaarda designed a one-off show car on a Corvette **Sting Ray** chassis. The car was built—with input from Pinin Farina himself—and shown at Paris and then at Geneva—with a revised rear window treatment. The basic design was subsequently adopted for the Pininfarina-designed Fiat 124 Spider. The Rondine (or Rondini as it is known in Italian) survives and is owned by Pininfarina.

Pink Slips, Pinks

These two slang terms refer to the title of ownership of a car, typically in California, although some other states have also used a pink title of ownership. Hardcore street racers of the late 1950s and early 1960s would sometimes race against each other for pink slips, with the loser surrendering his car to the winner.

Piston

A piston is a partly hollow cylinder that is closed at one end and moves in a cylinder. In an engine, a piston is fitted to each of the motor's cylinders and is attached to the **crankshaft** by a connecting rod. Each piston moves up

P

The **Pininfarina Corvette Sting Ray Rondine** was a one-off showcar.

A **piston** from a Corvette Mid-Year big block 427 cid engine with piston rings and connecting rod attached

and down in its cylinder transmitting the force of the combustion chamber's explosion to the crankshaft through the connecting rod. Pistons are fitted with **piston rings** that seal the piston to the cylinder. Brake systems also use pistons to convert the movement and force on the brake pedal through the hydraulic circuit into the motion of and pressure on the **disc brake**'s friction pad.

Piston Pin

Piston pins are cylindrical or tubular metal shafts that attach the pistons to the connecting rods in an engine. They are also called wrist pins.

Piston Rings

Piston rings are thin metal rings found at the top of the **piston** in an engine that form a seal against the cylinder to prevent oil from entering the combustion chamber. Typically, there are two compression rings and one oil control ring.

Pitman Arm

The Pitman arm is the lever connected to the steering box sector shaft that moves side-to-side to steer the wheels. Since the **C4**, **C5** and **C6** use rack-and-pinion steering, they don't have this part.

Plenum

A plenum is a container or chamber used to transport and distribute air or, sometimes, an air-fuel mixture. Typical examples are the engine intake plenum and the cockpit air plenum at the base of the windshield.

Plug

See *Spark Plug*.

Poehlmann, Chuck (N/A)

Chuck Poehlmann was a young designer working under **Bill Mitchell** who, along with **Peter Brock** and **Larry Shinoda**, was largely responsible for the basic **Sting Ray** body design. See also *Q Car*, *Q Corvette*.

Points

See *Breaker Points*.

Polo White

Polo White was the only color available for purchasers of the 1953 Corvette. While other colors were added in the next few years, Polo White remained available through the 1957 model year; it was replaced by Snowcrest White in 1958.

Poly Bushings, Polyurethane Bushings

These bushings are used predominantly in the front and rear suspension of Corvettes to replace the original rubber bushings. The polyurethane material retains its resiliency and is much more durable than the rubber bushings. Since they deflect less than rubber bushings, poly bushings improve vehicle handling somewhat although they contribute to a slightly harsher ride than rubber bushings.

Pony Express 100

The Pony Express 100 is a 100-mile race in Reno, Nevada, run by former Indianapolis 500 winner Rodger Ward. The race is in the spirit of the one featured in the early 1950s movie, *Johnny Dark*. Since the PE100 is a timed event, it is actually more of a high speed rally than a race. Independently owned and sponsored Corvettes are frequently entered and do well in this annual event. Winning cars must be capable of cruising at over 200 mph!

Pop Rivet

Pop rivets are metal fasteners made of aluminum that can be applied with access from only one side. A breakaway mandrel expands the rivet from the inside, thus securing it. Pop rivets are used for several fastening jobs on Corvettes such as securing the **VIN** plate and **trim plates** to the car, holding the stainless steel T-top molding in place on **Sharks** and several other applications.

Port Matching

This is the process of machining the exhaust and **intake ports** of the **cylinder head** so that their openings match the openings of the **intake manifold** and the exhaust manifolds to improve the flow of gases into and out of the head for increased power. It is also sometimes referred to as gasket matching or gasket porting.

Ported, Porting

Porting is the process of machining the exhaust and **intake ports** of the cylinder head and the **intake manifold** to improve the flow of gases into and out of the head to increase power.

Porterfield, Andy (1931–)

Andy Porterfield was a southern California Corvette racer of the late 1950s through early 1970s who was involved in upper management at the **SCCA**. He currently has a high-performance business specializing in brakes.

P

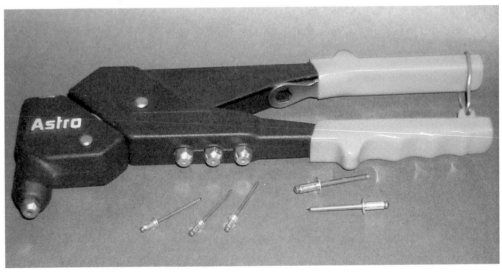

Assorted **pop rivets** with a pop rivet installation tool

A Corvette aluminum cylinder head showing the four round exhaust **ports**

Ports

Ports are openings in the heads of an engine that allow the air/fuel mixture to enter the combustion chamber (**intake ports**) and permit the spent gases resulting from combustion to exit the chamber (exhaust ports).

Posi, Positraction

See *Limited Slip Differential*.

Positive Crankcase Ventilation

See *PCV*.

Pound Feet

This is a measurement of torque. Think of tightening a bolt with a wrench. Torque is how hard you pull on the wrench times the distance from the bolt end of the wrench to the point where you're gripping the wrench. Thus, if you're pulling with 20 pounds of force on a wrench handle that is one foot long, you're exerting 20 pound feet of torque.

Pounds Per Square Inch (PSI)

Abbreviated psi, this is a unit of measure of pressure, commonly used for adjusting tire pressure, air conditioning refrigerant charges and other applications.

Power Band

The power band is the range, expressed in **rpm**, over which an engine delivers a major portion of its peak power.

Power Brakes

This describes a brake system that uses vacuum or hydraulic assist to augment the driver's effort to slow and stop a car. Power brakes were first offered as an option (J50) for the Corvette in 1963.

Power Door Locks

Power door locks permit both the driver and passenger doors to be locked or unlocked by flipping a switch. Power door locks were first offered as an option (AU3) on the 1978 Corvette.

Power Driver Seat

Height, tilt and forward/aft distance adjustments are made by moving switches on the left lower side of the power driver seat, first offered as an option (A42) on the 1981 Corvette.

Power Passenger Seat

The power passenger seat, which allowed adjustments via electrical switches, was first offered as an option (AC1) on the 1987 Corvette.

Power Steering

Power assisted steering, commonly known as power steering, uses hydraulic pressure to reduce the driver's effort in steering a car. The first Corvette on which it was offered as an option (N40) was the 1963 model. Many early Corvette enthusiasts showed disdain for power steering (and power brakes), forgetting that the responsiveness of the system could be increased dramatically with power assist.

Power Stroke

The power stroke is the third stroke of the engine's four-stroke cycle, in which the **piston** moves downward from **top dead center** to **bottom dead center** as a result of the force of combustion acting on the top of the piston.

Power Windows

Power windows permit lowering or raising the driver and/or passenger window by moving an electrical switch. Power windows were first offered as an option (**RPO** 426 through 1962 and A31 starting with 1963) on the 1956 Corvette.

Powerglide

The Powerglide was Chevrolet's two-speed **automatic transmission** available as standard equipment for 1953–1955 Corvettes and as an option (313) from 1956 through 1962 and (M35) from 1963–1967. It was replaced by the Turbo Hydra-Matic transmission in 1968. Early cars had a heavy cast iron case, which was later switched to aluminum. The transmission consisted of a three-element hydraulic **torque converter** and a planetary gear set that gave a low range and a 1:1 high gear.

Project Opel

Project Opel was the code name given to the prototype development of the Corvette in 1952 which ultimately resulted in the **EX-122 Motorama** show Corvette.

Protect-O-Plate

First included with Corvettes in 1965, the Protect-O-Plate was a metal warranty card which had the original purchaser's name on it in addition to some information on the original configuration of the car.

Pulley

A pulley is a wheel with a v-shaped groove around its circumference in which a belt is fitted to drive engine accessories such as the fan, **alternator** or other devices.

Pushrod

A pushrod is the rod positioned between the valve lifter and the rocker arm in an overhead-valve engine (**OHV**).

Protect-O-Plate

Q is for...

Quad Lights

Quad lights were an important identity
feature of all Corvettes from 1958
until C3 production ended with the
extended 1982 model year. These quad
headlamps belong to a 1976 Corvette.
See the full entry on page 154.

Q Car, Q Corvette

The Q cars were to be an entire line of new General Motors cars using a rear-mounted transaxle. The related transaxle-equipped Corvette, officially dubbed the XP-84, was a design exercise initiated by **Bill Mitchell** in 1957 to come up with a new body style originally intended for the 1960 Corvette. The end product, designed by **Peter Brock, Chuck Poehlmann** and **Larry Shinoda**, ultimately became the basis for the 1963 **Sting Ray**.

Quad Lights

Quad headlights, featuring dual high and dual low beams on each side of the car, were introduced on the 1958 Corvette and continued until the introduction of the **C4** in 1984. See *photo on page 153*.

QuadraJet, Q-Jet

The QuadraJet was a **Rochester** four-barrel **carburetor** with a spreadbore design where the front two barrels were smaller than the rear two, permitting better engine control for **emissions** reduction. The Q-Jet became the standard carburetor on Corvettes in 1968 except for high performance versions which used a **Holley** 4160.

Quarter Panel

The rear quarter panel (or fender) refers to the area of a car's body that starts behind the door and extends to the taillights.

Quartz Halogen Bulb

A quartz halogen bulb made of quartz glass, a tungsten filament and filled

A clay mockup of the XP-84 **Q Car**, which was the design basis for the 1963 Corvette Sting Ray

with an inert gas containing iodine or another of the five halogen gases. These bulbs produce a brilliant white light and are frequently used for headlights. The high filament temperature rapidly boils off the tungsten metal of the filament. The halogen combines with the boiled off tungsten atoms. When a tungsten halide molecule comes in contact with the white-hot filament it breaks down, redepositing the tungsten on the filament and sending the halogen atom off looking for another tungsten atom to capture, endlessly repeating the process.

Q

R is for...

Doug Rippie

After a long and successful racing career, **Doug Rippie** founded Doug Rippie Motorsports, known for its high-performance tuning and competition-quality modifications of Corvettes and Vipers. See the full entry on page 161.

R

R

Radiator

A radiator is a heat exchanging device connected to a car's engine through which a mixture of water and antifreeze circulates (usually a 50/50 mixture of water and ethylene glycol). Air passing through the radiator transfers heat from the coolant to the atmosphere before the coolant is returned to the engine. The **Harrison Radiator Company** manufactured aluminum radiators for Corvettes for many years.

Radio Delete

The option to delete the radio (UL5) and receive a credit became available with the 1980 Corvette and continued through the 1988 model year. This deletion of the radio primarily appealed to Corvette owners who intended to use their cars for road racing and rallies.

Rag Joint

Rag joint is a colloquial term for the flexible steering coupler disc usually made of layers of canvas sewn together that connects the steering shaft to the **steering box**. The canvas helps to prevent

Rag joint on the author's 1967 Corvette coupe

vibration and shocks caused by roadway irregularities from being transmitted to the **steering wheel**.

Ragtop

This is a slang term for a convertible.

Rally

Rallies are contests in which a driver and usually a navigator follow instruction sheets that guide them along a course to various checkpoints to the end. In most rallies, speeds are at or below the posted speed limits on public roads and are quite legal to run. Rallies are typically of the time/speed/distance type (TSD) or the "gimmick" type. The TSD type follows directions that indicate a predetermined average speed and points are accumulated for arriving too early or too late. The least number of points wins. The gimmick rally follows directions which may include pictures, counting the steps in front of a building, or other gimmicks and these rallies are designed primarily for fun and excitement; poker runs are typical gimmick rallies. Many Corvette and other clubs organize and run rallies for their members.

Professional rallying, on the other hand, is a worldwide sport involving factory sponsored teams racing against the clock on the worst roads imaginable or on no roads at all as in the Paris-to-Dakar Rally that crosses central Africa for 17 days every January.

Rally Wheels

Rally wheels were the steel 15 x 5.5-inch slotted steel wheels that were standard

Typical Corvette **rally wheel**

None of the design cues of the Bertone **Ramaro** gave away its Corvette heritage.

equipment on 1967–1982 Corvettes. These wheels were painted argent silver and had chrome trim rings and small cylindrical center hub caps.

Ram Horns
The exhaust manifolds on Chevrolet **small block** engines in the 1950s and 1960s had a design that looked similar to a ram's horns, going up and over the spark plugs. It came about as a result of the "book-fold" cylinder port arrangement of the small block **cylinder head** that lasted until the Generation III engine (1997), which reverted to the more conventional cadenced pattern. The "ram horn" style of manifold was used into the 1970s on Corvettes, although a different design was used on small block engines for other models in the Chevrolet line.

Ram Jet
Ram Jet was the name of the **Rochester** mechanical **fuel injection** system used on 1957 to 1965 Corvettes and 1957 Chevrolets.

Ramaro
The Ramaro was a C4-based concept car created by Carrozzeria Bertone, one of Italy's leading automotive design works. The basis for the Ramaro was a 1983 Corvette preproduction car updated to 1985 specifications.

Rat, Rat Motor
"Rat motor" is a slang name for Chevrolet **big block** motors. Since the **small block** Chevrolet motor is known as a "**mouse**" in slang terms, ostensibly the big block must then be a "rat".

Rear Wheel Drive
Rear wheel drive refers to an automotive propulsion system in which the rear wheels provide the power to drive the car. Corvettes have always been rear wheel drive.

Rear Window Defroster
The rear window defroster was first offered as an option (C50) on the 1968 Corvette.

Rebound Straps
On **straight-axle** Corvettes (1953–1962), a strap was attached between the frame

R

and the rear axle so that axle travel would be limited in rebound.

Redline

The redline is a mark or zone on most **tachometers** that indicates the maximum rotational speed at which the engine may be safely operated. Exceeding this limit can result in internal engine damage.

Redlines

This term is a slang term for the optional redlined **bias-ply tires** available in 1967 (QB1) and 1969 (PT6).

Regulator (Window)

The regulator is a mechanical device that raises and lowers the windows, either manually using a crank or via an electric motor controlled by a switch. See also *Voltage Regulator*.

Resistor Spark Plug

See *Suppressor Spark Plug*.

Restamp

To restamp an engine is to stamp either a new number and letter identifier in a blank pad or to deck an engine to remove the existing numbers and stamp in the desired numbers. Since grinding off the old numbers is easy to detect, the more sophisticated shops now cut the block deck so that the correct, factory style **broach marks** are left on the block to appear original. Because restamping is essentially counterfeiting, it is highly unethical.

This is really a rat's nest, since the NCRS actually allows restamping, calling them "restoration motors." If the owner affirms that this is the original motor then

everyone is happy. This is perhaps the most controversial area of NCRS judging.

Restoration

Restoration is the act of returning something to its original state. With Corvettes, it means building the Corvette to the specifications of either **NCRS** or the **Bloomington Gold** Corporation. Most view it as returning a Corvette to the condition in which it left the factory, although often the restored car is in much better condition. A restoration can be a frame-on restoration or a frame-off restoration, which indicates the state of disassembly the Corvette went through during its restoration.

Reverse Flow Cooling

Reverse flow cooling was introduced when the LT1 engine debuted in the 1992 Corvette.

The main concept behind reverse flow cooling is to cool the heads first, which greatly reduces the tendency for detonation. Reverse flow cooling is the primary reason that the LT1 could run 10.5:1 compression with a fairly significant ignition advance on modern **lead-free gasoline**. Reverse flow cooling is key to the Generation II LT1s increased power, durability and reliability over the earlier **small block** engines.

Reynolds Aluminum Corvette (XP-895)

The Reynolds Aluminum Corvette was designed by GM and built by Creative Industries in Detroit in 1974 in cooperation with Reynolds Aluminum on an extra **Aerovette/XP-882** chassis. The car had a transversely mounted 400

cid V-8 mated to a Turbo Hydra-Matic transmission and coil-spring suspension at all four corners. The body and structure were constructed entirely of aluminum, and were meant to convince GM of the practicality of aluminum as a body material. It anticipated the Accura NSX's use of aluminum some 20 years later.

Rippie, Doug (1950–)

Doug Rippie began racing as a teenager on small town streets in southern Minnesota. Once he moved to Minneapolis, he graduated from street racing to the Sports Car Club of America (**SCCA**). Rippie captured the 1972 Central Division Regional Championship. In 1977 he tried his hand at Group One Trans Am racing, and from 1980–82 raced a GT-1 Camaro.

By 1984 Rippie had twelve years of racing under his belt, most of which were in a modified stock chassis Corvette, and he had the opportunity to build a 1984 GT-1 Corvette race car from the ground up. He set three track records in 1984 and captured the Central Division Championship. The following year Rippie co-owned and managed the team and co-drove in the 1985 Playboy Series. In 1986 he continued this dual role in the Escort Showroom Stock Series. With a partner to share the driving and business responsibilities, he was able to expand his role in car setup. Those Corvettes were test beds for many of Rippie's brake and suspension development ideas. For the 1987 Escort Series, Rippie was on his own again, launching Rippie Racing, which would go on to become one of the most successful racing teams in Corvette history.

In 1988 Rippie Racing's Mark Dismore won the debut race of the **Corvette Challenge Series**. In 1989 Rippie Racing dominated with a four-car team. They won the opener, and went on to win five more races. They ended the season with Bill Cooper capturing the Championship. It was during these days that some of the best names in racing drove for Rippie including Mark Dismore, Shawn Hendricks, Jimmie Vasser, Jeff Andretti, Paul Tracy, Boris Said III and Bill Cooper. Also in 1989 Rippie began supplying Boris Said III's 1989 Camaro with competitive power plants. Said won the SCCA SS/GT National Run-Off Championship in 1989, 1990 and 1991. Rippie founded a company, **Doug Rippie Motorsports**, that provides high-performance components and performs competition-quality Corvette modifications. See *photo on page 157*. See the *Suppliers and Services Appendix.*

Riverside

Riverside was a road racing track in Riverside, California, that was the site of many early Corvette races and victories. In September 1962 the inaugural race of the **Sting Ray** and the **Cobra**—the Cobras were victorious—started a ferocious Chevy-Ford rivalry that would last for many years. The race track was demolished in 1989 and a shopping center was built on its location.

Roach

Roach is a slang term for a shabby or shoddy car.

R

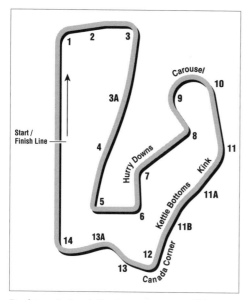

Road America is a challenging road course in Elkhart Lake, Wisconsin.

Road America

Road America is a road racing track in Elkhart Lake, Wisconsin, where many Indy Car, IMSA, and SCCA races are held. Corvettes have a long history at this track. The Chicago Region SCCA June Sprints have been the site of many Corvette championships over the years and the weekend event is usually marked with the traditional Corvette parade lap during the weekend where owners get to take their Corvettes out for a parade lap between sessions.

Road Atlanta

Road Atlanta is a road racing track near Gainesville, Georgia, 45 miles northeast of Atlanta, where the SCCA National Run Offs were held from 1970 until 1993. The track was the site of many Corvette victories for National Championships.

Roadster

Frequently the term roadster is wrongly used when referring to a convertible. A true roadster has side curtains rather than roll-down windows and a soft top that folds or detaches and is not permanently attached to the body. The 1953–1955 Corvettes were the only true Corvette roadsters.

Robinson, Doug (1945–)

Doug Robinson was the manager of Corvette development in the late 1980s who, with **Dave McLellan**, made the **ZR-1** a performance juggernaut. Doug also worked behind the scenes to make the Corvette successful in **SCCA** Showroom Stock racing. As a result of his efforts, Corvette never lost an endurance race during its three-year participation in the series. Doug also worked behind the scene to make the Chevrolet sponsored Corvette Challenge series successful.

Later, it was Doug's team in Chevrolet Research and Development (R&D) that conceived and executed the backbone structural design that became the basis for the **C5** Corvette's architecture.

Rochester

The complete and proper name of this company is the AC Rochester Division of General Motors, but it is often referred to simply as Rochester. This division of GM provides engine management subsystems, or matching sets of components, which interact to support automotive engine applications with top efficiency. **Spark plugs**, **fuel pumps**, **cruise controls**, positive crankcase ventilation valves (**PCV**), and air and

oil filters are but a few of the major engine management components produced by AC Rochester. In pre-1982 years, the division also manufactured **carburetors** and the original mechanical **fuel injection** units for the Corvette from 1957 through 1965.

Roll Bar, Roll Cage

A roll bar is a hoop made of welded tubular steel mounted behind the seats that protects the driver in the event of a roll over. Typically, a roll bar has four or five points of contact with the car; two are the ends of the hoop, two are the rearward braces that prevent it from bending over and the fifth, if used, is a forward brace into the passenger area footwell.

A roll cage is similar except that it offers more protection in that there are basically two hoops, a rear hoop behind the driver and a front hoop near the windshield that are connected over the top and on both sides. Cages typically have six points or eight points of contact and act to stiffen the chassis greatly.

Roll bars and roll cages are not factory installed. They are required for many racing activities and must meet the specifications of the sanctioning body that holds the races.

"Roll bar" is also the name given to the torsion anti-roll bar that is a suspension spring. This torsion bar spring is connected between the wheels on an axle and is linked to the wheel so as to stiffen the spring system only in roll.

Roller Cam

A roller cam is a **camshaft** specifically cut to be used with roller-equipped **hydraulic lifters**, which became standard on the Corvette in 1987. The ball bearing-equipped roller lifter reduces friction thus improving fuel economy. It also allows higher valve spring loads and more extreme cam lift profiles or higher **rpms**. Since each cam is cut to work with a specific type of lifter/rocker combination, serious damage to both the cam lobes and the lifters can result by intermixing incompatible cam curvatures and materials. See also *Hydraulic Cam, Solid Cam.*

Rosen, Joel (1939–)

Joel Rosen created and ran **Motion Performance** from 1966 through the early 1970s. The company specialized in building supercars in 1966, and by 1968 was the number two producer of specialty performance vehicles, behind the Ford-owned and run Shelby GT Mustang operation. Rosen created the "Fantastic Five:" the SS-427 Camaro, Chevrolet (Impala/Biscayne), Chevelle, Corvette and Chevy II (Nova), all powered by modified Chevrolet 427 engines. Rosen now owns and runs a Florida-based company that makes and sells scale models of ships and aircraft.

Rotary Engine

Rotary engine is a generic term for an engine in which combustion either spins a rotor or the compressing-expanding combustion chamber is formed by a rotating element as with the **Wankel Rotary Engine**. This is in contrast to the conventional reciprocating piston engine that generates large reciprocating forces as the **piston** and connecting rod move up and down. While these forces can be counteracted within the

engine, the result is never as smooth as the completely balanced rotary engine. The most common rotary engine is the Wankel. The 1973 **Aerovette/XP-882** and **XP-897GT** prototype Corvettes were equipped with Wankel Rotary Engines.

Route 66

US Route 66 was a United States Highway that originated in 1926 and stretched from downtown Chicago to Santa Monica (Los Angeles), California. For many, it was considered to be Main Street USA, as it was the primary highway west to California. In the 1970s the Interstate and National Defense Highway System (the I- highways, i.e., I-95, I-10, I-70, etc.) had duplicated US 66 in most areas and actually ran on the old highway in many sections. As such, US 66 was being decommissioned in many states and in 1985, the last section of US 66 was decommissioned and the signs were gone. Several Route 66 Associations have been created to keep the spirit of the old highway alive and have succeeded in getting old sections marked as "Historic 66" in many areas.

Route 66 (Television Series)

In the seven years since it was first introduced, the Corvette had become such a piece of Americana that a new television show featuring the Corvette, *Route 66*, debuted in October of 1960. The premise was simple: privileged and sheltered Tod Stiles' (played by Martin Milner) dad dies and leaves him an inheritance, so he and his buddy Buzz Murdock (played by George Maharis) take off in a shiny new Corvette to discover America. Along the way they encounter a host of outcasts and ordinary people entangled in conflicts. Eventually they travel to almost every city along the run of the historic highway the show was named after. The show aired through August 1964.

RPM (Revolutions Per Minute)

RPM is an abbreviation for revolutions per minute. It is the standard measure of rotational speed and expresses the speed of an engine's **crankshaft** and other rotating components in terms of the number of revolutions per minute.

RPO (Regular Production Option)

RPO is an abbreviation for Regular Production Option. An RPO was any listed option that could be added to the factory build order when the car was ordered from the dealership. In the 1950s, these option codes consisted of three numbers; in 1963 the RPO changed to a letter and number, such as C60 (air conditioning), L75 (300hp 327), etc.

A map showing the original US **Route 66** and the highways that made it obsolete

Rudd, Tony (1923–2003)

Tony Rudd was the managing director of Lotus Engineering. In June 1985 Rudd met with Chevrolet Chief Engineer Don Runkle to discuss creating four-valve heads for the L98 engine. These discussions led to the LT5 engine and the **CERV III**, a mid-engine technology showcase for Corvette and Chevrolet. Lotus was given the contract to develop the four-cam LT5 engine to power the **ZR-1** Corvette that debuted in 1989. Tony Rudd's autobiography, *It Was Fun*, documents the life of this extraordinary engineer who trained as an apprentice engineer on the Rolls Royce Merlin engine, was an important member of the BRM racing team and then contributed to the success of Colin Chapman's Lotus racing and car programs.

Rybicki, Irv (1921–)

In 1977 Irwin W. Rybicki became GM's third vice president of design (1977–1986) when **Bill Mitchell** retired. Rybicki was very different from Mitchell; he was a conservative, modest man who had directed the Buick-Oldsmobile-Cadillac studios through countless folded-edge designs that sold cars like mad. Rybicki inherited Mitchell's legacy as well as his staff. Rybicki was a 42-year GM veteran.

R

S
is for...

Sebring

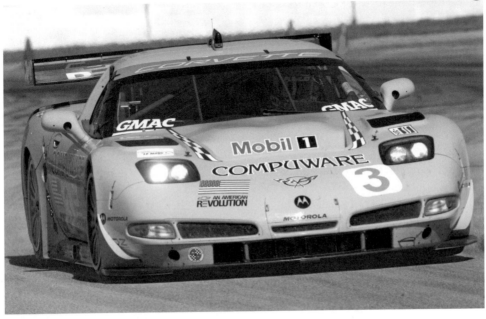

In the more than 50 years since the first endurance race at **Sebring**, many Corvettes have raced on the historic Florida circuit. Corvette teams have included such racing luminaries as John Fitch, Walt Hansgen and A.J. Foyt. Here, Ron Fellows, Johnny O'Connell and Franck Freon drive their C5R to win the GTS class at the 12 Hours of Sebring in 2004. See the full entry on page 170.

S

S

Safety Glass
See *Laminated Glass*.

Sail Panel
A sail panel is the rear-most roof member used to support the rear portion of the roof. It is also called a C-pillar or C-post or, in the case of the early **C3** Corvettes where it was unusually wide, the sail panel.

St. Catharines
St. Catharines, in Canada, is known as the Garden City throughout Ontario. It was the engine plant source for some 2000 model year Corvettes.

St. Louis
The second home of Corvette assembly, cars rolled out of St. Louis, Missouri, from December 1954 until August 1, 1981. The Corvette plant was located with the Chevrolet and Chevy truck assembly plants.

Assembly started in the new **Bowling Green**, Kentucky, plant on June 1, 1981, and continued concurrently with St. Louis through August 1, 1981.

Determining whether a 1981 Corvette was built in St. Louis or Bowling Green can be done using the **VIN** numbers (the ninth digit is a check code and varies):

- 1G1AY8764BS400001 through 1G1AY8764BS431611 (St. Louis)

- 1G1AY8764B5100001 through 1G1AY8764B5108995 (Bowling Green)

Salvage Yard
A salvage yards is an auto parts recycling yard, also called a junkyard or **boneyard**.

The **sail panels** on a 1976 C3 Shark coupe

SBC (Small Block Chevy)
SBC is an abbreviation for Small Block Chevy motors—the 265 cid, 283 cid, 305 cid (in California), 327 cid and 350 cid engines used in Corvettes.

Scaglietti Corvette
After a bad Ferrari experience, amateur racer, oil man and Chevy dealership owner Gary Laughlin approached Italian coachbuilder Sergio Scaglietti to body a trio of special Corvettes for competition purposes. The only design constraint that Laughlin imposed was that the Italian retain the Corvette grilles. By 1960, three Corvette chassis were in Modena; eighteen months later, Laughlin had his cars, but his interest in the project had waned.

SCCA (Sports Car Club of America)
SCCA is an abbreviation for the Sports Car Club of America, Inc., the sanctioning body and club which holds road races and autocrosses for all types of sports cars in the United States. Formed in 1944, the SCCA has a long history in which the Corvette has played a part since the 1950s.

Contemporary Corvette in Bristol, Pennsylvania, is a
salvage yard for C3s, C4s and C5s.

One of three **Scaglietti Corvettes**

Scott, Myron (1907–1998)

Myron E. "Scottie" Scott is most
recognized as the man who gave the
Corvette its name. For 22 years he
served as an artist, photographer and art
director with the *Dayton Daily News*.

In June 1933 he photographed six boys
racing wooden contraptions down Big
Hill Road in Oakwood, Ohio. Scott got
the idea for the soap box derby, attracting
330 participants and a crowd of 40,000.
After the 1934 derby at Burkhardt Hill,
Chevrolet decided to sponsor the event

nationally with Scott in charge of the Akron race. Chevrolet sponsored the derby until 1972.

In 1937, Chevrolet hired him as an assistant director for the public relations department, where he was responsible for photography of new cars, among other duties. In 1953 a special executive meeting was arranged to find a name for a new Chevrolet sports car then in the developmental stage. The company wanted a name that began with a "C" and a review of over 300 names began.

That night Scott searched the "C" section of the dictionary and stopped at the definition of "corvette"—a speedy pursuit ship in the British Royal Navy. Scott suggested "Corvette" the next day and the group loved it. He retired in 1971 with over three decades of service to Chevrolet, and he died on October 4, 1998, at the age of 91. He was inducted into the **National Corvette Museum**'s Hall of Fame in 2002.

Myron Scott, the man who gave the Corvette its name

Seat Belt

A seat belt is a device in a vehicle that restrains the driver or passenger in the event of a collision. Seat belts typically consist of a lap belt attached across the hips and a shoulder belt running diagonally across the chest and connecting to the seat belt assembly.

Sebring

Sebring is a small town in central Florida on U.S. 27 well known for its race track on an airfield. Sebring has been the site of a twelve-hour endurance race for over 40 years. It was also the venue for the first ever **Trans Am** race and is the site of much **SCCA** road racing. See *photo on page 167*.

Second Flight

The Second Flight is the second highest of the **NCRS** Flight Awards, and it is bestowed on Corvettes achieving a point score of 85–93.9 percent. See also *Third Flight* and *Top Flight*.

Selective Ride & Handling Package

An option (FX3) first offered in the 1989 Corvette, the Selective Ride & Handling Package allowed the driver to select from three levels of suspension damper control: "touring," "sport" or "performance." The Selective Ride computer then set the front and rear damper settings as a function of speed and driver setting. Damper settings generally increased with speed in all three modes.

Sending Unit

A sending unit can be a mechanical, electronic or electromechanical sensing

device that measures a physical property such as temperature, pressure or fluid level and transmits a signal to a gauge or warning light. It is also sometimes called a sensor unit.

Serpentine Belt

A serpentine belt is a flat, grooved drive belt that follows a path over, under and around a number of pulleys to drive several engine accessories such as the fan, **alternator** and **water pump**, thus taking the place of several discrete fan belts. The serpentine belt was first used on the Corvette in 1984.

Setting Codes

Setting codes are stored parameters in the computers of newer cars, including Corvettes, that are compared against current engine conditions. Deviations from the setting codes result in error codes that are stored in the computer's memory and can be retrieved by service technicians who can make adjustments or take appropriate actions to correct the indicated problems.

Shackle

A shackle is a swinging support that attaches to the car's frame and to one end of a leaf spring in order to accommodate the change in the spring's length as it deforms in response to wheel deflections. Shackles are found on the rear springs of all **solid axle** Corvettes (1953–1962).

Shark, The

The Shark was the original name of the **Mako Shark I (XP-755)** showcar built by **Bill Mitchell** before the 1963 Corvette came out.

Sharks

Corvettes built from 1968–1982 are nicknamed Sharks.

The original Bill Mitchell **Shark** before it was later rechristened the Mako Shark I

S

Shift Linkage

The shift linkage refers to the rods, levers and cables that cause a shaft to slide or rotate, thus selecting a gear in the transmission.

Shinoda, Larry (1930–1997)

Larry Shinoda has been closely associated with the stunning design of the 1963 Corvette **Sting Ray**. Larry played a major role in the execution of that design—from the original **Q Corvette** to the 1963 **Split Window**.

Born in Los Angeles of Japanese parents, Shinoda started drawing images of cars when he was a young boy using broken pencil stubs. During World War II, Larry and his family, along with thousands of other Japanese Americans, were interned at Manzanar in California. While humiliating, the experience allowed Larry to showcase the benefit of a positive attitude. He amazed others in the camp by designing a reclining armchair out of some old crates.

Besides design, his other love was racing. He joined the crew for the John

The creator and his creation: designer **Larry Shinoda**, standing next to the author's 1963 Corvette Sting Ray Split Window coupe in 1997, two months before his death

Zink Special at the 1956 Indianapolis 500. The Offenhauser-powered Watson racer sported Shinoda-designed bodywork and a distinctive dark-pink-and-white paint scheme. It also won, driven by Pat Flaherty. In 1968 Shinoda followed then-Chevy General Manager Bunkie Knudsen to Ford, and there he designed the Boss 302 Mustang. Later he established his own design company and designed everything from **Roger Penske's** race trailers to the Goodyear blimp. He also created a sleek aftermarket body treatment for the fourth-generation Corvette called the Rick Mears Special Edition. He even designed motorhomes for Monaco Motor Coach.

Larry succumbed to kidney problems in 1996 and was the subject of a massive fundraising effort for a kidney transplant. Despite his handicap, he maintained a vigorous schedule. He died November 13, 1997, at age 67, before the transplant could take place. Larry was inducted into the **National Corvette Museum's** Hall of Fame in 1998.

Shock Absorber

Often simply called a shock or shocks, these devices are more correctly called dampers. They provide mostly viscous damping of the body and suspension resonances. Dampers are connected between the wheel and the body. They operate on the velocity component of the motion between the wheel and the body, generating a force in opposition to the velocity, turning the flow of oil through an orifice into heat.

Short

Short is a shortened form for short circuit, which is a defect in an electric

circuit that permits current to take an alternate (usually shorter, hence the name) path to ground instead of the originally intended path. This usually results in a burned out circuit and/or failure of an electrical device.

Short Block

Often called a partial engine, a short block is a replacement engine that usually includes only the block, **crankshaft**, connecting rods, **pistons**, **camshaft**, **timing gears** and **timing chain**. All other components and assemblies must be added to it before installing it in the vehicle.

Shoulder Belt, Shoulder Harness

A shoulder belt is a safety belt running diagonally across the chest and connecting to the **seat belt** assembly as added protection for the driver or passenger in the event of a collision. The shoulder belt option (A85) first became available in the 1966 Corvette. A shoulder harness is part of a racing safety harness. This harness is typically two shoulder and two lap belts coming together at about your belt buckle location in a special quick connect/disconnect receiver.

Side Exhaust, Side Pipes

The side exhaust and side pipes refer to the side exhaust systems that run along the side of the Corvette just under the doors. Factory side pipes were available from 1965 to 1967 and again in 1969. The 1965 to 1967 design is a single pipe on each side that is "pinched" into chambers to baffle the noise and has a brushed slotted aluminum shield. The 1969 design had two pipes, one over the other, to

muffle the exhaust. This version used a chrome-plated pot metal ribbed shield.

Skelton, Betty (1926–)

Betty Skelton Frankman, frequently referred to as the "first lady of firsts", worked side-by-side with some of the biggest names in Corvette, and established records of her own in racing, aviation and automotive history. She was the first woman in the world to drive racing cars to new records through the famous NASCAR measured mile on the sands of **Daytona Beach**. Skelton established records for Chevrolet behind the wheel of the Corvette, and appeared at major auto shows, as well as in national ads and TV commercials.

Working as the first woman technical narrator for GM at major shows, Skelton attended and participated in many major races where Corvettes were showcased. She was on the committee that originated *Corvette News* and worked as the agency's editor for many years. **Harley Earl** and **Bill Mitchell** had a special Corvette designed for her in 1956–57. Skelton drove the translucent gold Corvette to Daytona for Speed Week

S

Betty Skelton (Frankman), Corvette racer and multiple record holder

and then paced all the NASCAR races with it in 1957. In 1959 she was invited by NASA to become the first woman to undergo physical and psychological testing for the first seven astronauts, and was directly involved with arranging for America's first astronauts to become Corvette owners. She was inducted into the **National Corvette Museum**'s Hall of Fame in 2001.

Slalom

A slalom is a maneuverability test or event in which several cones or markers are placed in a straight line at equal intervals. The objective is to negotiate the slalom course by steering the left and right of the successive markers as quickly as possible. See also *Autocrossing*.

Slick

A slick is a wide and treadless tire made of soft rubber used for racing on dry, smooth surfaces. These were first developed for the Can Am cars.

Sloan, Alfred P. (1875–1966)

The first of five children of Alfred Pritchard Sloan, Sr., and Katherine Mead Sloan, Alfred, Jr., excelled as a student both in public schools and at Brooklyn Polytechnic Institute. After being admitted to the Massachusetts Institute of Technology, he matriculated in 1892 and took a degree in electrical engineering in three years as the youngest member of his graduating class.

Sloan began his working career as a draftsman in a small machine shop, the Hyatt Roller Bearing Company of Newark, New Jersey. At his urging, Hyatt was soon producing new antifriction bearings for automobiles. In 1899, at age 24, he became the president of Hyatt, where he supervised all aspects of the company's business. Hyatt bearings became a standard in the automobile industry, and the company grew rapidly under his leadership. In 1916 the company merged with the United Motors Corporation, of which Sloan became president. Two years later that company became part of the General Motors Corporation, and Sloan was named Vice President in Charge of Accessories and a member of the Executive Committee.

By the time he became President of General Motors in 1923, Sloan had developed his system of disciplined, professional management that provided for decentralized operations with coordinated centralized policy control. Applying it to General Motors, he set the corporation on its course of industrial leadership. The next 23 years, with Sloan as Chief Executive Officer, were years of enormous expansion for the corporation and of a steady increase in its share of the automobile market.

Alfred Sloan shaped and built the modern General Motors.

In 1937 Sloan was elected Chairman of the Board of General Motors. He continued as Chief Executive Officer until 1946. When he resigned from the chairmanship in 1956, he was named Honorary Chairman of the Board, a title he retained until his death on February 17, 1966.

Slush Box

Slush box is a slang term for an **automatic transmission**.

Small Block

This term refers to the 265 cid, 283 cid, 305 cid (in California only), 327 cid and 350 cid engines used in Corvettes over the years.

- 265 cubic inches was the displacement of the first Chevrolet V-8 engine used in the 1955 and 1956 Corvette. This motor was the original **SBC** (small block Chevrolet) engine.

- The 283 was the second generation SBC engine used in Corvettes from 1957 through 1961.

- The 305 cid engine was used in 1980 Corvettes sold in California only to comply with that state's more stringent **emissions** requirements.

- The 327 cid engine debuted on Corvettes in 1962 and lasted through the 1968 model year.

- The original 350 cid engine was used in Corvettes from 1969 to 1991. The LT1 used in the 1992 to 1996 Corvettes is also a 350, although it is a different generation and design, as are the LT4 and LS1.

See also *L Series Engines.*

This 327 **small block** has been dressed up with extra chrome.

Small Journal

Small journal is a reference to the rod and main journals of the **crankshaft** in the **small block** Chevrolet engines. The small journal engines were produced from 1955 to 1967, and the large journal engines started in 1968.

Smog Pump

See *AIR.*

Snyder, Charles (1949-1968)

Charlie Snyder, or "Astoria Chas" as he was popularly known, hailed from Astoria, New York. He raced his highly modified **big block** Corvette, named **Ko-Motion**, regularly turning winning 11.5-second times at 124 mph. Snyder was killed in Vietnam in August, 1968. See also *Baldwin Chevrolet, Motion Performance, Rosen, Joel.*

SOHC (Single Overhead Cam)

This stands for single overhead cam engine. In a SOHC, there is only one cam over the head and often only two **valves** per cylinder—an exhaust and an intake. The advantages are only that of higher rev limits than a **pushrod** engine. Often it is referred to as an overhead cam (**OHC**).

S

Solenoid

A solenoid is a device with an iron core surrounded by a coil of wire that is activated by magnetic attraction when electric current is fed to the coil. The movement of the core can be used to open or close a valve or as a switch. See also *Starter Solenoid*.

Solid Axle

This is a slang term for 1953–1962 Corvettes which did not have **independent rear suspensions** and **half shafts**.

Solid Cam

A solid cam is a **camshaft** specifically cut to be used with solid valve lifters. Since each cam is cut to work with a specific type of lifter/rocker combination, serious damage to both the cam lobes and the lifters can result by intermixing them. See also *Hydraulic Cam, Roller Cam*.

Solid Lifters

Solid lifters are small solid cylindrical objects that ride on the lobes of the **camshaft** and push the **pushrods** up to open the **valves**. Solid lifters are more noisy than hydraulic or roller lifters, but their lighter weight makes them desirable in high-performance applications. See also *Valve Train*.

Solo, Solo II

Solo and Solo II are the SCCA's names for **autocrossing**. These events are held on closed parking lot courses and speeds are limited to 70 mph. Only one car runs the course at a time, thus eliminating the possibility of hitting or being hit by another car. The only safety equipment required normally is a helmet and the car's seat belt, making it possible for just about any street car to compete.

Solo I

Solo I is the SCCA's name for a high speed event, similar to an **autocross**, that is run on a wide open race track or parking lot course where the speeds can become much higher than expected on a public road. Only one car at a time runs the course, except on long courses where cars are spaced so far apart that one car can never pass another. Car preparation rules require driver safety equipment and car equipment beyond that found on street cars. **Roll bars**, safety harnesses and fuel cells are usually required.

Spare Tire Delete

On the 1995 and 1996 Corvette, selecting the N84 option would delete the spare tire in exchange for a $100 credit. This was actually a test for the C5. GM wanted to eliminate the spare in the C5 and they tested it on the C4. This was known as a pull-through. In its last couple of years the C4 used 35 different ideas that were to be utilized in the C5 Corvette.

Spark Plug

A spark plug is an electrical device inserted into the engine's combustion chamber(s) that ignites the air/fuel mixture. High-tension voltage jumps across a gap formed by two electrodes to create a spark that ignites the combustible mixture.

Speedometer

A speedometer, often referred to as a speedo, is an instrument for measuring

and indicating the rate of speed at which a car is traveling.

Spielman, Joseph (1945–)

Joseph Spielman became the proud owner of his first Corvette as a 19-year-old engineering student at General Motors Institute, now Kettering University. Over 37 years, Spielman has had 33 Corvettes. A member of the **NCRS**, Spielman is currently a GM vice president and general manager of GM Metal Fabricating Division. Spielman was also a member of the team that moved the fifth generation Corvette (**C5**), along with the revolutionary LS1 aluminum engine, into the future.

He is a member of the National Society of Professional Engineers and the Society of Automotive Engineers. He was inducted into the **National Corvette Museum**'s Hall of Fame in 2001.

Split Window

Split window refers to the rear windows of the 1963 Corvette **Sting Ray** coupe, which were split by a narrow spine at the insistence of **Bill Mitchell**. Because it interfered with the driver's rearward vision, it was discontinued with the 1964 model. The split window of the 1963 coupe makes it the singularly most distinguishable of all Corvettes and, subsequently, one of the most desirable.

Spool

A spool is a solid hub that connects the inner ends of both rear axles in place of the differential so that both axles are connected as though they were solid. This is desirable in **drag racing** to give both tires equal traction.

GM vice president and avid Corvette enthusiast **Joseph Spielman**

Spooner, Bob (1945–)

Bob Spooner was a Corvette racer from the St. Louis area in the late 1950s and the early 1960s. He raced numerous types of cars throughout his career.

Sports Car Club Of America

See *SCCA*.

Sprung Weight

Sprung weight refers to the parts of a car that are supported by its springs including the frame, engine and body.

S

Squat

Squat is the compression of a car's rear end under hard acceleration. It occurs because the center of gravity is some 18 inches above the ground. The tractive force at the rear wheels pushes on the car at the ground plane. This force is resisted at the center of gravity, which generates a pitch moment that is itself resisted by the springs, causing the rear to squat and the front to rise. Beginning with the

C4, the rear suspension **trailing arms** were aimed in side view to introduce a counteracting moment that would reduce (but not eliminate) squat.

Squeeze
Squeeze is a slang term for a **nitrous oxide** boost.

SR-2
Legend has it that Jerry Earl, son of GM Styling chief **Harley Earl**, yearned to race a Ferrari. Chevrolet already had the 1956 **Sebring** racers but, to keep Jerry from jumping on the Ferrari bandwagon, Harley Earl had his designers come up with a hotter looking Corvette for his son to race. The SR-2 was the result.

Ssnake-Oyl Products, Inc.
Ssnake-Oyl is the leading restoration house for **seat belts** for Corvettes and

other marques. See the *Suppliers and Services Appendix*.

Stainless Steel Brakes Corp.
Stainless Steel Brakes is a leading supplier of stainless steel brake components and conversion kits for Corvettes and other marques. See the *Suppliers and Services Appendix*.

Starter
The starter is a small, high-torque electric motor that engages teeth on the engine **flywheel** and causes the engine to turn over until it begins to run under its own power. It is also called a starter motor.

Starter Solenoid
The starter solenoid is an electrical switch that transfers electricity from the battery to the starter when the ignition key is turned.

The 1956 **SR-2** Corvette racer

Steering Arm

The steering arm is the crank arm output of the steering gear box. It connects to the steering linkage, which imparts steering motion to the wheel. This type of steering was used from 1953 to 1982. The steering arm was eliminated when rack and pinion steering was introduced with the **C4**.

Steering Box

The steering box is a gearbox located at the lower end of the steering column that converts the rotary motion of the **steering wheel** into the angular motion of the **steering arms** and **steering knuckles**. This was eliminated in the 1984 conversion to rack and pinion steering.

Steering Column

The steering column is a shaft that connects the **steering wheel** to the **steering box** or the steering rack.

Steering Knuckle

The steering knuckle consists of a **universal joint** on the lower steering column that allows for a change of angle and movement in all directions.

Steering Linkage

The steering linkage consists of the rods, arms and other links and ball joints that carry movement of the **steering arm** to the **steering knuckles**.

With the introduction of rack and pinion steering with the **C4** Corvette, the steering rack and the pinion box became elements of the steering linkage. See also *Pitman Arm*.

Steering Lock

Steering lock refers to the turns of the steering wheel needed to reach the turn stops (as in three turns lock to lock).

Steering Wheel

The steering wheel is the primary control the driver uses to aim and position the vehicle as it moves along the road. Corvettes have had several optional steering wheels over the years, including a wood-grained plastic steering wheel (N34) available in 1964 and one made of teakwood (N32) available in 1965 and 1966.

Stick Shift

Stick shift is a common term for a car equipped with a **manual transmission**.

Sting Ray

Sting Ray is the model name for the 1963–1967 Corvettes (**C2** or **Mid-Years**).

Stinger, Stinger Hood

The 1967 **big block** 427 cid Corvettes were outfitted with a unique hood that had distinctive striping along its bulge and points at the front that became

The **stinger hood** of the author's 1967 big block coupe

S

known as a stinger. The 427 emblems adorned both sides of the stinger to identify the Corvette as a big block. Some **small block** 1967 Corvettes were also outfitted with the stinger hood sans 427 emblems when a fallen screwdriver inadvertently caused damage to the regular hood mold.

Stingray

Also known as the XP-87, the Stingray was a 1959 race car owned by **Bill Mitchell**, built on a discarded **Corvette SS** chassis (the Mule) and raced extensively by **Dr. Dick Thompson**. Thompson raced his way to a championship with the Stingray. Mitchell used the Stingray as the basis for the 1963 **Sting Ray** body, after which the Stingray was once again welcomed at Chevrolet. It subsequently toured the show circuit with Chevrolet and Stingray emblems.

The Stingray name (all one word) was again used on 1969 through 1976 Corvettes, before being dropped.

Storage Battery

Also simply called the battery, a storage battery is an electrochemical device for converting chemical energy into electrical energy. For 1953 and 1954, Corvettes used six-volt batteries and from 1955 to present, twelve-volt batteries are used.

Straight Axles

Like **solid axle**, the term straight axle commonly refers to the rear axle of 1953 to 1962 Corvettes. The term came about because it was perceived that a straight axle kept the wheels running straight ahead as they moved up and down as opposed to an **independent rear suspension** where the wheels

The 1959 XP-87 **Stingray** racer owned by Bill Mitchell

toed in and out as the wheels moved up and down.

Stroke

The stroke is the distance the **piston** moves from **bottom dead center** to **top dead center** in an engine.

Strut Rod

Strut rod is another common name for the **camber rod** in a 1963 to 1996 **independent rear suspension** assembly. It controls the **camber** of the rear wheels. See also *Half-Shaft*.

Stud

A stud is a headless bolt threaded at both ends. Studs are commonly used to attach **cylinder heads** to engine blocks, but never on a stock Corvette.

Studio X

Studio X was **Bill Mitchell**'s private (and relatively secret) studio where **Larry Shinoda** and his other designers worked on new concepts and special projects.

Summit Point Raceway (SPR)

SPR is a race track near Charlestown, West Virginia. Mainly a club track owned by Bill Scott, a former Formula Vee champion, it is the site of club and SCCA events. Many high performance driving schools also run here. SPR holds its own open track days where individuals can run their own street cars and race cars for testing.

Suppressor Spark Plug

A suppressor **spark plug** incorporates radio frequency interference (RFI) suppression so that the ignition does not create static in the radio reception. It is also sometimes called a resistor spark plug.

Surge Tank

See *Expansion Tank*.

Survivor

A survivor is any unrestored, mostly original (80 percent), Corvette. It is also a **Bloomington** award bestowed on Corvettes that meet this criteria. A survivor Corvette is generally considered more valuable than a restored Corvette.

Sway Bar

Also called an anti-roll bar, **roll bar** or stabilizer bar, a sway bar is a transverse bar linking both sides of a suspension system. Its function is to reduce body roll in cornering, and in so doing transfer weight from one wheel to another, influencing overall limit handling.

Synchromesh Transmission

Many **manual transmissions** use synchronizers so that downshifting of gears may be done smoothly without grinding. The synchronizers spin to get the gear rotating at the same speed as the input shaft. This eliminates any grinding when the gears are engaged since they are already spinning at the required speed, rather than having to play "catch up."

Synthetic Oil

Synthetic oil is an artificially produced lubricant as opposed to being refined from naturally occurring organic petroleum. This generally refers to the newer motor oils engineered to resist breakdown and loss of lubricity under extreme heat and friction. Mobil 1 synthetic oil has been the factory fill oil in the LT1 engines.

S

T
is for…

Trans Am

The SCCA began a race series in 1966 for stock sedans which ran in the under-5.0-liter and under-2.0-liter classes. This **Trans Am** series still exists and Corvettes are still active in the series. See page the full entry on page 188.

T-10

The Borg-Warner T-10 **manual transmission** was used in 1957 to mid-1963 Corvettes. The first ones were close ratio only but a wide-ratio box was available with the 327 cid engine in 1962.

Tach Drive Distributor

The tach drive distributor was used on Corvettes from 1962 through 1974. It had a mechanical drive from a cross gear under the **distributor** breaker plate housing that ran a cable (similar to a **speedometer** cable) to the car's mechanical **tachometer**. In some **fuel injection** cars, the drive also drove the mechanical high pressure pump.

Tach Drive Generator

From 1956 through 1961 the mechanical tachometer on Corvettes was driven from the back of the **generator**, which had a special rear housing to accommodate the drive cable.

Tachometer

A tachometer, often simply called a tach, is an instrument that measures and indicates the speed at which the engine's **crankshaft** is turning in revolutions per minute (**rpm**). See also *Redline*.

Tank Sticker

Starting in 1967, the **build sheet** with the dealer number, zone number and the options on the Corvette was glued to the top of the gas tank during assembly. Tank stickers today serve as a good reference as to what that Corvette was equipped with when it was built.

Tanker

Mid-Year Corvettes equipped with the large 36-gallon fuel tank option (N03) are sometimes called tankers. This option was only available for coupes from 1963 through 1967. In 1963 it was installed in 63 Corvette coupes; in 1964 it was installed in 38 coupes; in 1965 it was installed in 41 coupes; in 1966 it was installed in 66 coupes; and in 1967 it was installed in 2 coupes.

Targa Roof

A Targa roof refers to a semi-convertible coupe design that was introduced in the mid-1960s by Porsche. In this design, the forward portion of the roof was opened by removing a full-width panel that attached to the windshield header at the front and to a **roll bar** at the rear. All **C4** and **C5** Corvette fastback

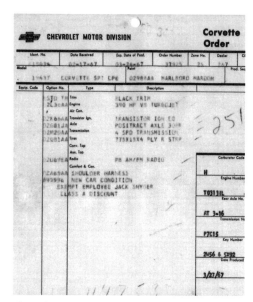

The **tank sticker**/build sheet from the author's 1967 Corvette 427 coupe

coupes are Targas. The Targa top stores in a specially designed receiver under the **hatchback** glass. The Corvette used **T-Tops** from 1968 through 1982. These were a variation on the Targa concept, but utilized two panels instead of one. See also *T-Bar Roof*.

T-Bar Roof

The T-Bar roof was a semi-convertible coupe design—first used on the 1968 Corvette and used through the 1982 model year—in which the forward portion of the roof can be removed. The T-bar roof consists of two removable panels attached to a central longitudinal member that extends from the windshield header to the rear roof structure. The windshield and longitudinal member are T-shaped and the panels attach using clamping levers at the front and rear of the panels. The panels are stored in bags or on specially designed receivers attached to the luggage rack. The panels can be of **fiberglass**, finished the same color as the car's body or they can be transparent and made of tempered glass. Aftermarket roof panels made of acrylic plastic were also available.

Teeters, K. Scott (1954–)

K. Scott Teeters is an automotive illustrator whose work regularly appears in several magazines. His *Illustrated Corvette Series* provides images and facts about Corvettes and his prints are

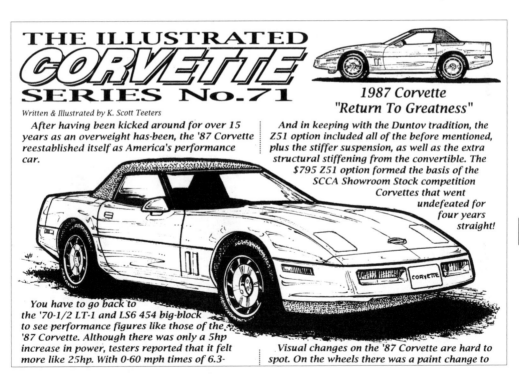

THE ILLUSTRATED

CORVETTE

SERIES No. 71

Written & Illustrated by K. Scott Teeters

1987 Corvette
"Return To Greatness"

After having been kicked around for over 15 years as an overweight has-been, the '87 Corvette reestablished itself as America's performance car.

And in keeping with the Duntov tradition, the Z51 option included all of the before mentioned, plus the stiffer suspension, as well as the extra structural stiffening from the convertible. The $795 Z51 option formed the basis of the SCCA Showroom Stock competition Corvettes that went undefeated for four years straight!

You have to go back to the '70-1/2 LT-1 and LS6 454 big-block to see performance figures like those of the '87 Corvette. Although there was only a 5hp increase in power, testers reported that it felt more like 25hp. With 0-60 mph times of 6.3-

Visual changes on the '87 Corvette are hard to spot. On the wheels there was a paint change to

Detail from a drawing of the 1987 Corvette (number 71 in *The Illustrated Corvette Series*) by **K. Scott Teeters**

available for sale. See the *Suppliers and Services Appendix*.

TH700R4

The four-speed **automatic transmission** (three speeds with one overdrive gear) that debuted in the 1982 Corvette was designated TH700R4. It was also the only transmission available, since no **manual transmission** option was offered that year.

Thermostat

A thermostat is a temperature-controlled valve used in an engine's cooling system to regulate the flow of coolant between the engine block and the **radiator**.

Third Flight

The Third Flight Award is bestowed on Corvettes achieving a point score of 75 to 84.9 percent in the **NCRS**. See also *Second Flight, Top Flight*.

Thomas, Bill (N/A)

Bill Thomas was a race enthusiast and car builder who, with Don Edmunds, conceived and created the **Cheetah**, a lightweight, high-performance, limited-edition sports car meant to be a Corvette killer. Due mainly to Thomas' connections at Chevrolet, the most recent Corvette technology was available for almost every component.

Thompson Astro Tops & Performance Products

Thompson is a leading supplier of aftermarket roof panels for Corvettes as well as other products for the marque. See the *Suppliers and Services Appendix*.

Thompson, Dr. Dick (1931–)

Dick Thompson, a dentist by profession, started racing Corvettes in 1956 with the support of **Zora Arkus-Duntov**. Thompson won numerous races in the late 1950s and 1960s and took the **SCCA** championship in 1956, 1957, 1960, 1961 and 1962 in Classes A, B and C. In 1963 he won at Watkins Glen driving a Corvette **Grand Sport** and was class winner at **Sebring** in 1957. He also took third place at **Daytona** in 1963, and took the win in 1970 in the GT class. Thompson used his knowledge of the

A typical **thermostat** with housing gasket

Corvette racing legend **Dr. Dick Thompson:** "The Flying Dentist"

Corvette to write *The Corvette Guide* in 1958. Thompson was distinguished with the moniker "The Flying Dentist," and he brought credibility to the Corvette as a world class sports car. He was inducted into the **National Corvette Museum**'s Hall of Fame in 2000.

Thompson, Jerry (1937–)
Jerry Thompson was a Corvette racer in the 1960s who won the **SCCA** National championship in 1969 in A-Production.

Thompson, Mickey (1928–1988)
Mickey Thompson was a racer who set several land speed records, mainly with his Challenger series of cars. In fact, he held more speed and endurance records than any man in the world, including the distinction of having been the first American to break the 400 mph mark. In 1963 he built a special lightweight Corvette for use at **Daytona** that was closer to the production Corvette than were the **Grand Sports**. Later on, he developed a high-performance parts empire. Thompson's life ended tragically when he and his wife were gunned-down in their driveway on March 16, 1988.

Three Deuces
Three deuces is a slang term for a **carburetor** setup using three two-barrel carburetors. This is also known as a **tri-power** setup. It was available on the 1967 Corvette with the 427 cid engine, and on the 1968 and 1969 **C3**s with the 427 engine.

Throttle-Body
The throttle-body is the section of an engine's intake system in which the throttle valve (also called the butterfly) is

located. This was first used in 1984 and it is still used on the **C6**.

Throw-Out Bearing
The **clutch** throw-out bearing is located at the hub of the **clutch pressure plate**. Pushing on the clutch pedal disengages the spinning clutch driven disk through the clutch throw-out bearing, thus disconnecting the engine from the **drivetrain**. It is also called the clutch release bearing.

Tilt/Telescopic Steering Wheel
A tilt/telescopic **steering wheel** provides adjustments to move the steering wheel toward or away from the driver and to change the angle of the steering wheel all for optimal driver comfort. The telescopic steering column option (N36) was first offered in the 1965 Corvette, and the tilt/telescopic option (N37) became available in 1969.

Timing
Timing refers to the **crankshaft** angles at which the **valves** and **breaker points** begin to open or close.

Timing Belt
A timing belt is a toothed belt by which the **crankshaft** drives the **camshaft**(s). It is an alternative to a **timing chain**. The Corvette has never used a timing belt.

Timing Chain
Used on all Corvettes, a timing chain is a chain by which the **crankshaft** drives the **camshaft**(s) at half crankshaft speed.

Timing Gears
Timing gears are a set of gears by which the **crankshaft** drives the **camshaft**(s).

While timing gears will yield long life under extra-hard service, timing gears are noisier in operation than a timing belt or chain. These replace the **timing chain** or the **timing belt**. Corvettes were not originally built with timing gears.

Title

The certificate of ownership for a motor vehicle is known as a title in most states.

Top Dead Center (TDC)

Top dead center is the highest point the piston and connecting rod reach in a cylinder in an engine. It occurs at the ends of the compression and exhaust strokes.

Top Flight

The Top Flight is the highest of the **NCRS** Flight Awards, and it is bestowed on Corvettes achieving a point score of 94 to 100 percent. See also *Second Flight, Third Flight*.

Torque Converter

The torque converter is the assembly at the front of an **automatic transmission**. It contains three vaned elements: the pump or impeller, the turbine and the stator. The pump is connected to the engine. The turbine is connected to the gears of the transmission and the stator is connected to the output shaft of the transmission. These elements rotate in a fluid-filled housing and serve as a hydraulic coupling that transmits and multiplies engine torque and also cushions the flow of power.

Tow Bar

The tow bar refers to a portable trailer tongue that attaches to a towed car on one end and to the trailer hitch ball of the towing vehicle on the other. This device enables towing a car on its own wheels, which is known as flat towing.

Tow Car, Tow Vehicle

The tow car or the tow vehicle is the vehicle in front that tows a trailer or car behind it. See *Trailering*.

TPI

See *Tuned-Port Injection*.

Trailering

This refers to transporting a Corvette or other car on a trailer, usually to events like a race or a car show.

Trailer Queen

Trailer Queen is a slang term for a restored Corvette or other collector vehicle that is trailered to shows and never driven. This term doesn't apply to trailered race cars, however, since they are driven many harsh miles on the race track under a significantly more demanding environment than ordinary street driving.

Trailing Arm

The trailing arm provides the fore/aft location and brake reaction for the rear axle wheel hub spindle of the 1963 through 1982 Corvette. The trailing arm transmits all braking and acceleration forces to the chassis. A similar concept utilizing links was used on the 1984 to 1996 Corvettes. The links, by their side view attitude, introduce an element of anti-**squat** into the suspension.

Trans Am

The **SCCA** began a race series in 1966 for stock sedans which ran in the under-5.0-

liter and under-2.0-liter classes. In the 1970s these cars were no longer stock and by the late 1970s they were tube frame GT cars. Corvettes ran in the Trans Am as tube-frame GT cars. This series still exists and Corvettes are still active in the series—even if they don't resemble any Corvette ever built by GM. See *photo on page 183*.

Transistorized Ignition

A transistorized breakerless **distributor** and **ignition system** was an option (K66) on 1964–1969 Corvettes. The distributor used a magnetic pick up and differed from the transistor ignition designs used in other GM vehicles.

Transverse Leaf Spring

See *Leaf Spring*.

Trick, Tricked-Out

Something extra special or really out of the ordinary might be referred to as "trick paint" or a "really tricked-out engine."

Trim Parts Company

Trim Parts Company is a leading supplier of emblems and other restoration trim parts officially licensed by General Motors for Corvettes and other marques. See the *Suppliers and Services Appendix*.

Trim Plate

Starting in 1963, a trim plate was attached to each Corvette. It contained data about the interior, exterior paint, body style and body build date stamped into it. In **Sting Rays (Mid-Years)** it is located under the dash next to the **VIN** plate on the passenger side. In **Sharks** (1968 to 1982) it is inside the drivers door hinge area.

Tri-Power

The three two-barrel **carburetor** setups available on Corvettes in 1967–1969 on the 400 hp (L68) and 435 hp (L71) versions of the 427 were known as "tri-power." This induction system is easily identified by the huge triangular-shaped air cleaner.

Trunk

Corvettes had functional trunks from 1953 through 1962. An opening rear hatchback window on the 1982 Corvette provided exterior access to the storage area behind the seats. A true trunk returned to the Corvette with the 1998 convertible model after a 36-year hiatus.

TSD (Time/Speed/Distance)

TSD refers to time/speed/distance, which denotes a type of road rally where the participants are instructed to travel at a given average speed which must be adhered to so they don't arrive too early or too late at each checkpoint. Points are scored by seconds off in time and the lowest number of points (seconds) is the winner. See *Rally*.

T-Tops

T-tops are the two roof panels that can be removed on 1968–1982 Corvette coupes. The name comes from the design of the top (**Targa Roof**), not the common notion that the open area formed a T.

Tuned-Port Injection (TPI)

TPI was the name given to the electronic **fuel injection** system used on Corvettes from 1985 to 1996.

Turbine Wheels

Corvette **bolt-on wheels** are also known as turbine wheels because of their vaned pattern. The bolt-on version of this style of wheel was first used in 1967. A similar wheel was also used on late **C3** Corvettes.

Turbo, Turbocharger

A turbocharger, also called a turbo, consists of a turbine wheel in the stream of the exhaust that spins a similar compressor wheel in the intake stream, thus compressing the air in the intake and forcing this extra charge of air into the combustion chamber to produce additional power. Turbochargers spin at upwards of 100,000 rpm and must be able to survive the extreme heat of the exhaust. Boost pressures of ½ to 1 atmosphere are common. Turbo lag, the transient time required to bring the turbocharger up to speed, is the frustrating down side of turbocharger-enhanced performance. Corvettes have never been turbocharged from the factory but there were several aftermarket kits and complete cars available in the mid 1970s and 1980s (**Callaway**) as well as twin-turbo conversion kits that are available today. A turbocharged V-6 was explored by Chevrolet, but it was never seriously considered for production.

This **turbocharger** installation is on a Chevrolet small-block V-8.

Turbo 350, Turbo 400

These two designations are abbreviations for Turbo Hydra-Matic 350 and Turbo Hydra-Matic 400, the two **automatic transmissions** that replaced the **Powerglide** in Corvettes. Both are popular with racers, since they are relatively easy to modify with shift kits.

Turbo Fire

Turbo Fire was the name given to the **small block** engines during the 1960s, and they often had Turbo Fire decals on their valve covers.

Turbo Jet

Turbo Jet was the name given to the **big block** engines during the 1960s, and a decal on the air cleaner usually identified the engine as such.

Two-Tone Paint

Two-tone paint is, as the name implies, a paint job that uses a primary color for the body and a secondary color for accents.

The two-tone paint option (440) was first offered on the 1956 Corvette and was available through the 1961 model year. It reappeared for one year only as standard on the **big block** 1967 Corvettes, where the **stinger** on the hood was painted a color contrasting with the body (e.g., Marlboro Maroon body with a black stinger, Goodwood Green body with a white stinger). Two-tone paint again reappeared for a single year in 1978 with the **Pace Car** option (1YZ87/78) and the Silver Anniversary Paint option (B2Z). In 1981 two-tone paint was again offered as an option (D84) on Corvette coupes and was available through the 1987 model year. The next instance of two-tone paint was in 1996 with the **Grand Sport** option (Z16) which featured an Admiral Blue body with a white racing stripe on the hood and rear deck and two red hashes on the left front fender. The 2004 C5, the last of the series, was also available in two-tone paint when the Le Mans Commemorative Edition was ordered.

T

U is for...

When a five-mph bumper first found its way onto the nose of a 1973 Corvette (1974 Corvette pictured here), it was manufactured of **urethane** plastic. The 1973 model year cars retained chrome rear bumpers, which also gave way to urethane in 1974. See the full entry on page 195.

Underdrive Pulley

An underdrive pulley is a smaller-than-normal pulley mounted on the **crankshaft** in order to slow the speed of the belts. This is done to save **horsepower**, since it causes the **alternator** and **water pump** to spin more slowly. Underdrive pulleys are commonly found on race cars, but they are undesirable for street use because they tend to undercharge the battery and don't circulate enough coolant to adequately cool the engine. The only factory application of an underdrive pulley was on the L88 Corvette.

Understeer

Understeer is a steady-state handling characteristic characterized by requiring increased **steering wheel** input as speed is increased in a constant-radius turn.

Ultimately, understeer means the front wheels break away first and you'll get to see what you're going to hit. Most American cars understeer—they're designed that way since it's safer. The Corvette is a classic understeer car, although it can be made to handle neutrally or oversteer under power. **Active handling**, introduced in 1998, changes the paradigm of understeer/**oversteer**. This sophisticated electronic control system makes it possible for even an average driver to manage the car at its limit of control.

Universal Joint, U-Joint

A universal joint or U-joint is a double-pivoted joint that allows driving power to be transmitted through two shafts at an angle to each other. U-joints are typically used to connect the **driveshaft** to the

A **U-joint** being installed in a Corvette half shaft

transmission and the rear differential. U-joints are also used to connect the **half shafts** to the rear differential and rear wheel spindles on Corvettes and other cars with **independent rear suspension**.

Unleaded Gasoline
Unleaded gasoline is gasoline that contains no tetraethyl lead.

Unsprung Weight
Unsprung weight is the weight of those parts of a car not supported by the car's suspension. These parts include the wheels and tires, outboard brake assemblies, the rear live axle assembly, and parts of the suspension control arms, springs, **shock absorbers** and anti-sway bars.

Upshift
An upshift is the process of changing from a lower gear to a higher gear as the vehicle accelerates (e.g., shifting from first to second gear).

Urethane
Urethane is a firm but pliable plastic commonly used for suspension bushings. Urethane front bumpers first appeared on Corvettes on the 1973 model, and urethane replaced chrome on rear bumpers in 1974. See *photo on page 193*.

U

V is for...

Valance Panel

The **valance panel** is a panel under the rear bumpers that covers the frame and undercarriage. During the years that side exhausts were available for C2 and C3 Corvettes, two different versions of the panels were used. The valance panel shown here is for a Corvette with side exhausts. See the full entry on page 198.

V

Vacuum Advance

A vacuum advance is a mechanism on a **distributor** that automatically varies the instant at which the spark occurs as a function of the **intake manifold** vacuum.

Valance Panel

Also called a modesty panel or modesty skirt, the valance panel is a panel under the rear bumpers that covers the frame and undercarriage. On many cars, the panel under the front bumper is also called a valance. During the years side exhausts were available for **C2** and **C3** Corvettes, two separate versions of the panel were used. A valance panel with holes was used for Corvettes with the standard dual rear exhausts, and a panel without holes was used on Corvettes with side exhausts. See *photo on page 197.*

Valve

A valve is a device that controls or restricts the flow of a gas or liquid. Tires have valves for inflating or deflating them, and a four-cycle engine has intake and exhaust valves that admit the air/fuel mixture into the combustion chambers and expel the resulting spent exhaust gases after combustion.

Valve Guide

A valve guide is the cylindrical hole in the **cylinder head** or engine block that keeps the valve moving up and down in a straight line. A valve guide usually contains a bushing that functions as a bearing surface. Some engines use replaceable valve guides, although Chevrolet never used them. This means that if your cylinder head has separate valve guides the head has been rebuilt.

Valve Lifter

See *Lifters.*

Valve Train

The valve train is the assembly of parts that open and close the valves. The **camshaft**, **valves**, valve springs, retainers, **pushrods**, belt and other components comprise the valve train.

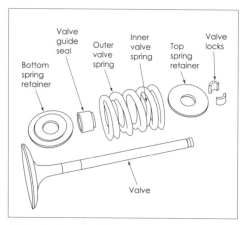

A typical **valve** and ancillary components

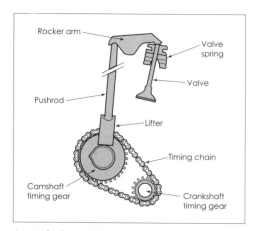

A typical **valve train**'s components

Vanacor's Corvette

Vanacor's is a major supplier of aftermarket **fiberglass** Corvette replacement parts. See the *Supplier and Service Appendix.*

V-Belt

Also called a fan belt, a V-belt is a tapered belt that runs in the grooves of two or more pulleys. These haven't been used on the Corvette since 1982; **serpentine belts** with automatic spring tensioners have been used since 1984 on Corvettes. This removed one of the most common failure modes of the fixed-tension V-belt: belts losing tension and flying off at high revs. One belt coming off invariably took the rest of the belts with it.

Vehicle Identification Number (VIN)

The vehicle identification number (VIN) is a car's identification code that carries its serial number, model, year of manufacture and basic equipment information. See also *VIN Plate.*

Vette Brakes & Products

Vette Brakes & Products is a major supplier of brake, suspension and running gear components for Corvettes. See the *Suppliers and Services Appendix.*

Vette Magazine

Vette is a monthly magazine devoted to Corvettes published by Primedia Specialty Group. See the *Magazine Appendix.*

Vette Vues Magazine

Vette Vues is a monthly magazine devoted to Corvettes published by Vette Vues Incorporated. See the *Magazine Appendix.*

Vettenet.org

Vettenet.org is a large and comprehensive Corvette website with multiple links to other Corvette sites.

Vietro, "Corvette Mike" (1955–)

"Corvette Mike" Vietro is one of the best known and most successful Corvette brokers in the hobby. He has "**Corvette Mike**" locations on both coasts and always has at least 100 Corvettes available at each site. His Corvettes are often unique and rare examples of the marque. See the *Suppliers and Services Appendix.*

VIN

See *Vehicle Identification Number.*

VIN Plate

The VIN plate is a metal plate that carries a car's **vehicle identification number** (VIN). Since the late 1960s the VIN plate has been required by law to be affixed to the top of the dashboard to make it visible from the outside of the vehicle.

Voltage Regulator

The voltage regulator is an electrical device that maintains a constant and safe voltage within the car's **electrical system**. It also controls the recharging of the car's battery from the **alternator**. Early Corvettes (1953–1968) used an external voltage regulator and in 1969 the voltage regulator was integrated into the alternator.

V-Shield

The term V-shield refers to the ignition shielding on the lower side of the engine block.

 **W** is for...

Washboard Hood

For one year, in 1958, the Corvette hood was fitted with false louvers. With only 9,168 Corvettes built for that year, the so-called **washboard hood** is quite rare. See the full entry on page 202.

Wankel Rotary Engine

The Wankel is a rotary internal combustion engine developed in Germany by Felix Wankel. The engine consists of an equilateral triangular member with curved sides orbiting an eccentric on a shaft inside a stationary housing. The Wankel's advantages are its compact size, light weight and smooth operation. The Wankel was seriously considered as a power plant for the Corvette, but emissions and oil seal problems prevented it from ever getting past the prototype stages in the **Aerovette/XP-882** and the **XP-897** Corvette show cars.

Washboard Hood

Washboard hood is a nickname for the faux louvers found on the hood of the 1958 Corvette. See *photo on page 201*.

Water Pump

The water pump is a pump driven by a pulley and belt from the **crankshaft**. Its purpose is to circulate coolant throughout the engine's cooling system.

Waterfall

The waterfall is the area between the driver and passenger seats on a Corvette convertible.

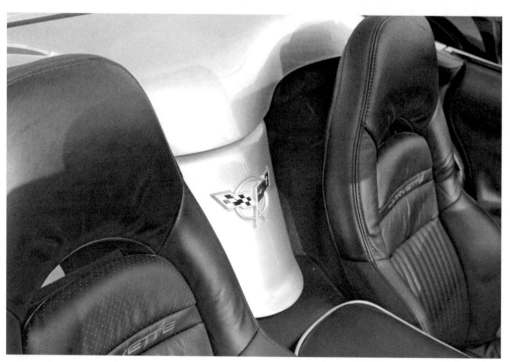

The **waterfall** of a Corvette C5 convertible

WCFB
See *Carter WCFB*.

Weight Distribution
Weight distribution is the proportions of a car's total weight carried by the front and rear wheels, typically expressed as front/rear percentages. Weight distribution is an important factor in a car's handling, with the best distribution being as close as possible to 50/50.

Wheel Base
The wheel base is the measured distance from the center of the front wheel to the center of the rear wheel on the same side of the car. Generally, cars with long wheel bases are more stable but less nimble than those with shorter wheel bases.

Window Sticker
The window sticker is the paper label affixed to a new vehicle by the manufacturer that provides information on the car including its **Vehicle Identification Number** (VIN), its standard and optional equipment, its color, EPA information, delivery charges and other pertinent data. Formally known as a Monroney label, it was named after Oklahoma congressman Mike Monroney, sponsor of the bill resulting in the label. In 1958 the Automobile Information Disclosure Act was passed based on Monroney's bill.

Windshield Wipers
Windshield wipers are mechanical arms with replaceable rubber blades that sweep across the windshield to clear water or snow. From 1953 through 1967 Corvette windshield wipers were exposed. In 1968 a vacuum-operated retractable cowl was added to the Corvette to conceal the windshield wipers when not in use. In 1973 the hood was redesigned to conceal the wipers in a slot between the rear edge of the hood, and the windshield and the retractable cowl was eliminated.

Wobble Plate
The wobble plate, also known as a swash plate, was a component of the piston pump used in early Rochester **Ram Jet** fuel injection systems. The wobble plate, along with the piston pump, was eliminated as the design evolved.

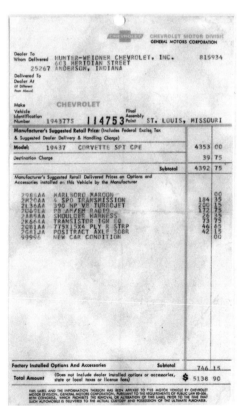

The **window sticker** from the author's 1967 Corvette big-block coupe

Woodward Avenue

Woodward Avenue is a street heading north by northwest out of Detroit, Michigan. During the 1960s it gained a reputation as a weekend and late night "drag strip," and many auto executives tested new performance ideas there prior to revealing them to the public. Heightened police awareness and presence made street racing on Woodward Avenue less popular, relegating performance tests to the test tracks and **drag strips**. Today, every August, Woodward Avenue between 12 Mile Road and 15 Mile Road is the scene of a major nostalgia cruise attracting thousands of hot-rod-era cars and tens of thousands of spectators.

WOT (Wide Open Throttle)

WOT is an abbreviation for wide open throttle, or having the accelerator pushed to the floor.

X is for…

XP-700 Phantom

The **XP-700 Phantom** was one of GM design chief Bill Mitchell's pet projects. It first received a special "duck tail" rear end which was later incorporated into the 1961 Corvette. The XP-700 started as Bill Mitchell's personal car but evolved into a full GM showcar. See the full entry on page 206.

X-Brace

The structure of the C4 convertible required an "X" brace bolted to it to locally stiffen the frame. Since the convertible was not as stiff torsionally as the C4 coupe (with the roof on), only the coupe was available with the optional performance handling package.

X-Member

In **straight-axle** Corvettes, a section of the frame formed an "X" which added strength and rigidity to the chassis. An X-member is not the same as a crossmember and should not be confused with it. A crossmember is a transverse girder or tube that connects each side of the frame, while an X-member runs diagonally through the center of the 1953 through 1962 Corvette frame connecting the two side rails.

XP-700 Phantom

Bill Mitchell had a 1958 Corvette modified to be his personal car. It first received a special "duck tail" rear end which was later incorporated into the 1961 Corvette, and the front end was redesigned to closely resemble the nose of the 1954 Oldsmobile F88 show car. The car received further modifications in 1959 including a longer rear end, a new front end with smaller air intake, new transparent roof with a periscope in the middle of the two bubbles. The car thus became a true showcar rather than Mitchell's personal **Woodward Avenue** cruiser. See *additional photo on page 205*.

XP-755

See *Mako Shark I.*

XP-87

See *Stingray.*

XP-880/Astro II

See *Astro II/XP-880.*

XP-882/Aerovette

See *Aerovette/Four-Rotor Corvette/ XP-882.*

XP-895

See *Reynolds Aluminum Corvette.*

XP-897 GT

Built on an early Porsche 914 platform by Pininfarina in Italy to GM's design, the XP-897 GT "Two-Rotor Car" was built to prove (or disprove) the viability of a Corvette powered by the two-rotor engine. It proved to be under-powered

Front end of the **XP-700 Phantom** show Corvette, which was redesigned to closely resemble the nose of the 1954 Oldsmobile F88 show car

The two-rotor Wankel-engined **XP-897 GT** show Corvette

and convinced **Ed Cole** that a **Wankel**-powered Corvette would have to use a four-rotor engine. Still, it was shown in 1973 as a showcase for GM's then-imminent Wankel-type rotary engine. Like the original **Aerovette/XP-882**, it was widely believed to be a precursor of the next generation Corvette.

XP-898

The one-off 1973 XP-898 showcar was to test feasibility of a new "sandwich" **fiberglass** body construction using a foam filler that could be varied in thickness to provide desired strength in specific areas. The construction technique was never put into production.

The **XP-898** showcar

Y

is for...

Don Yenko

In addition to the Yenko Corvettes, Chevrolet dealer **Don Yenko** was responsible for many other super Chevrolets built on Camaro, Chevelle and Nova platforms. For 1969, Yenko ordered Camaros with the L72 engine, and added emblems, stripes and decals at the dealership. The result was this 427 cid/425 hp Camaro. See the full entry on page 210.

Yager, Mike (1949–)

Mike Yager is the "chief cheerleader" (C.E.O.) of **Mid America Motorworks**, a catalog mail order company that supplies parts and accessories for Corvettes, and has recently expanded to supply the Volkswagen and Porsche markets as well. Yager's company was a major sponsor of the **Corvette Challenge Series** and he has been actively involved with Corvettes for three decades. Mike has an extensive collection of Corvettes including the **CERV I** and the *Corvette Summer* Shark. He is currently the chairman of the board of directors of the **National Corvette Museum**. See the *Suppliers and Services Appendix.*

Y-Body

This is a GM term that refers to the body of the **C4** Corvette.

Y-Car

Y-car is the General Motors internal designation for the automotive platform that the Corvette is built on. This designation has existed for the Corvette platform since 1953. Prior to 1953, the Y-job designation was used to denote experimental platforms and models, the most notable of which was **Harley Earl**'s Buick Y-job show car.

Yenko, Don (1927–1987)

Don Yenko was a Chevrolet dealer and Corvette racer of the 1950s and 1960s who won several championships for Chevrolet. Using COPOs (**Central Office Production Options**) through his dealership, he later created several "special" Chevrolets including the Yenko Stinger Corvair and the Yenko Camaro. See *additional photo on page 209.*

Y-Pipe

The Y-pipe is the front exhaust pipe that connects to both exhaust manifolds and then comes together as it enters the **catalytic converter**. Exiting the catalytic converter, another Y-pipe resplit the

All C4 models use the **Y-Body**.

The Yenko Camaro, created by **Don Yenko**

exhaust into two mufflers, though this was not a true dual exhaust. The **ZR1** Corvettes and the **C5s** eliminated the Y-pipe by using two discrete catalytic converters. There was, however, still a connection made downstream between the two halves of the system. It is important acoustically to couple the right and left exhausts, otherwise the two exhausts sound like a pair of unequal firing four-cylinder engines. Carburetted V-8s had an exhaust passage connecting the right and left banks that ran through the base of the **intake manifold**. This could be modulated to provide manifold heat to improve fuel atomization.

Z is for...

The **Z06** was an option for the C5 Corvette available from 2001 through 2004 only on the hardtop model. At its heart was a 350 cid/385 hp (increased to 405 hp in 2002) engine mated to a six-speed manual transmission and a special suspension. The Z06 was the lightest, most rigid and most potent C5. See the full entry on page 214.

Z

Z RPO Codes

RPO codes beginning with Z (**ZL1**, **Z06**, etc.) designate special performance packages for Corvettes. These packages were comprised of several components, such as stiffer suspension and bigger brakes, rather than a single part.

Z06

Z06 was a high-performance option package available for the 1963 Corvette coupe only. It consisted of heavy-duty suspension and brakes, the 327 cid/ 360 hp fuel-injected engine and a four-speed transmission. Early production Z06s were equipped with a 36-gallon fuel tank, although later versions could be ordered with a standard fuel tank. Of the 199 Z06s built, fewer than 90 were "big tank" versions (**tankers**).

The Z06 reemerged as an option for the 2001 **C5** Corvette. This package was only available on the hardtop model and it included a 350 cid/385 hp engine, six-speed **manual transmission**, dual-zone **air conditioning** and special suspension (FE4). In 2002 the **horsepower** output was increased to 405 and a **heads-up display** was included in the package. The Z06 option remained available through the 2004 model year, the last year of the C5. See *additional photo on page 213*.

Z07

Z07 was the **RPO** for the special offroad brake and suspension package available from 1973 through 1975. It was available only with the 350 cid/250 hp or 454 cid/275 hp engines and it required power brakes and a four-speed **manual transmission** to be ordered with it. The package consisted of special front and rear suspension and heavy duty brakes. It was not available with **air conditioning**.

Available from 2001 through 2004, the **Z06** option was only offered with the hardtop coupe body style.

This RPO appeared again in 1991 as the option code for the adjustable suspension package that was available through the 1995 model year.

Z51

Z51 was a special performance handling option package available from 1984 through 1990 on coupes only. It consisted of heavy-duty front and rear springs, **shock absorbers**, larger stabilizer bars, fast steering ratio, engine oil cooler, extra "pusher" radiator fan, P255/65R16 tires and directional alloy wheels. The front control arm bushings are also stiffer.

This **RPO** appeared again as the code for the performance handling package in 1996 and remained available through the 2004 model year.

Zip Products

Zip is a major supplier of Corvette **restoration**, performance and accessory parts. See the *Suppliers and Services Appendix*.

ZL1

ZL1 was a performance option package available only in 1969 that consisted of the L88 engine with aluminum **cylinder heads** and a special aluminum block, **transistorized ignition**, special front and rear suspension, special heavy-duty brakes and positraction. Neither a radio nor **air conditioning** was available when this option was ordered. Costing $4,718.35 on top of the base price of $4,781.00 for a Corvette coupe, only two cars were so equipped in 1969.

The ultimate big-block was the 1969 aluminum **ZL1** 427.

Z

ZR-1s were offered from 1990 through 1995; the distinctive wheels and higher 405 hp rating distinguish this as a 1994 or 1995 model.

Zora Arkus-Duntov

See *Arkus-Duntov, Zora*.

ZR1

ZR1 was a performance option package available from 1970 through 1972 that was not recommended for normal traffic situations. It consisted of the 350 cid/ 370 hp engine, special four-speed close-ratio transmission, heavy-duty power brakes, full **transistorized ignition** system, aluminum radiator, special springs with matching **shock absorbers**, special larger front and rear stabilizer bars and metal **fan shrouds**.

The ZR1 was resurrected as a special high-performance 1990–1995 model with an all-aluminum engine designed jointly by Lotus and Chevrolet. See also *ZR-1*.

ZR-1

The ZR-1 option package was introduced in 1990 and was available through the 1995 model year for Corvette coupes only. The package consisted of the Lotus-developed LT5 350 cid double-overhead-cam engine, six-speed transmission, a wider body to accommodate larger tires, sport leather seats, power driver and passenger seats, **selective ride and handling package**, Delco-Bose stereo **system** with CD, **low tire pressure warning indicator** and a specially laminated "solar" windshield. The ZR-1 Corvette was codenamed "**The King of the Hill.**"

ZR2

ZR2 was a performance option package available in 1971 only. It was the same as the ZR1 package except that it was based on the LS6 454 cid/425 hp engine.

Appendix 1:
Year-by-Year Specifications

1953 Base Corvette Convertible

Total Produced: 300   **List Price:** $3,498.00

Dimensions

Weight	2,886.0 lb.	Tire Size	6.70x15 in.
Length	167.3 in.	Front Track	57.0 in.
Width	69.8 in.	Rear Track	58.8 in.
Height	51.5 in.		

Engines

235 cid/150 hp "Blue Flame Special" six-cylinder

Options	Qty	Price
AM radio, signal seeking	300	$145.15
Heater	300	$91.40

Exterior Colors	Qty
Polo White	300

1954 Base Corvette Convertible

Total Produced: 3,640   **List Price:** $2,774.00

Dimensions

Weight	2,886.0 lb.	Tire size	6.70x15 in.
Length	167.3 in.	Front Track	57.0 in.
Width	69.8 in.	Rear Track	58.8 in.
Height	51.5 in.		

Engines

235 cid/155 hp "Blue Flame Special" six-cylinder

Options	Qty	Price
Courtesy lights	3,640	$4.05
Windshield washer	3,640	$11.85
Parking brake alarm	3,640	$5.65
Powerglide automatic transmission	3,640	$178.55
Whitewall tires	3,640	$26.90
Directional signal	3,640	$16.75
AM radio, signal seeking	3,640	$145.15
Heater	3,640	$91.40

Exterior Colors	Qty
Polo White	3,230
Pennant Blue	300
Sportsman Red	100
Black	4

1955 Base Corvette Convertible

Total Produced: 700   **List Price**

Base Convertible, six-cylinder	7	$2,774.00
Base Convertible, V-8	693	$2,909.00

Dimensions

Weight	2,805.0 lb.	Tire Size	6.70x15 in.
Length	167.3 in.	Front Track	57.0 in.
Width	69.8 in.	Rear Track	58.8 in.
Height	51.5 in.		

Engines	Qty	Price
235 cid/155 hp "Blue Flame Special" six-cylinder	N/A	N/A
265 cid/195 hp V-8	N/A	N/A

Options	Qty	Price
Courtesy lights	700	$4.05
Windshield washer	700	$11.85
Parking brake alarm	700	$5.65
Powerglide automatic transmission	700	$178.35
Whitewall tires	700	$26.90
Directional signal	700	$16.75
AM radio, signal seeking	700	$145.15
Heater	700	$91.40

Exterior Colors	Qty
Polo White	325
Pennant Blue	45
Corvette Copper	15
Gypsy Red	180
Harvest Gold	120

1956 Base Corvette Convertible

Total Produced: 3,467   **List Price:** $3,120.00

Dimensions

Weight	2,875.0 lb.	Tire Size	6.70x15 in.
Length	168.0 in.	Front Track	57.0 in.
Width	70.5 in.	Rear Track	58.8 in.
Height	51.0 in.		

Engines	Qty	Price
265 cid/210 hp V-8 (standard)	N/A	—
265 cid/225 hp V-8 (two four-barrel carbs)	3,080	$172.20
265 cid/240 hp V-8 (Duntov high-lift camshaft)	N/A	N/A

Options	Qty	Price
Courtesy lights	2,775	$8.65
AM radio, signal seeking	2,717	$198.90
Parking brake alarm	2,685	$5.40
Windshield washers	2,815	$11.85
Whitewall tires, 6.70x15	N/A	$32.30
Powerglide automatic transmission	N/A	$188.50
Auxiliary hardtop	2,076	$215.20
Power windows	547	$64.60
Two-tone paint combination	1,259	$19.40
Special high-lift camshaft	111	$188.30
Rear axle, 3.27:1 ratio	N/A	$0.00
Power-operated folding top	2,682	$107.60
Heater	N/A	$123.65

Exterior Colors	Qty
Polo White	532
Arctic Blue	390
Aztec Copper	402
Venetian Red	1,043
Onyx Black	810
Cascade Green	290

1957 Base Corvette Convertible

Total Produced: 6,339   **List Price:** $3,176.32

Dimensions

Weight	2,849.0 lb.	Tire Size	6.70x15 in.
Length	168.0 in.	Front Track	57.0 in.
Width	70.5 in.	Rear Track	58.8 in.
Height	51.0 in.		

Engines	Qty	Price
283 cid/ 220 hp (standard)	1,633	—
283 cid/245 hp (two four-barrel carbs)	2,045	$150.65
283 cid/270 hp (two four-barrel carbs)	1,621	$182.95
283 cid/250 hp (fuel injection)	182	$484.20
283 cid/283 hp (fuel injection)	713	$484.20
283 cid/250 hp (fuel injection)	102	$484.20
283 cid/283 hp (fuel injection, tachometer and fresh-air intake included)	43	$726.30

Options	Qty	Price
Courtesy lights	2,489	$8.65
Heater	5,373	$118.40
AM radio, signal seeking	3,635	$199.10
Parking brake alarm	1,873	$5.40
Windshield washers	2,555	$11.85
Wheels, 15x5.5 (set of five)	51	$15.10
Whitewall tires, 6.70x15	5,019	$31.60
Three-speed manual transmission (close ratio)	2,886	$0.00
Four-speed manual transmission	664	$188.30
Powerglide automatic transmission	1,393	$188.30
Auxiliary hardtop	4,055	$215.20
Power windows	379	$59.20
Two-tone paint combination	2,797	$19.40

Power-operating folding top	1,336	$139.90
Positraction rear axle, 3.70:1	327	$48.45
Positraction rear axle, 4.11:1	1,772	$48.45
Positraction rear axle, 4.56:1	N/A	$48.45
Heavy duty racing suspension	51	$780.10

Exterior Colors	**Qty**
Polo White	1,273
Arctic Blue	487
Aztec Copper	452
Venetian Red	1,320
Onyx Black	2,189
Cascade Green	550
Inca Silver	65

1958 Base Corvette Convertible

Total Produced: 9,168   **List Price:** $3,591.00

Dimensions

Weight	2,926.0 lb.	Tire Size	6.70x15 in.
Length	177.2 in.	Front Track	57.0 in.
Width	72.8 in.	Rear Track	58.8 in.
Height	51.0 in.		

Engines

Engines	Qty	Price
283 cid/220 hp (standard)	4,243	—
283 cid/245 hp (two four-barrel carbs)	2,436	$150.65
283 cid/270 hp (two four-barrel carbs)	978	$182.95
283 cid/250 hp (fuel injection)	504	$484.20
283 cid/290 hp (fuel injection)	1,007	$484.20

Options	Qty	Price
Courtesy lights	4,600	$6.50
Heater	8,014	$96.85
AM radio, signal seeking	6,142	$144.45
Parking brake alarm	2,883	$5.40
Windshield washers	3,834	$16.15
Wheels, 15x5.5 (set of five)	404	$0.00
Whitewall tires, 6.70x15	7,428	$31.55
Powerglide automatic transmission	2,057	$188.30
Auxiliary hardtop	5,607	$215.20
Power windows	649	$59.20
Two-tone paint	3,422	$16.15
Power-operated folding top	1,090	$139.90
Positraction rear axle, 3.70:1	1,123	$48.45
Positraction rear axle, 4.11:1	2,518	$48.45
Positraction rear axle, 4.56:1	370	$48.45
Heavy duty brakes and suspension	144	$780.10
Four-speed manual transmission	3,764	$215.20

Exterior Colors	Qty
Snowcrest White	2,447
Silver Blue	2,006
Charcoal	1,631
Regal Turquoise	510
Panama Yellow	455
Signet Red	1,399
Silver	193
Black	493

1959 Base Corvette Convertible

Total Produced: 9,670   **List Price:** $3,875.00

Dimensions

Weight	2,975.0 lb.	Tire Size	6.70x15 in.
Length	177.2 in.	Front Track	57.0 in.
Width	72.8 in.	Rear Track	58.8 in.
Height	51.0 in.		

Engines	Qty	Price
283 cid/230 hp V-8 (standard)	5,487	—
283 cid/245 hp (two four-barrel carbs)	1,417	$150.65
283 cid/270 hp (two four-barrel carbs)	1,846	$182.95
283 cid/250 hp (fuel injection)	175	$484.20
283 cid/290 hp (fuel injection)	745	$484.20

Options	Qty	Price
Courtesy lights	3,601	$6.50
Heater	8,909	$102.25
AM radio, signal seeking	7,001	$149.80
Parking brake alarm	3,601	$5.40
Windshield washers	7,929	$16.15
Radiator fan clutch	67	$21.55
Sunshades	3,722	$10.80
Wheels, 15x5.5 (set of five)	214	$0.00
Whitewall tires, 6.70x15	8,173	$31.55
Powerglide automatic transmission	1,878	$199.10
Auxiliary hardtop	5,481	$236.75
Power windows	587	$59.20
Power-operated folding top	661	$139.90
Two-tone exterior paint	2,931	$16.15
Positraction rear axle	4,170	$48.45
Heavy duty brakes and suspension	142	$425.05

	Qty	Price
Four-speed manual transmission	4,175	$188.30
Metallic brakes	333	$26.90
Blackwall tires, 6.70x15 nylon	N/A	N/A
24-gallon fuel tank	N/A	N/A

Exterior Colors	Qty			Qty
Snowcrest White	3,354		Inca Silver	957
Frost Blue	1,024		Regal Turquoise	510
Crown Sapphire	888		Panama Yellow	455
Tuxedo Black	1,594		Signet Red	1,399
Classic Cream	223		Silver	193
Roman Red	1,542		Black	493

1960 Base Corvette Convertible

Total Produced: 10,261   **List Price:** $3,872.00

Dimensions

Weight	2,985.0 lb.	Tire Size:	6.70x15 in.
Length	177.2 in.	Front Track:	57.0 in.
Width	72.8 in.	Rear Track	58.8 in.
Height	51.0 in.		

Engines	Qty	Price
283 cid/230 hp V-8 (standard)	5,827	—
283 cid/245 hp V-8 (two four-barrel carbs)	1,211	$150.65
283 cid/270 hp V-8 (two four-barrel carbs)	2,364	$182.95
283 cid/250 hp V-8 (fuel injection)	100	$484.20
283 cid/290 hp V-8 (fuel injection)	759	$484.20

Options	Qty	Price
Courtesy lights	6,774	$6.50
Heater	9,808	$102.25
AM radio, signal seeking	8,166	$137.75
Parking brake alarm	4,051	$5.40
Windshield washers	7,205	$16.15
Temperature-controlled radiator fan	2,711	$21.55
Sunshades	5,276	$10.80
Wheels, 15x5.5 (set of five)	246	$0.00
Whitewall tires, 6.70x15	9,104	$31.55
Powerglide automatic transmission	1,766	$199.10
Auxiliary hardtop	5,147	$236.75
Power windows	544	$59.20
Power-operated folding top	512	$139.90
Two-tone exterior paint	3,309	$16.15
Positraction rear axle	5,231	$43.05
Heavy duty brakes and steering	119	$333.60
Four-speed manual transmission	5,328	$188.30
Metallic brakes	920	$26.90
Blackwall tires, 6.70x15 nylon	N/A	$15.75
24-gallon fuel tank	N/A	$161.40

Exterior Colors	Qty
Tuxedo Black	1,268
Tasco Turquoise	635
Horizon Blue	766
Honduras Maroon	1,202
Roman Red	1,529
Ermine White	3,717
Cascade Green	140
Sateen Silver	989

1961 Base Corvette Convertible

Total Produced: 10,939   **List Price:** $3,934.00

Dimensions

Weight	3,035.0 lb.	Tire Size	6.70x15 in.
Length	177.2 in.	Front Track	57.0 in.
Width	70.4 in.	Rear Track	58.8 in.
Height	51.5 in.		

Engines	Qty	Price
283 cid/230 hp V-8 (standard)	5,357	—
283 cid/245 hp (two four-barrel carbs)	2,827	$150.65
283 cid/270 hp (two four-barrel carbs)	1,175	$182.95
283 cid/275 hp (fuel injection)	118	$484.20
283 cid/315 hp (fuel injection)	1,462	$484.20

Options	Qty	Price
Heater	10,671	$102.25
AM radio, signal seeking	9,316	$137.75
Positive crankcase ventilation	N/A	$5.40
Wheels, 15x5.5 (set of five)	337	$0.00
Whitewall tires, 6.70x15	9,730	$31.55
Powerglide automatic transmission	1,458	$199.10
Auxiliary hardtop	5,680	$236.75
Power windows	698	$59.20
Power-operated folding top	442	$161.40
Two-tone exterior paint	3,368	$16.15
Positraction rear axle	6,915	$43.05
Heavy duty brakes and steering	233	$333.60
Four-speed manual transmission	7,013	$188.30
Metallic brakes	1,402	$37.70
Blackwall tires, 6.70x15 nylon	N/A	$15.75
24-gallon fuel tank	N/A	$161.40

Exterior Colors	Qty
Tuxedo Black	1,340
Jewel Blue	855
Honduras Maroon	1,645
Roman Red	1,794
Ermine White	3,178
Fawn Beige	1,363
Sateen Silver	747

1962 Base Corvette Convertible

Total Produced: 14,531   **List Price:** $4,038.00

Dimensions

Weight	3,065.0 lb.	Tire Size	6.70x15 in.
Length	177.2 in.	Front Track	57.0 in.
Width	70.4 in.	Rear Track	58.8 in.
Height	51.5 in.		

Engines

	Qty	Price
327 cid/250 hp V-8 (standard)	4,907	—
327 cid/340 hp	4,412	$107.65
327 cid/300 hp	3,294	$53.80
327 cid/360 hp (fuel injection)	1,918	$484.20

Options

	Qty	Price
AM radio, signal seeking	13,076	$137.75
Positive crankcase ventilation	N/A	$5.40
Rear axle, 3.08:1	N/A	$0.00
Wheels, 15x5.5 (set of five)	561	$0.00
Whitewall tires, 6.70x15	N/A	$31.55
Blackwall tires, 6.70x15 nylon	N/A	$15.70

Powerglide automatic transmission	1,532	$199.10
Auxiliary hardtop	8,074	$236.75
Power windows	995	$59.20
Direct flow exhaust system	2,934	$0.00
Power-operated folding top	350	$139.00
Positraction rear axle	14,232	$43.05
Heavy duty brakes and steering	246	$333.60
Four-speed manual transmission	11,318	$188.30
Metallic brakes	2,799	$37.70
24-gallon fuel tank	65	$118.40

Exterior Colors	Qty
Tuxedo Black	N/A
Almond Beige	820
Honduras Maroon	N/A
Roman Red	N/A
Ermine White	N/A
Fawn Beige	1,851
Sateen Silver	N/A

1963 Corvette

Total Produced: 21,513   **List Price**

Base Corvette Coupe	10,594	$4,257.00
Base Corvette Convertible	10,919	$4,037.00

Dimensions

Weight	3,015.0 lb.	Tire Size	6.70x15 in.
Length	175.1 in.	Front Track	56.25 in.
Width	69.6 in.	Rear Track	57.00 in.
Height	49.8 in.		

Engines

Engines	Qty	Price
327 cid/250 hp V-8 (standard)	3,892	—
327 cid/300 hp	8,033	$53.80
327 cid/340 hp	6,978	$107.60
327 cid/360 hp (fuel injection)	2,610	$430.40

Options

Options	Qty	Price
Genuine leather seats	1,114	$80.70
Sebring Silver exterior paint	3,516	$80.70
Soft Ray tinted glass, all windows	629	$16.15
Soft Ray tinted glass, windshield	470	$10.80
Power windows	3,742	$59.20
Auxiliary hardtop (convertible)	5,739	$236.75
Heater/Defroster Delete	124	−$100.00
Air conditioning	278	$421.80
Positraction rear axle	17,554	$43.05
Special highway axle, 3.08:1	211	$2.20
Aluminum knock-off wheels (set of five)	N/A	$322.80
Blackwall tires, 6.70x15 (nylon)	412	$15.70
Whitewall tires, 6.70x15 (rayon)	19,383	$31.55
Power brakes	3,336	$43.05
Sintered metallic brakes	5,310	$37.70

Four-speed manual transmission	17,973	$188.30
Powerglide automatic transmission	2,621	$199.10
36-gallon fuel tank (for coupe)	63	$202.30
Off-road exhaust system	N/A	$37.70
Woodgrained plastic steering wheel	130	$16.15
Power steering	3,063	$75.35
Back-up lamps	318	$10.80
AM radio, signal seeking (early)	11,368	$137.75
AM-FM radio (later)	9,178	$174.35
Special performance equipment	199	$1,818.45

Exterior Colors	Qty
Tuxedo Black	N/A
Ermine White	N/A
Riverside Red	4,612
Silver Blue	N/A
Daytona Blue	3,475
Sebring Silver	3,516
Saddle Tan	N/A

1964 Corvette

Total Produced: 22,229   **List Price**

	Qty	List Price
Base Corvette Coupe	8,304	$4,252.00
Base Corvette Convertible	13,925	$4,037.00

Dimensions

Weight	3,125.0 lb.	Tire Size	6.70x15 in.
Length	175.1 in.	Front Track	56.25 in.
Width	69.6 in.	Rear Track	57.00 in.
Height	49.8 in.		

Engines

	Qty	Price
327 cid/250 hp V-8 (standard)	3,262	—
327 cid/300 hp	10,471	$53.80
327 cid/365 hp	7,171	$107.60
327 cid/375 hp (fuel injection)	1,325	$538.00

Options

	Qty	Price
Auxiliary hardtop (convertible)	7,023	$236.75
Heater/Defroster Delete	60	–$100.00
Air conditioning	1,988	$421.80
Genuine leather seats	1,334	$80.70
Tinted glass, all windows	6,031	$16.15
Tinted glass, windshield	6,387	$10.80
Power windows	3,706	$59.20
Special front and rear suspension	82	$37.70
Positraction rear axle	18,279	$43.05
Special highway axle, 3.08:1	2,310	$2.20
Power brakes	2,270	$43.05
Special sintered metallic brake package	29	$629.50
Sintered metallic brakes, power	4,780	$53.80
Transistor ignition system	552	$75.35

Four-speed manual transmission	19,034	$188.30
Powerglide automatic transmission	2,480	$199.10
36-gallon fuel tank (coupe)	38	$202.30
Off-road exhaust system	1,953	$37.70
Power steering	3,126	$75.35
Aluminum knock-off wheels (set of five)	806	$322.80
Blackwall tires, 6.70x15 (nylon)	372	$15.70
Whitewall tires, 6.70x15 (rayon)	19,977	$31.85
Back-up lamps	11,085	$10.80
AM-FM radio	20,934	$176.50

Exterior Colors	**Qty**
Tuxedo Black	1,897
Ermine White	3,909
Riverside Red	5,274
Silver Blue	3,121
Saddle Tan	1,765
Daytona Blue	3,454
Satin Silver	2,785

1965 Corvette

Total Produced: 23,564		**List Price**
Base Corvette Coupe	8,186	$4,321.00
Base Corvette Convertible	15,378	$4,106.00

Dimensions

Weight	3,135.0 lb.	Tire Size	7.75x15 in.
Length	175.1 in.	Front Track	56.80 in.
Width	69.6 in.	Rear Track	57.60 in.
Height	49.8 in.		

Engines

	Qty	Price
327 cid/250 hp V-8 (standard)	2,551	—
327 cid/300 hp	8,358	$53.80
327 cid/350 hp	4,716	$107.60
327 cid/365 hp	5,011	$129.15
327 cid/375 hp (fuel injection)	771	$538.00
396 cid/425 hp	2,157	$292.00

Options

	Qty	Price
Auxiliary hardtop (convertible)	7,787	$236.75
Heater/Defroster Delete	39	−$100.00
Air conditioning	2,423	$421.80
Genuine leather seats	2,128	$80.70
Tinted glass, all windows	8,752	$16.15
Tinted glass, windshield	7,624	$10.80
Power windows	3,809	$59.20
Special front and rear suspension	975	$37.70
Positraction rear axle	19,965	$43.05
Special highway axle, 3.08:1	1,886	$2.20
Power brakes	4,044	$43.05
Drum brakes (substitution credit)	316	−$64.50
Transistor ignition system	3,686	$75.35

Four-speed manual transmission	21,107	$188.30
Powerglide automatic transmission	2,021	$199.10
36-gallon fuel tank (coupe)	41	$202.30
Off-road exhaust system	2,468	$37.70
Side-mount exhaust system	759	$134.50
Power steering	3,236	$96.85
Teakwood steering wheel	2,259	$48.45
Telescopic steering column	3,917	$43.05
Aluminum knock-off wheels (five)	1,116	$322.80
Blackwall tires, 7.75x15 (nylon)	168	$15.70
Whitewall tires, 7.75x15 (rayon)	19,300	$31.85
Goldwall tires, 7.75x15 (rayon)	989	$50.05
Comfort and Convenience Group	15,397	$16.15
AM-FM radio	22,113	$203.40

Exterior Colors	**Qty**
Tuxedo Black	1,191
Ermine White	2,216
Rally Red	3,688
Glen Green	3,782
Milano Maroon	2,831
Silver Pearl	2,552
Goldwood Yellow	1,275
Nassau Blue	6,022

1966 Corvette

Total Produced: 27,720

List Price

Base Corvette Coupe	9,958	$4,295.00
Base Corvette Convertible	17,762	$4,084.00

Dimensions

Weight	3,140.0 lb.	Tire Size	7.75x15 in.
Length	175.1 in.	Front Track	56.80 in.
Width	69.6 in.	Rear Track	57.60 in.
Height	49.8 in.		

Engines

	Qty	Price
327 cid/300 hp V-8 (standard)	9,755	—
327 cid/350 hp	7,591	$105.35
427 cid/390 hp	5,116	$181.20
427 cid/425 hp	5,258	$312.85

Options

	Qty	Price
Auxiliary hardtop (convertible)	8,463	$231.75
Heater/Defroster Delete	54	−$97.85
Air conditioning	3,520	$412.90
Genuine leather seats	2,002	$79.00
Tinted glass, all windows	11,270	$15.80
Tinted glass, windshield	9,270	$10.55
Headrests	1,033	$42.15
Shoulder belts	37	$26.35
Power windows	4,562	$57.95
Special front and rear suspension	2,705	$36.90
Positraction rear axle	24,056	$42.15
Power brakes	5,464	$42.15
Special heavy duty brakes	382	$342.30
Transistor ignition system	7,146	$73.75
Air Injection Reactor	2,380	$44.75

Four-speed manual transmission	10,837	$184.35
Four-speed manual transmission, close ratio	13,903	$184.35
Four-speed manual transmission, close ratio, heavy duty	15	$237.00
Powerglide automatic transmission	2,401	$194.85
36-gallon fuel tank (coupe)	66	$198.05
Off-road exhaust system	2,795	$36.90
Side-mount exhaust system	3,617	$131.65
Power steering	5,611	$94.80
Teakwood steering wheel	3,941	$47.40
Telescopic steering column	3,670	$42.15
Aluminum knock-off wheels (set of five)	1,194	$316.00
Whitewall tires, 7.75x15 (rayon)	17,969	$31.30
Goldwall tires, 7.75x15 (rayon)	5,557	$46.55
Traffic hazard lamp switch	5,764	$11.60
AM-FM radio	26,363	$199.10

Exterior Colors	**Qty**
Tuxedo Black	1,190
Ermine White	2,120
Rally Red	3,366
Milano Maroon	3,799
Silver Pearl	2,967
Sunfire Yellow	2,339
Nassau Blue	6,100
Laguna Blue	2,054
Trophy Blue	1,463
Mosport Green	2,311

1967 Corvette

Total Produced: 22,940

List Price

Base Corvette Coupe	8,504	$4,388.75
Base Corvette Convertible	14,436	$4,240.75

Dimensions

Weight	3,155.0 lb.	Tire Size	7.75x15 in.
Length	175.1 in.	Front Track	56.80 in.
Width	69.6 in.	Rear Track	57.60 in.
Height	49.8 in.		

Engines

	Qty	Price
327 cid/300 hp V-8 (standard)	6,858	—
327 cid/350 hp	6,375	$105.35
427 cid/390 hp	3,832	$200.15
427 cid/400 hp	2,101	$305.50
427 cid/430 hp	20	$947.90
427 cid/435 hp	3,754	$437.10

Options

	Qty	Price
Auxiliary hardtop (convertible)	6,880	$231.75
Auxiliary hardtop vinyl covering	1,966	$52.70
Heater/Defroster Delete	35	−$97.85
Air conditioning	3,788	$412.90
Genuine leather seats	1,601	$79.00
Tinted glass, all windows	11,331	$15.80
Tinted Glass, windshield	6,558	$10.55
Headrests	1,762	$42.15
Shoulder belts	1,426	$26.35
Power windows	4,036	$57.95
Special front and rear suspension	2,198	$36.90
Positraction rear axle	20,308	$42.15
Power brakes	4,766	$42.15

Special heavy duty brakes	267	$342.30
Transistor ignition system	5,769	$73.75
Air Injection Reactor	2,573	$44.75
Four-speed manual transmission	9,157	$184.35
Four-speed manual transmission, close ratio	11,015	$184.35
Four-speed manual transmission, close ratio, heavy duty	20	$237.00
Powerglide automatic transmission	2,324	$194.35
36-gallon fuel tank (coupe)	2	$198.05
Off-road exhaust system	2,326	$36.90
Side-mount exhaust system	4,209	$131.65
Power steering	5,747	$94.80
Telescopic steering column	2,415	$42.15
Cast aluminum bolt-on wheels (set of five)	720	$263.30
Whitewall tires, 7.75x15	13,445	$31.35
Redline tires, 7.75x15	4,230	$46.65
Speed warning indicator	2,108	$10.55
AM-FM radio	22,193	$172.75
Aluminum cylinder heads (427 cid/435 hp)	16	$368.65

Exterior Colors	**Qty**
Tuxedo Black	815
Ermine White	1,423
Rally Red	2,341
Marina Blue	3,840
Lynndale Blue	1,381
Elkhart Blue	1,096
Goodwood Green	4,293
Sunfire Yellow	2,325
Silver Pearl	1,952
Marlboro Maroon	3,464

1968 Corvette

Total Produced: 28,566

		List Price
Base Corvette Coupe	9,936	$4,663.00
Base Corvette Convertible	18,630	$4,320.00

Dimensions

Weight	3,210.0 lb.	Tire Size	F70x15
Length	182.5 in.	Front Track	58.30 in.
Width	69.0 in.	Rear Track	59.00 in.
Height	47.8 in.		

Engines

	Qty	Price
327 cid/300 hp V-8 (standard)	6,499	—
327 cid/350 hp	9,440	$105.35
427 cid/390 hp	7,717	$200.15
427 cid/400 hp	1,932	$305.50
427 cid/430 hp	80	$947.90
427 cid/435 hp	2,898	$437.10

Options

	Qty	Price
Auxiliary hardtop (convertible)	8,735	$231.75
Auxiliary hardtop vinyl covering	3,050	$52.70
Rear window defroster	693	$31.60
Air conditioning	5,664	$412.90
Genuine leather seats	2,429	$79.00
Tinted glass, all windows	17,635	$15.80
Tinted glass, windshield	5,509	$10.55
Headrests	3,197	$42.15
Custom shoulder belts (standard on coupe)	350	$26.35
Power windows	7,065	$57.95
Special front and rear suspension	1,758	$36.90
Positraction rear axle	27,008	$46.35

Power brakes	9,559	$42.15
Special heavy duty brakes	81	$384.45
Transistor ignition system	5,457	$73.75
Four-speed manual transmission	10,760	$184.35
Four-speed manual transmission, close ratio	12,337	$184.35
Four-speed manual transmission, close ratio, heavy duty	80	$263.30
Turbo Hydra-Matic transmission	5,063	$226.45
Alarm system	388	$26.35
Off-road exhaust system	4,695	$36.90
Power steering	12,364	$94.80
Telescopic steering column	6,477	$42.15
Bright metal wheel covers	8,971	$57.95
White stripe tires, F70x15 (nylon)	9,692	$31.30
Red stripe tires, F70x15 (nylon)	11,686	$31.30
Speed warning indicator	3,453	$10.55
AM-FM radio	24,609	$172.75
AM-FM radio, stereo	3,311	$278.10
Aluminum cylinder heads (427 cid/435 hp)	624	$805.75

Exterior Colors	Qty
Tuxedo Black	708
Polar White	1,868
Rally Red	2,918
Le Mans Blue	4,722
International Blue	2,473
British Green	4,779
Safari Yellow	3,133
Silverstone Silver	3,435
Cordovan Maroon	1,155
Corvette Bronze	3,374

1969 Corvette

Total Produced: 38,762

		List Price
Base Corvette Coupe	22,129	$4,781.00
Base Corvette Convertible	16,633	$4,438.00

Dimensions

Weight	3,245.0 lb.	Tire Size	F70x15
Length	182.5 in.	Front Track	58.70 in.
Width	69.0 in.	Rear Track	59.40 in.
Height	47.8 in.		

Engines

	Qty	Price
350 cid/300 hp V-8 (standard)	10,473	—
350 cid/350 hp	12,846	$131.65
427 cid/390 hp	10,531	$221.20
427 cid/400 hp	2,072	$326.55
427 cid/430 hp	116	$1,032.15
427 cid/430 hp (special L88/ZL1)	2	$4,718.35
427 cid/435 hp	2,722	$437.10

Options

	Qty	Price
Auxiliary hardtop (convertible)	7,878	$252.80
Auxiliary hardtop vinyl covering	3,266	$57.95
Rear window defroster	2,485	$32.65
Air conditioning	11,859	$428.70
Genuine leather seats	3,729	$79.00
Tinted glass, all windows	31,270	$16.90
Headrests	38,762	$17.95
Custom shoulder belts (standard on coupe)	600	$42.15
Power windows	9,816	$63.20
Special front and rear suspension	1,661	$36.90
Positraction rear axle	36,965	$46.35
Power brakes	16,876	$42.15
Special heavy duty brakes	115	$384.45

Transistor ignition system	5,702	$81.10
Engine block heater	824	$10.55
Four-speed manual transmission	16,507	$184.80
Four-speed manual transmission, close ratio	13,741	$184.80
Four-speed manual transmission, close ratio, heavy duty	101	$290.40
Turbo Hydra-Matic transmission	8,161	$221.80
Heavy duty clutch	102	$79.00
Alarm system	12,436	$26.35
Side-mount exhaust system	4,355	$147.45
Power steering	22,866	$105.35
Tilt/telescopic steering column	10,325	$84.30
Deluxe wheel covers	8,073	$57.95
Front fender louver trim	11,962	$21.10
White stripe tires, F70x15 (nylon)	21,379	$31.30
White letter tires, F70x15 (nylon)	2,398	$33.15
Red stripe tires, F70x15 (nylon)	5,210	$31.30
Speed warning indicator	3,561	$11.60
AM-FM radio	33,871	$172.75
AM-FM radio, stereo	4,114	$278.10
Aluminum cylinder heads (427 cid/435 hp)	390	$832.05

Exterior Colors	**Qty**
Tuxedo Black	N/A
Can Am White	N/A
Monza Red	N/A
Le Mans Blue	N/A
Riverside Gold	N/A
Fathom Green	N/A
Daytona Yellow	N/A
Cortez Silver	N/A
Burgundy	N/A
Monaco Orange	N/A

1970 Corvette

Total Produced: 17,316   **List Price**

Base Corvette Coupe	10,668	$5,192.00
Base Corvette Convertible	6,648	$4,849.00

Dimensions

Weight	3,285.0 lb.	Tire Size	F70x15
Length	182.5 in.	Front Track	58.70 in.
Width	69.0 in.	Rear Track	59.40 in.
Height	47.8 in.		

Engines

Engines	Qty	Price
350 cid/300 hp V-8 (standard)	6,646	—
350 cid/350 hp	4,910	$158.00
350 cid/370 hp	1,287	$447.60
454 cid/390 hp	4,473	$289.65

Options

Options	Qty	Price
Auxiliary hardtop (convertible)	2,556	$273.85
Auxiliary hardtop vinyl covering	832	$63.20
Custom interior trim	3,191	$158.00
Rear window defroster	1,281	$36.90
Air conditioning	6,659	$447.65
Custom shoulder belts (standard on coupe)	475	$42.15
Power windows	4,813	$63.20
Optional rear axle ratios	2,862	$12.65
Power brakes	8,984	$47.40
Four-speed manual transmission, close ratio	4,383	$0.00
Four-speed manual transmission, close ratio, heavy duty	25	$95.00
Turbo Hydra-Matic transmission	5,102	$0.00
Alarm system	6,727	$31.60

Power steering	11,907	$105.35
Tilt/telescopic steering column	5,803	$84.30
Deluxe wheel covers	3,467	$57.95
White stripe tires, F70x15 (nylon)	6,589	$31.30
White letter tires, F70x15 (nylon)	7,985	$33.15
Heavy duty battery (standard with 454 cid)	165	$15.80
AM-FM radio	14,529	$172.75
AM-FM radio, stereo	2,462	$278.10
California emission test	1,758	$36.90
ZR1 secial purpose package	25	$968.95

Exterior Colors	Qty
Classic White	N/A
Monza Red	N/A
Marlboro Maroon	N/A
Mulsanne Blue	N/A
Bridgehampton Blue	N/A
Donnybrooke Green	N/A
Daytona Yellow	N/A
Cortez Silver	N/A
Laguna Gray	N/A
Ontario Orange	N/A
Corvette Bronze	N/A

1971 Corvette

Total Produced: 21,801   **List Price**

Base Corvette Coupe	14,680	$5,496.00
Base Corvette Convertible	7,121	$5,259.00

Dimensions

Weight	3,202.0 lb.	Tire Size	F70x15
Length	182.5 in.	Front Track	58.70 in.
Width	69.0 in.	Rear Track	59.40 in.
Height	47.8 in.		

Engines

Engines	Qty	Price
350 cid/270 hp V-8 (standard)	14,567	—
350 cid/330 hp	1,949	$483.00
454 cid/365 hp	5,097	$295.00
454 cid/425 hp	188	$1,221.00

Options

Options	Qty	Price
Auxiliary hardtop (convertible)	2,619	$274.00
Auxiliary hardtop vinyl covering	832	$63.00
Custom interior trim	2,602	$158.00
Rear window defroster	1,598	$42.00
Air conditioning	11,481	$459.00
Custom shoulder belts (standard on coupe)	677	$42.00
Power windows	6,192	$79.00
Optional rear axle ratio	2,395	$13.00
Power brakes	13,558	$47.00
Four-speed manual tranmission, close ratio	2,387	$0.00
Four-speed manual transmission, close ratio, heavy duty	130	$100.00
Turbo Hydra-Matic transmission	10,060	$0.00
Alarm system	8,501	$31.60
Power steering	17,904	$115.90

Tilt/telescopic steering column	8,130	$84.30
Deluxe wheel covers	3,007	$63.00
White stripe tires, F70x15 (nylon)	6,711	$28.00
White letter tires, F70x15 (nylon)	12,449	$42.00
Heavy duty battery (standard with 454 cid)	1,455	$15.80
AM-FM radio	18,078	$178.00
AM-FM radio, stereo	3,431	$283.00
ZR1 special purpose package (350 cid/330 hp)	8	$1,010.00
ZR2 special purpose package (454 cid/425 hp)	12	$1,747.00

Exterior Colors	Qty	Exterior Colors	Qty
Nevada Silver	1,177	Bridgehampton Blue	1,417
Sunflower Yellow	1,177	Brands Hatch Green	3,445
Classic White	1,875	Ontario Orange	2,269
Mille Miglia Red	2,180	Steel Cities Gray	1,591
Mulsanne Blue	2,465	War Bonnet Yellow	3,706

1972 Corvette

Total Produced: 27,004   **List Price**

Base Corvette Coupe	20,496	$5,533.00
Base Corvette Convertible	6,508	$5,296.00

Dimensions

Weight	3,205.0 lb.	Tire Size	F70x15
Length	182.5 in.	Front Track	58.70 in.
Width	69.0 in.	Rear Track	59.40 in.
Height	47.8 in.		

Engines

Engines	Qty	Price
350 cid/200 hp V-8 (standard)	21,350	—
350 cid/255 hp	1,741	$483.45
454 cid/270 hp	3,913	$294.90

Options	Qty	Price
Auxiliary hardtop (convertible)	2,646	$273.85
Vinyl covering (for auxiliary hardtop)	811	$158.00
Custom interior trim	8,709	$158.00
Three-point seat belts	17,693	N/A
Air Injection Reactor	3,912	N/A
Rear window defroster	2,221	$42.15
Air conditioning	17,011	$464.50
Custom shoulder belts (standard on coupe)	749	$42.15
Power windows	9,495	$83.35
Optional rear axle ratio	1,986	$12.65
Power brakes	18,770	$47.40
Four-speed manual transmission, close ratio	1,638	$0.00
Turbo Hydra-Matic transmission	14,543	$0.00
Power steering	24,794	$115.90
Tilt/telescopic steering column	12,992	$84.30
Deluxe wheel covers	3,593	$63.20
White stripe tires, F70x15 (nylon)	6,666	$30.95
White letter tires, F70x15 (nylon)	16,623	$43.65
Heavy duty battery (standard with 454 cid)	2,969	$15.80
AM-FM radio	19,480	$178.00
AM-FM radio, stereo	7,189	$283.35
California emission test	1,967	$15.80
ZR1 special purpose package (350 cid/255 hp)	20	$1,010.05

Exterior Colors	Qty	Exterior Colors	Qty
Pewter Silver	1,372	Bryar Blue	1,617
Sunflower Yellow	1,543	Elkhart Green	4,200
Classic White	2,763	Ontario Orange	4,891
Mille Miglia Red	2,478	Steel Cities Gray	2,346
Targa Blue	3,198	War Bonnet Yellow	2,550

1973 Corvette

Total Produced: 30,464

		List Price
Base Corvette Coupe	25,521	$5,561.50
Base Corvette Convertible	4,943	$5,398.50

Dimensions

Weight	3,416.0 lb.	Tire Size	GR70x15
Length	184.6 in.	Front Track	58.70 in.
Width	69.0 in.	Rear Track	59.50 in.
Height	47.8 in.		

Engines	Qty	Price
350 cid/190 hp V-8 (standard)	20,342	—
350 cid/250 hp	5,710	$299.00
454 cid/275 hp	4,412	$250.00

Options	Qty	Price
Auxiliary hardtop (convertible)	1,328	$267.00
Auxiliary hardtop, vinyl covering	323	$62.00
Custom interior trim	13,434	$154.00
Rear window defroster	4,412	$41.00
Air conditioning	21,578	$452.00
Custom shoulder belts (standard on coupe)	788	$41.00
Power windows	14,024	$83.00
Optional rear axle ratio	1,791	$12.00
Power brakes	24,168	$46.00
Four-speed manual transmission, close ratio	3,704	$0.00
Turbo Hydra-Matic transmission	17,927	$0.00
Power steering	27,872	$113.00
Tilt/telescopic steering column	17,949	$82.00
Deluxe wheel covers	1,739	$62.00
White stripe tires, GR70x15	19,903	$32.00
White letter tires, GR70x15	4,541	$45.00

Cast aluminum wheels (set of four)	4	$175.00
Off-road suspension and brake package	45	$369.00
Heavy duty battery (standard with 454 cid)	4,912	$15.00
AM-FM radio	17,598	$173.00
AM-FM radio, stereo	12,482	$276.00
Rear-view mirror map light	8,186	$5.00
California emission test	3,008	$15.00

Exterior Colors	Qty	Exterior Colors	Qty
Classic White	N/A	Elkhart Green	N/A
Silver	N/A	Yellow	N/A
Medium Blue	N/A	Metallic Yellow	N/A
Dark Blue	N/A	Mille Miglia Red	N/A
Blue-Green	N/A	Orange	N/A

1974 Corvette

Total Produced: 37,502

List Price

Base Corvette Coupe	32,028	$6,001.50
Base Corvette Convertible	5,474	$5,765.50

Dimensions

Weight	3,388.0 lb.	Tire Size	GR70x15
Length	185.5 in.	Front Track	58.70 in.
Width	69.0 in.	Rear Track	59.50 in.
Height	47.8 in.		

Engines

	Qty	Price
350 cid/195 hp V-8 (standard)	27,318	—
350 cid/250 hp	6,690	$299.00
454 cid/275 hp	3,494	$250.00

Options	Qty	Price
Auxiliary hardtop (convertible)	2,612	$267.00
Auxiliary hardtop, vinyl covering	367	$62.00
Custom interior trim	19,959	$154.00
Custom shoulder belts (standard on coupe)	618	$41.00
Tilt/telescopic steering column	27,700	$82.00
Rear-view mirror map light	16,101	$5.00
Air conditioning	29,397	$467.00
Power steering	35,944	$117.00
Power brakes	33,306	$49.00
Power windows	23,940	$86.00
AM-FM radio	17,374	$173.00
AM-FM radio, stereo	19,581	$276.00
Dual horns	5,258	$4.00
Rear window defroster	9,322	$43.00
White stripe tires, GR70x15	9,140	$32.00
White letter tires, GR70x15	24,102	$45.00
Turbo Hydra-Matic transmission	25,146	$0.00
Four-speed manual transmission, close ratio	3,494	$0.00
Optional rear axle ratio	1,219	$12.00
Gymkhana suspension	1,905	$7.00
Off-road suspension and brake package	47	$400.00
Heavy duty battery (standard with 454 cid)	9,169	$15.00
California emission test	N/A	$20.00

Exterior Colors	Qty	Exterior Colors	Qty
Classic White	N/A	Bright Yellow	N/A
Silver Mist	N/A	Dark Brown	N/A
Corvette Gray	N/A	Medium Red	N/A
Corvette Medium Blue	N/A	Mille Miglia Red	N/A
Dark Green	N/A	Corvette Orange	N/A

1975 Corvette

Total Produced: 38,465   **List Price**

Base Corvette Coupe	33,836	$6,810.10
Base Corvette Convertible	4,629	$6,550.10

Dimensions

Weight	3,529.0 lb.	Tire Size	GR70x15	
Length	185.2 in.	Front Track	58.70 in.	
Width	69.0 in.	Rear Track	59.50 in.	
Height	48.1 in.			

Engines

Engines	Qty	Price
350 cid/165 hp V-8 (standard)	36,093	—
350 cid/205 hp	2,372	$336.00

Options

Options	Qty	Price
Auxiliary hardtop (convertible)	2,407	$267.00
Auxiliary hardtop, vinyl covering	279	$83.00
Custom interior trim	N/A	$154.00
Custom shoulder belts (standard on coupe)	646	$41.00
Tilt/telescopic steering column	31,830	$82.00
Rear-view mirror map light	21,676	$5.00
Air conditioning	31,914	$490.00
Power steering	37,591	$129.00
Power brakes	35,842	$50.00
Power windows	28,745	$93.00
AM-FM radio	12,902	$178.00
AM-FM radio, stereo	24,701	$284.00
Dual horns	22,011	$4.00
Rear window defroster	13,760	$46.00
White stripe tires, GR70x15	5,233	$35.00
White letter tires, GR70x15	30,407	$48.00
Turbo Hydra-Matic transmission	28,473	$0.00

Four-speed manual transmission, close ratio	1,057	$0.00
Optional rear axle ratios	1,969	$12.00
Gymkhana suspension	3,194	$7.00
Off-road suspension and brake package	144	$400.00
Heavy duty battery	16,778	$15.00
California emission test	3,037	$20.00

Exterior Colors	Qty	Exterior Colors	Qty
Classic White	8,007	Bright Yellow	2,883
Silver	4,710	Medium Saddle	3,403
Bright Blue	2,869	Orange Flame	3,030
Steel Blue	1,268	Dark Red	3,342
Bright Green	1,664	Mille Miglia Red	3,355

1976 Base Corvette Coupe

Total Produced: 46,558   **List Price:** $7,604.85

Dimensions

Weight	3,541.0 lb.	Tire Size	GR70x15
Length	185.2 in.	Front Track	58.70 in.
Width	69.0 in.	Rear Track	59.50 in.
Height	48.1 in.		

Engines	Qty	Price
350 cid/180 hp V-8 (standard)	40,838	—
350 cid/210 hp	5,720	$481.00

Options	Qty	Price
Custom interior trim	N/A	$164.00
Tilt/telescopic steering column	41,797	$95.00
Rear-view mirror map light	35,361	$10.00
Air conditioning	40,787	$523.00

Power steering	46,385	$151.00
Power brakes	46,558	$59.00
Power windows	38,700	$107.00
AM-FM radio	11,083	$187.00
AM-FM radio, stereo	34,272	$281.00
Rear window defroster	24,960	$78.00
Aluminum wheels (set of four)	6,253	$299.00
White stripe tires, GR70x15	3,992	$37.00
White letter tires, GR70x15	39,923	$51.00
Turbo Hydra-Matic transmission	36,625	$0.00
Four-speed manual transmission, close ratio	2,088	$0.00
Optional rear axle Ratios	1,371	$13.00
Gymkhana suspension	5,368	$35.00
Heavy duty battery	25,909	$16.00
California emission test	3,527	$50.00

Exterior Colors	**Qty**
Classic White	10,764
Silver	6,934
Bright Blue	3,268
Dark Green	2,038
Mahogany	4,182
Bright Yellow	3,389
Buckskin	2,954
Dark Brown	4,447
Orange Flame	4,073
Red	4,590

1977 Base Corvette Coupe

Total Produced: 49,213   **List Price:** $8,647.65

Dimensions

Weight	3,534.0 lb.	Tire Size	GR70x15
Length	185.2 in.	Front Track	58.70 in.
Width	69.0 in.	Rear Track	59.50 in.
Height	48.1 in.		

Engines

350 cid/180 hp V-8 (standard)	43,065	—
350 cid/210 hp V-8	6,148	$495.00

Options	Qty	Price
Tilt/telescopic steering column	46,487	$165.00
Convenience group	40,872	$22.00
Color-keyed floor mats	36,763	$22.00
Sport mirrors	20,206	$36.00
Air conditioning	45,249	$553.00
Cruise control	29,161	$88.00
Power windows	44,341	$116.00
AM-FM radio	4,700	$187.00
AM-FM radio, stereo	18,483	$281.00
AM-FM radio, stereo with eight-track tape	24,603	$414.00
Luggage and roof panel rack	16,860	$73.00
Rear window defogger	30,411	$84.00
Aluminum wheels (set of four)	12,646	$321.00
Trailer package	289	$83.00
White letter tires, GR70x15	46,227	$57.00
Turbo Hydra-Matic transmission	41,231	$0.00
Four-speed manual transmission, close ratio	2,060	$0.00
Optional rear axle ratios	972	$14.00
Gymkhana suspension	7,269	$38.00

Heavy duty battery	32,882	$17.00
High altitude emission equipment	854	$22.00
California emission test	4,084	$70.00

Exterior Colors	Qty	Exterior Colors	Qty
Classic White	9,408	Yellow	71
Silver	5,518	Bright Yellow	1,942
Black	6,070	Orange	4,012
Light Blue	5,967	Tan	4,588
Dark Blue	4,065	Medium Red	4,057
Chartreuse	1	Dark Red	3,434

1978 Corvette Coupe

Total Produced: 46,776   **List Price**

	Qty	List Price
Base Corvette Coupe	40,274	$9,351.89
Limited Edition Pace Car	6,502	$13,653.21

Dimensions

Weight	3,572.0 lb.	Tire Size	P255/70R15
Length	185.2 in.	Front Track	58.70 in.
Width	69.0 in.	Rear Track	59.50 in.
Height	48.0 in.		

Engines	Qty	Price
350 cid/185 hp V-8 (standard)	34,037	—
350 cid/220 hp	12,739	$525.00

Options	Qty	Price
Silver Anniversary paint	15,283	$399.00
Removable glass roof panels	972	$349.00
Tilt/telescopic steering column	37,858	$175.00
Convenience group	37,222	$84.00
Sport mirrors	38,405	$40.00

Air conditioning	37,638	$605.00
Cruise control	31,608	$99.00
Power windows	36,931	$130.00
Power door locks	12,187	$120.00
AM-FM radio	2,057	$199.00
AM-FM radio, stereo	10,189	$286.00
AM-FM radio, stereo with eight-track tape	20,899	$419.00
AM-FM radio, stereo with CB radio	7,138	$638.00
Dual rear speakers	12,340	$49.00
Power antenna	23,069	$49.00
Rear window defogger	30,912	$95.00
Aluminum wheels (set of four)	28,008	$340.00
Trailer package	972	$89.00
White letter tires, P225/70R15	26,203	$51.00
White letter tires, P255/60R15	18,296	$216.32
Automatic transmission	38,614	$0.00
Four-speed manual transmission, close ratio	3,385	$0.00
Optional rear axle ratios	382	$15.00
Gymkhana suspension	12,590	$41.00
Heavy duty battery	28,243	$18.00
High altitude emission equipment	260	$33.00
California emission test	3,405	$75.00

Exterior Colors	Qty	Exterior Colors	Qty
Classic White	4,150	Yellow	1,243
Silver	3,232	Light Beige	1,686
Silver Anniversary	15,283	Red	2,074
Black	4,573	Mahogany	2,121
Black/Silver Pace	6,502	Dark Blue	2,084
Light Blue	1,960	Dark Brown	1,991

1979 Base Corvette Coupe

Total Produced: 53,807   **List Price:** $10,220.23

Dimensions

Weight	3,503.0 lb.	Tire Size	P255/70R15
Length	185.2 in.	Front Track	58.70 in.
Width	69.0 in.	Rear Track	59.50 in.
Height	48.0 in.		

Engines	Qty	Price
350 cid/195 hp V-8 (standard)	39,291	—
350 cid/225 hp	14,516	$565.00

Options	Qty	Price
Removable glass roof panels	14,480	$365.00
Tilt/telescopic steering column	47,463	$190.00
Convenience group	41,530	$94.00
Sport mirrors	48,211	$45.00
Spoilers, front and rear	6,853	$265.00
Air conditioning	47,136	$635.00
Cruise control	34,445	$113.00
Power windows	20,631	$141.00
Power door locks	9,054	$131.00
AM-FM radio, stereo	9,256	$90.00
AM-FM radio, stereo with eight-track tape	21,435	$228.00
AM-FM radio, stereo with cassette tape	12,110	$234.00
AM-FM radio, stereo with CB radio	4,483	$439.00
Dual rear speakers	37,754	$52.00
Power antenna	35,730	$52.00
Rear window defogger	41,587	$102.00
Aluminum wheels (set of four)	33,741	$380.00
Trailer package	1,001	$98.00
White letter tires, P225/70R15	29,603	$54.00

White letter tires, P255/60R15	17,920	$226.00
Automatic transmission	41,454	$0.00
Four-speed manual transmission, close ratio	4,062	$0.00
Optional rear axle ratios	428	$19.00
Gymkhana suspension	12,321	$49.00
Heavy duty shock absorbers	2,164	$33.00
Heavy duty battery	3,405	$21.00
High altitude emission equipment	56	$35.00
California emission test	3,798	$83.00

Exterior Colors	Qty	Exterior Colors	Qty
Classic White	8,629	Dark Green	2,426
Silver	7,331	Light Beige	2,951
Black	10,465	Dark Brown	4,053
Light Blue	3,203	Dark Blue	5,670
Yellow	2,357	Red	6,707

1980 Base Corvette Coupe

Total Produced: 40,614   **List Price:** $13,140.24

Dimensions

Weight	3,336.0 lb.	Tire Size	P255/70R15
Length	185.2 in.	Front Track	58.70 in.
Width	69.0 in.	Rear Track	59.50 in.
Height	48.0 in.		

Engines	Qty	Price
350 cid/190 hp V-8 (standard)	32,324	—
305 cid/180 hp (California)	3,221	–$50.00
350 cid/230 hp	5,069	$595.00

Options	Qty	Price
Removable glass roof panels	19,695	$391.00
Roof panel carrier	3,755	$125.00
Cruise control	30,821	$123.00
Power door locks	32,692	$140.00
AM-FM radio, stereo	6,138	$46.00
AM-FM radio, stereo with eight-track tape	15,708	$155.00
AM-FM radio, stereo with cassette tape	15,148	$168.00
AM-FM radio, stereo with CB radio	2,434	$391.00
Radio Delete	201	−$126.00
Dual rear speakers	36,650	$52.00
Power antenna	32,863	$56.00
Rear window defogger	36,589	$109.00
Aluminum wheels (set of four)	34,128	$407.00
Trailer package	796	$105.00
White letter tires, P225/70R15	26,208	$62.00
White letter tires, P255/60R15	13,140	$426.00
Automatic transmission	34,838	$0.00
Four-speed manual transmission	5,726	$0.00
Gymkhana suspension	9,907	$55.00
Heavy duty shock absorbers	1,695	$35.00
Heavy duty battery	1,337	$22.00
California emission test	3,221	$250.00

Exterior Colors	Qty	Exterior Colors	Qty
White	7,780	Yellow	2,077
Silver	4,341	Dark Green	844
Black	7,250	Frost Beige	3,070
Dark Blue	4,135	Dark Claret	3,451
Dark Brown	2,300	Red	5,714

1981 Base Corvette Coupe

Total Produced: 40,606   **List Price:** $16,258.52

Dimensions

Weight	3,307.0 lb.	Tire Size	P255/70R15
Length	185.2 in.	Front Track	58.70 in.
Width	69.0 in.	Rear Track	59.50 in.
Height	48.0 in.		

Engines

350 cid/190 hp V-8 (standard, no options)

Options	Qty	Price
Removable glass roof panels	29,095	$414.00
Roof panel carrier	3,303	$135.00
Cruise control	32,522	$155.00
Power door locks	36,322	$145.00
Power driver seat	29,200	$183.00
AM-FM radio, stereo	5,145	$95.00
AM-FM radio, stereo with eight-track tape	8,262	$386.00
AM-FM radio, stereo with eight-track tape and CB radio	792	$712.00
AM-FM radio, stereo with cassette tape	22,892	$423.00
AM-FM radio, stereo with cassette tape and CB radio	2,349	$750.00
Radio Delete	315	–$118.00
Power antenna	32,903	$55.00
Rear window defogger	36,893	$119.00
Electric sport mirrors	13,567	$117.00
Two-tone paint	5,352	$399.00
Aluminum wheels (set of four)	36,485	$428.00
Trailer package	916	$110.00
White letter tires, P225/70R15	21,939	$72.00
White letter tires P255/60R15	18,004	$491.92

Automatic transmission	34,888	$0.00
Four-speed manual transmission	5,757	$0.00
Performance axle ratio	2,400	$20.00
Gymkhana suspension	7,803	$57.00
Heavy duty shock absorbers	1,128	$37.00
California emission test	4,951	$46.00

Exterior Colors	Qty	Exterior Colors	Qty
Mahogany Metallic	1,092	Dark Blue Metallic	2,522
White	6,387	Beige/Dark Bronze	N/A
Silver Metallic	2,590	Yellow	1,031
Charcoal Metallic	3,485	Autumn Red/Dark Claret	N/A
Black	4,712	Beige	3,842
Silver/Dark Blue	N/A	Red	4,310
Bright Blue Metallic	1	Maroon Metallic	1,618
Silver/Charcoal	N/A		

1982 Corvette Coupe

Total Produced: 25,407   **List Price**

Base Corvette Coupe	18,648	$18,290.07
Collector Edition Hatchback	6,759	$22,537.59

Dimensions

Weight	3,342.0 lb.	Tire Size	P255/70R15
Length	185.2 in.	Front Track	58.70 in.
Width	69.0 in.	Rear Track	59.50 in.
Height	48.0 in.		

Engines

350 cid/200 hp V-8 (cross-fire injection, no options)

Options	Qty	Price
Removable glass roof panels	14,763	$443.00
Roof panel carrier	1,992	$144.00
Heavy duty cooling	6,006	$57.00
Cruise control	24,313	$165.00
Power door locks	23,936	$155.00
Power driver seat	22,585	$197.00
AM-FM radio, stereo	1,533	$101.00
AM-FM radio, stereo with eight-track tape	923	$386.00
AM-FM radio, stereo with cassette tape	20,355	$423.00
AM-FM radio, stereo with cassette and CB radio	1,987	$755.00
Radio Delete	150	−$124.00
Power antenna	15,557	$60.00
Rear window defogger	16,886	$129.00
Electric sport mirrors	20,301	$125.00
Two-tone paint	4,871	$428.00
Aluminum wheels	16,844	$458.00
White letter tires, P225/70R15	5,932	$80.00
White letter tires, P255/60R15	19,070	$542.52
Gymkhana suspension	5,457	$61.00
California emission test	4,951	$46.00

Exterior Colors	Qty	Exterior Colors	Qty
White	2,975	Dark Blue	562
Gold	648	White/Silver	664
Silver	711	Bright Blue	567
Silver Beige	6,759	Silver Charcoal	1,239
Black	2,357	Charcoal	1,093
Red	2,155	Silver/Dark Claret	1,301
Silver Blue	1,124	Silver Green	723
Dark Claret	853	Silver Blue/Blue	1,667

1983 Corvette

GM produced 83 Corvettes, but none was offered to the public.

1984 Base Corvette Coupe

Total Produced: 51,547   **List Price:** $21,800.00

Dimensions

Weight	3,192.0 lb.	Tire Size	P255/50VR16
Length	176.5 in.	Front Track	59.60 in.
Width	71.0 in.	Rear Track	60.40 in.
Height	46.7 in.		

Engines

350 cid/205 hp V-8 (cross-fire injection, no options)

Options	Qty	Price
Transparent roof panel	15,767	$595.00
Sport seat, cloth	4,003	$625.00
Base seats, leather	40,568	$400.00
Cruise control	49,832	$185.00
Power door locks	49,545	$165.00
Power driver seat	48,702	$210.00
AM-FM radio, stereo with cassette tape	6,689	$153.00
AM-FM radio, stereo with CB radio	178	$215.00
Delco-Bose stereo system	43,607	$895.00
Radio Delete	104	−$331.00
Rear window/side mirror defogger	47,680	$160.00
Two-tone paint	8,755	$428.00
Automatic transmission	45,104	$0.00
Four-speed manual transmission	6,443	$0.00
Heavy duty radiator	12,008	$57.00
P255/50VR16 tires/16-inch wheels	51,547	$561.20

Delco-Bilstein shock absorbers	3,729	$189.00
Performance axle ratio	410	$22.00
Performance handling package	25,995	$600.00
Engine oil cooler	4,295	$158.00
California emission test	6,833	$75.00

Exterior Colors	Qty	Exterior Colors	Qty
White	6,417	Bright Red	12,942
Bright Silver Metallic	3,109	Light Bronze Metallic	2,452
Medium Gray Metallic	3,147	Silver/Medium Gray	3,629
Black	7,906	Dark Bronze Metallic	1,371
Light Blue Metallic	1,196	Light Blue/Medium Blue	1,433
Medium Blue Metallic	1,822	Light Bronze/Dark Bronze	3,693
Gold Metallic	2,430		

1985 Base Corvette Coupe

Total Produced: 39,729   **List Price:** $24,403.00

Dimensions

Weight	3,224.0 lb.	Tire Size	P255/50VR16
Length	176.5 in.	Front Track	59.60 in.
Width	71.0 in.	Rear Track	60.40 in.
Height	46.7 in.		

Engines

350 cid/230 hp V-8 (tuned-port injection, no options)

Options	Qty	Price
Transparent roof panel	28,143	$595.00
Sport seat, leather	N/A	$1,025.00
Sport seat, cloth	5,661	$625.00
Base seats, leather	N/A	$400.00

Cruise control	38,369	$185.00
Power door locks	38,294	$170.00
Power driver seat	37,856	$215.00
AM-FM radio, stereo with CB radio	16	$215.00
Delco-Bose stereo system	35,998	$895.00
Radio Delete	172	–$256.00
Rear window/side mirror defogger	37,720	$160.00
Two-tone paint	6,033	$428.00
Four-speed manual transmission	9,576	$0.00
Heavy duty cooling	17,539	$225.00
Delco-Bilstein shock absorbers	9,333	$189.00
Performance axle ratio	5,447	$22.00
Performance handling package	14,802	$470.00
California emission test	6,583	$99.00

Exterior Colors	Qty
White	4,455
Silver Metallic	1,752
Medium Gray Metallic	2,519
Black	7,603
Light Blue Metallic	1,021
Medium Blue Metallic	2,041
Gold Metallic	1,411
Bright Red	10,424
Light Bronze Metallic	1,440
Silver/Gray	2,170
Dark Bronze Metallic	1,030
Light Blue/Medium Blue	1,470
Light Bronze/Dark Bronze	2,393

1986 Corvette

Total Produced: 35,109

		List Price
Base Corvette Coupe	27,794	$27,027.00
Base Corvette Convertible	7,315	$32,032.00

Dimensions

Weight	3,239.0 lb.	Tire Size	P255/50VR16
Length	176.5 in.	Front Track	59.60 in.
Width	71.0 in.	Rear Track	60.40 in.
Height	46.7 in.		

Engines

350 cid/230 hp V-8 (standard with iron heads)

350 cid/235 hp V-8 (standard with aluminum heads)

Options	Qty	Price
Removable roof panel, blue tint	12,021	$595.00
Removable roof panel, bronze tint	7,819	$595.00
Dual removable roof panels	6,242	$895.00
Electronic AC control	16,646	$150.00
Custom feature package	4,832	$195.00
Sport seat, leather	13,372	$1,025.00
Base seats, leather	N/A	$400.00
Cruise control	34,197	$185.00
Power door locks	34,215	$175.00
Power driver seat	33,983	$225.00
AM-FM radio, stereo cassette tape	2,039	$122.00
Delco-Bose stereo system	32,478	$895.00
Radio Delete	166	–$256.00
Rear window/side mirror defogger	21,837	$165.00
Two-tone paint	3,897	$428.00
Automatic transmission	28,274	$0.00
Four-speed manual transmission	6,835	$0.00

Heavy duty radiator	10,423	$40.00
Engine oil cooler	7,394	$110.00
Radiator boost fan	8,216	$75.00
Delco-Bilstein shock absorbers	5,521	$189.00
Performance axle ratio	4,879	$22.00
Performance handling package	12,821	$470.00
California emission test	5,697	$99.00
Malcolm Konner Special Edition paint	50	$500.00

Exterior Colors	**Qty**
White	4,176
Silver Metallic	1,209
Copper Metallic	4
Medium Gray Metallic	1,603
Black	5,464
Silver Beige Metallic	1,383
Medium Blue Metallic	128
Gold Metallic	777
Silver Beige/Black	50
Yellow	1,464
Bright Red	9,466
Medium Brown Metallic	488
Silver/Gray	1,049
Dark Red Metallic	5,002
Gray/Black	1,138
White/Silver	693
Silver Beige/Med. Brown	1,014

1987 Corvette

Total Produced: 30,632

		List Price
Base Corvette Coupe	20,007	$27,999.00
Base Corvette Convertible	10,625	$33,172.00

Dimensions

Weight	3,216.0 lb.	Tire Size	P255/50VR16
Length	176.5 in.	Front Track	59.60 in.
Width	71.0 in.	Rear Track	60.40 in.
Height	46.7 in.		

Engines

350 cid/240 hp V-8 (standard, no options)

Options	Qty	Price
Removable roof panel, blue tint	8,883	$615.00
Removable roof panel, bronze tint	5,766	$615.00
Dual removable roof panels	5,017	$915.00
Electronic AC control	20,875	$150.00
Sport seat, leather	14,119	$1,025.00
Base seats, leather	14,579	$400.00
Cruise control	29,594	$185.00
Power door locks	29,748	$190.00
Power driver seat	29,561	$240.00
Power passenger seat	17,124	$240.00
AM-FM radio, stereo cassette tape	2,182	$132.00
Delco-Bose stereo system	27,721	$905.00
Radio Delete	247	–$256.00
Twin remote heated mirrors	6,840	$35.00
Illuminated driver vanity mirror	14,992	$58.00
Rear window/side mirror defogger	19,043	$165.00
Two-tone paint	1,361	$428.00
Automatic transmission	26,403	$0.00

Four-speed manual transmission	4,229	$0.00
Heavy duty radiator	7,871	$40.00
Engine oil cooler	6,679	$110.00
Radiator boost fan	7,291	$75.00
Delco-Bilstein shock absorbers	1,957	$189.00
Performance axle ratio	7,285	$22.00
Performance handling package	1,596	$795.00
Sport handling package	12,662	$470.00
California emission test	5,423	$99.00
Callaway Twin Turbo (non-GM)	184	$19,995.00

Exterior Colors	**Qty**
Silver Metallic	767
Copper Metallic	87
Medium Gray Metallic	1,035
White Silver	195
Medium Blue Metallic	2,677
Medium Brown Metallic	245
Yellow	1,051
Dark Red Metallic	5,578
White	3,097
Bright Red	8,285
Black	5,101
Silver/Gray	403
Gold Metallic	397
Gray/Black	316
Silver Beige Metallic	950
Silver Beige/Medium Brown	447

1988 Corvette

Total Produced: 22,789		List Price
Base Corvette Coupe	15,382	$29,489.00
Base Corvette Convertible	7,407	$34,820.00

Dimensions

Weight	3,245.0 lb.	Tire Size	P255/50ZR16
Length	176.5 in.	Front Track	59.60 in.
Width	71.0 in.	Rear Track	60.40 in.
Height	46.7 in.		

Engines	Qty	Price
350 cid/240 hp V-8 (standard)	N/A	—
350 cid/245 hp (coupe with 3.07:1 axle ratio only)	N/A	N/A

Options	Qty	Price
Removable roof panel, blue tint	8,332	$615.00
Removable roof panel, bronze tint	3,337	$615.00
Dual removable roof panels	5,091	$915.00
Electronic AC control	19,372	$150.00
Sport seat, leather	12,724	$1,025.00
Base seats, leather	9,043	$400.00
Power driver seat	22,084	$240.00
Power passenger seat	18,779	$240.00
Delco-Bose stereo system	20,304	$773.00
Radio Delete	179	–$297.00
Twin remote heated mirrors	6,582	$35.00
Illuminated driver vanity mirror	14,249	$58.00
Rear window/side mirror defogger	14,648	$165.00
Automatic transmission	18,507	$0.00
Four-speed manual transmission	4,282	$0.00
Heavy duty radiator	19,271	$40.00

Engine oil cooler	18,877	$110.00
Radiator boost fan	19,035	$75.00
Delco-Bilstein shock absorbers	18,437	$189.00
Performance axle ratio	4,497	$22.00
Performance handling package	1,309	$1,295.00
Sport handling package	16,017	$970.00
California emission test	3,882	$99.00
35th Special Edition package	2,050	$4,795.00
Callaway Twin Turbo (non-GM)	124	$25,895.00

Exterior Colors	Qty	Exterior Colors	Qty
Silver Metallic	385	White	3,620
Dark Blue Metallic	1,675	Black	3,420
Medium Blue Metallic	1,148	Gray Metallic	644
Dark Red Metallic	2,878	White/Black	2,050
Yellow	578	Charcoal Metallic	1,046
Bright Red	5,340		

1989 Corvette

Total Produced: 26,412

		List Price
Base Corvette Coupe	16,663	$31,545.00
Base Corvette Convertible	9,749	$36,785.00

Dimensions

Weight	3,238.0 lb.	Tire Size	P275/40ZR17
Length	176.5 in.	Front Track	59.60 in.
Width	71.0 in.	Rear Track	60.40 in.
Height	46.7 in.		

Engines

	Qty	Price
350 cid/240 hp V-8 (standard)	N/A	—
350 cid/245 hp (coupe w/ 3.07:1 axle ratio only)	N/A	N/A

Options	Qty	Price
Auxiliary hardtop	1,573	$1,995.00
Removable roof panel, blue tint	8,748	$615.00
Removable roof panel, bronze tint	4,042	$615.00
Dual removable roof panels	5,274	$915.00
Electronic AC control	24,675	$150.00
Sport seat, leather	1,777	$1,025.00
Base seats, leather	23,364	$400.00
Power driver seat	25,606	$240.00
Power passenger seat	20,578	$240.00
Delco-Bose stereo system	24,145	$773.00
Luggage rack (convertible)	616	$140.00
Illuminated driver vanity mirror	17,414	$58.00
Low tire pressure warning indicator	6,976	$325.00
Six-speed manual transmission	4,113	$0.00
Heavy duty radiator	20,888	$40.00
Engine oil cooler	20,162	$110.00
Engine block heater	2,182	$20.00
Radiator boost fan	20,281	$75.00
Selective ride and handling package	1,573	$1,695.00
Performance axle ratio	10,211	$22.00
Performance handling package	2,224	$575.00
California emission test	4,501	$100.00
Callaway Twin Turbo (not-GM)	69	$25,895.00

Exterior Colors	Qty	Exterior Colors	Qty
Dark Blue Metallic	1,931	Black	4,855
Bright Red	7,663	Arctic Pearl	27
Medium Blue Metallic	1,428	Yellow	6
Dark Red Metallic	3,409	Gray Metallic	225
White	5,426	Charcoal Metallic	1,440

1990 Corvette

Total Produced: 23,646

List Price

Base Corvette Coupe	16,016	$31,979.00
Base Corvette Convertible	7,630	$37,264.00

Dimensions

Weight	3,288.0 lb.	Tire Size	P275/40ZR17	
Length	176.5 in.	Front Track	59.60 in.	
Width	71.0 in.	Rear Track	60.40 in.	
Height	46.7 in.			

Engines

Engines	Qty	Price
350 cid/245 hp V-8 (standard)	N/A	—
350 cid/250 hp V-8 (standard)	N/A	—
350 cid/375 hp V-8 (ZR-1 only)	N/A	N/A

Options

Options	Qty	Price
Electronic AC	22,497	$180.00
Engine block heater	1,585	$20.00
Engine oil cooler	16,220	$110.00
Performance axle ratio	9,362	$22.00
Performance handling package	5,446	$460.00
Six-speed manual transmission	8,100	$0.00
Low tire pressure warning indicator	8,432	$325.00
Delco-Bose stereo system	6,401	$823.00
Delco-Bose stereo system with CD player	15,716	$1,219.00
Luggage rack (convertible)	1,284	$140.00
Sport seats, leather	11,457	$1,050.00
Base seats, leather	11,649	$425.00
Power passenger seat	20,419	$270.00
Power driver seat	23,109	$270.00
Auxiliary hardtop (convertible)	2,371	$1,995.00
Dual removable roof panels	6,422	$915.00

Removable roof panel, blue tint	7,852	$615.00
Removable roof panel, bronze tint	4,340	$615.00
California emission test	4,035	$100.00
Selective ride and handling	7,576	$1,695.00
Callaway Twin Turbo (non-GM)	58	$26,895.00
ZR-1 performance package	3,049	$27,016.00

Exterior Colors	**Qty**
Steel Blue Metallic	13
Bright Red	6,956
Competition Yellow	278
Turquoise Metallic	589
Quasar Blue Metallic	474
Dark Red Metallic	2,353
Artic White	4,872
Black	4,759
Polo Green Metallic	1,674
Charcoal Metallic	878

1991 Corvette

Total Produced: 20,639		**List Price**
Base Corvette Coupe	14,967	$32,455.00
Base Corvette Convertible	5,672	$38,770.00

Dimensions

Weight	3,288.0 lb.	Tire Size	P275/40ZR17
Length	176.5 in.	Front Track	59.60 in.
Width	71.0 in.	Rear Track	60.40 in.
Height	46.7 in.		

Engines	Qty	Price
350 cid/245 hp V-8 (standard)	N/A	—
350 cid/250 hp V-8 (standard)	N/A	—
350 cid/375 hp V-8 (ZR-1 only)	N/A	N/A

Options	Qty	Price
Electronic AC control	19,233	$180.00
Engine oil cooler	7,525	$110.00
Performance axle ratio	3,453	$22.00
Six-speed manual transmission	5,875	$0.00
Low tire pressure warning indicator	5,175	$325.00
Delco-Bose stereo system	3,786	$823.00
Delco-Bose stereo system with CD player	15,345	$1,219.00
Luggage rack (convertible)	886	$140.00
Sport seats, leather	10,650	$1,050.00
Base seats, leather	9,505	$425.00
Power passenger seat	17,267	$290.00
Power driver seat	19,937	$290.00
Auxiliary hardtop (convertible)	1,230	$1,995.00
Dual removable roof panels	5,031	$915.00
Removable roof panel, blue tint	6,991	$615.00
Removable roof panel, bronze tint	3,036	$615.00
California emission test	3,050	$100.00
Adjustable suspension package	733	$2,155.00
Callaway Twin Turbo (non-GM)	62	$33,000.00
ZR-1 performance package	2,044	$31,683.00

Exterior Colors	Qty	Exterior Colors	Qty
Steel Blue Metallic	835	Dark Red Metallic	1,311
Bright Red	5,318	White	4,305
Yellow	650	Black	3,909
Turquoise Metallic	1,621	Polo Green Metallic	1,230
Quasar Blue	1,038	Charcoal Metallic	417

1992 Corvette

Total Produced: 20,479		List Price
Base Corvette Coupe	14,604	$33,635.00
Base Corvette Convertible	5,875	$40,145.00

Dimensions

Weight	3,388.0 lb.	Tire Size	P275/40ZR17
Length	178.5 in.	Front Track	57.70 in.
Width	70.7 in.	Rear Track	59.10 in.
Height	46.3 in.		

Engines	Qty	Price
350 cid/300 hp V-8 (standard)	N/A	—
350 cid/375 hp V-8 (ZR-1 coupe only)	N/A	N/A

Options	Qty	Price
Electronic AC control	18,460	$205.00
Selective ride and handling	5,840	$1,695.00
Performance axle ratio	2,283	$50.00
Six-speed manual transmission	5,487	$0.00
Delco-Bose stereo system	3,241	$823.00
Delco-Bose stereo system with CD player	15,199	$1,219.00
Luggage rack (convertible)	845	$140.00
Sport seats, leather	7,973	$1,100.00
Sport seats, white leather	709	$1,180.00
Low tire pressure warning indicator	3,416	$325.00
Base seats, leather	10,565	$475.00
Base seats, white leather	752	$555.00
Power passenger seat	16,179	$305.00
Power driver seat	19,378	$305.00
Auxiliary hardtop (convertible)	915	$1,995.00
Dual removable roof panels	3,739	$950.00
Removable roof panel, blue tint	6,424	$650.00

Removable roof panel, bronze tint	3,005	$650.00
California emission test	3,092	$100.00
Adjustable suspension package	738	$2,045.00
ZR-1 performance package (coupe)	502	$31,683.00

Exterior Colors	Qty
Bright Red	4,466
Yellow	678
Bright Aqua Metallic	1,953
Quasar Blue	1,043
Dark Red Metallic	1,148
White	4,101
Black	3,209
Polo Green Metallic	1,995
Black Rose Metallic	1,886

1993 Corvette

Total Produced: 21,590

		List Price
Base Corvette Coupe	15,898	$34,595.00
Base Corvette Convertible	5,692	$41,195.00

Dimensions

Weight	3,333.0 lb.	Front Tire Size	P275/40ZR17
Length	178.5 in.	Rear Tire Size	P285/40ZR17
Width	70.7 in.	Front Track	57.70 in.
Height	46.3 in.	Rear Track	59.10 in.

Engines

	Qty	Price
350 cid/300 hp V-8 (standard)	N/A	—
350 cid/405 hp V-8 (ZR-1 coupe only)	N/A	N/A

Options	Qty	Price
Electronic AC control	19,550	$205.00
Selective ride and handling	5,740	$1,695.00
Performance axle ratio	2,630	$50.00
Six-speed manual transmission	5,330	$0.00
Delco-Bose stereo system	2,685	$823.00
Delco-Bose stereo system with CD player	16,794	$1,219.00
Luggage rack (convertible)	765	$140.00
Sport seats, leather	11,267	$1,100.00
Sport seats, white leather	622	$1,180.00
Low tire pressure warning indicator	3,353	$325.00
Base seats, leather	8,935	$475.00
Base seats, white leather	766	$555.00
Power passenger seat	18,067	$305.00
Power driver seat	20,626	$305.00
Auxiliary hardtop (convertible)	976	$1,995.00
Dual removable roof panels	4,204	$950.00
Removable roof panel, blue tint	6,203	$650.00
Removable roof panel, bronze tint	4,288	$650.00
California emission test	2,401	$100.00
Adjustable suspension package	824	$2,045.00
40th Anniversary package	6,749	$1,455.00
ZR-1 performance package (coupe)	448	$31,683.00

Exterior Colors	Qty	Exterior Colors	Qty
Black Rose Metallic	935	Dark Red Metallic	325
Ruby Red	6,749	Arctic White	3,031
Competition Yellow	517	Black	2,684
Bright Aqua Metallic	1,305	Polo Green Metallic	2,189
Quasar Blue Metallic	683	Torch Red	3,172

1994 Corvette

Total Produced: 23,330

List Price

Base Corvette Coupe	17,984	$36,185.00
Base Corvette Convertible	5,346	$42,960.00

Dimensions

Weight	3,309.0 lb.	Front Tire Size	P255/45ZR17	
Length	178.5 in.	Rear Tire Size	P285/40ZR17	
Width	70.7 in.	Front Track		57.70 in.
Height	46.3 in.	Rear Track		59.10 in.

Engines

	Qty	Price
350 cid/300 hp V-8 (standard)	N/A	—
350 cid/405 hp V-8 (ZR-1 coupe only)	N/A	N/A

Options

	Qty	Price
Selective ride and handling	4,570	$1,695.00
Performance axle ratio	9,019	$50.00
Six-speed manual transmission	6,012	$0.00
Low tire pressure warning indicator	5,097	$325.00
Delco-Bose stereo system with CD player	17,579	$396.00
Sport seats	9,023	$625.00
Power passenger seat	17,863	$305.00
Power driver seat	21,592	$305.00
Auxiliary hardtop (convertible)	682	$1,995.00
Dual removable roof panels	3,875	$950.00
Removable roof panel, blue tint	7,064	$650.00
Removable roof panel, bronze tint	3,979	$650.00
Tires, extended mobility	2,781	$70.00
California emission test	2,372	$100.00
New York emission test	1,363	$100.00
Adjustable suspension package (coupe)	887	$2,045.00

ZR-1 performance package (coupe)	448	$31,258.00
Preferred Equipment Group One (electronic AC control, Delco-Bose stereo, power driver seat)	N/A	$1,333.00

Exterior Colors	Qty
Black Rose Metallic	1,267
Copper Metallic	116
Competition Yellow	834
Bright Aqua Metallic	1,209
Admiral Blue	1,584
Dark Red Metallic	1,511
Arctic White	4,066
Black	4,136
Polo Green Metallic	3,534
Torch Red	5,073

1995 Corvette

Total Produced: 20,742		List Price
Base Corvette Coupe	15,771	$36,785.00
Base Corvette Convertible	4,971	$43,665.00

Dimensions

Weight	3,203.0 lb.	Front Tire Size	P255/45ZR17
Length	178.5 in.	Rear Tire Size	P285/40ZR17
Width	70.7 in.	Front Track	57.70 in.
Height	46.3 in.	Rear Track	59.10 in.

Engines	Qty	Price
350 cid/300 hp V-8 (standard)	N/A	—
350 cid/405 hp V-8 (ZR-1 coupe only)	N/A	N/A

Options	Qty	Price
Selective ride and handling	3,421	$1,695.00
Performance axle ratio	10,056	$50.00
Six-speed manual transmission	4,784	$0.00
Spare Tire Delete	418	−$100.00
Low tire pressure warning indicator	5,300	$325.00
Power driver seat	19,012	$305.00
Power passenger seat	15,323	$305.00
Sport seats	7,908	$625.00
Auxiliary hardtop (convertible)	459	$1,995.00
Dual removable roof panels	2,979	$950.00
Removable roof panel, blue tint	4,688	$650.00
Removable roof panel, bronze tint	2,871	$650.00
Delco-Bose stereo system with CD player	15,528	$396.00
Tires, extended mobility	3,783	$70.00
California emission test	2,026	$100.00
New York emission test	268	$100.00
Adjustable suspension package (coupe)	753	$2,045.00
Indy 500 Pace Car replica	527	$2,816.00
ZR-1 performance package (coupe)	448	$31,258.00
Preferred Equipment Group One (AC, Delco-Bose stereo, power driver seat)	N/A	$1,333.00

Exterior Colors	Qty
Dark Purple/White	527
Dark Purple	1,049
Competition Yellow	1,003
Bright Aqua Metallic	909
Admiral Blue	1,006
Dark Red Metallic	1,437
Arctic White	3,381
Black	3,959
Polo Green Metallic	2,940
Torch Red	4,531

1996 Corvette

Total Produced: 21,536

		List Price
Base Corvette Coupe	17,167	$37,225.00
Base Corvette Convertible	4,369	$45,060.00

Dimensions

Weight	3,298.0 lb.	Front Tire Size	P255/45ZR17
Length	178.5 in.	Rear Tire Size	P285/40ZR17
Width	70.7 in.	Front Track	57.70 in.
Height	46.3 in.	Rear Track	59.10 in.

Engines

Engines	Qty	Price
350 cid/300 hp V-8 (standard)	15,177	—
350 cid/330 hp V-8 (LT4 package)	6,359	$1,450.00

Options

Options	Qty	Price
Selective real time damping	2,896	$1,695.00
Performance axle ratio	9,801	$50.00
Six-speed manual transmission	6,359	$0.00
Spare Tire Delete	986	−$100.00
Low tire pressure warning indicator	6,865	$325.00
Power driver seat	19,798	$305.00
Power passenger seat	17,060	$305.00
Sport seats	12,016	$625.00
Auxiliary hardtop (convertible)	429	$1,995.00
Dual removable roof panels	3,983	$950.00
Removable roof panel, blue tint	6,626	$650.00
Removable roof panel, bronze tint	2,492	$650.00
Delco-Bose stereo system with CD player	17,037	$396.00
Tires, extended mobility	4,945	$70.00
Collectors Edition	5,412	$1,250.00
Grand Sport package	746	$3,250.00
Grand Sport package (convertible)	254	$2,880.00
Performance handling package	1,869	$350.00

Exterior Colors	Qty
Dark Purple Metallic	320
Sebring Silver Metallic	5,412
Competition Yellow	488
Bright Aqua Metallic	357
Admiral Blue	1,000
Arctic White	3,210
Black	3,917
Polo Green Metallic	2,414
Torch Red	4,418

1997 Base Corvette Coupe

Total Produced: 9,752   **List Price:** $37,495.00

Dimensions

Weight	3,250.0 lb.	Front Tire Size	P245/45ZR17
Length	179.7 in.	Rear Tire Size	P275/40ZR18
Width	73.6 in.	Front Track	62.00 in.
Height	47.7 in.	Rear Track	62.10 in.

Engines

350 cid/345 hp V-8 (standard, no options)

Options	Qty	Price
Memory package	6,186	$150.00
Air conditioning (dual zone)	7,999	$365.00
Selective real time damping	3,094	$1,695.00
Six-speed manual transmission	2,809	$815.00
Automatic transmission	6,943	N/A
Body side moldings	4,366	$75.00
Dual halogen fog lamps	8,829	$69.00
Power passenger seat	8,951	$305.00

Sport seats	6,711	$625.00
Base roof	2,078	N/A
Removable roof panel, blue tint	7,213	$650.00
Dual removable roof panels	416	$950.00
Stereo with CD player, ATC, TheftLock	6,282	$100.00
Remote twelve-disc CD changer	4,496	$600.00
Floor mats	9,371	$25.00
Luggage shade and parcel net	8,315	$50.00
Performance axle ratio	2,739	$100.00
Z51 performance handling package	1,077	$350.00
Front license plate frame	2,258	$15.00
California emission test	885	$170.00
Massachusetts/New York emission test	677	$170.00
Canadian options	325	$170.00
Mexico	46	N/A
Export	426	N/A
Customer pick up	9	N/A

Exterior Colors	**Qty**
Light Carmine Red Metallic	381
Sebring Silver Metallic	2,164
Arctic White	1,341
Black	2,393
Fairway Green Metallic	155
Torch Red	3,026
Nassau Blue Metallic	292

Interior Colors	**Qty**
Black	6,481
Light Gray	2,543
Firethorn Red	728
Light Oak	N/A

1998 Corvette

Total Produced: 31,084   **List Price**

Base Corvette Coupe	19,235	$37,495.00*
Base Corvette Convertible	11,849	$44,425.00

*GM increased the price on the 1998 Corvette Coupe on January 19, 1998, by $500: From $37,495 to $37,995.

Dimensions

Weight	3,250.0 lb.	Front Tire Size	P245/45ZR17
Length	179.7 in.	Rear Tire Size	P275/40ZR18
Width	73.6 in.	Front Track	62.00 in.
Height	47.7 in.	Rear Track	62.10 in.

Engines

350 cid/345 hp V-8 (standard, no options)

Options	Qty	Price
Indy Pace Car replica ($5,804.00 w/ manual)	1,163	$5,039.00
Destination charge	N/A	$565.00
Preferred Equipment Group	11,500	$0.00
Memory package (required with dual-zone AC)	24,234	$150.00
Power passenger seat	28,575	$305.00
Sport seats	22,675	$625.00
Sport seats, European style	8,409	N/A
Floor mats	30,592	$25.00
Body side moldings	17,070	$75.00
Removable roof panel, blue tint	6,957	$650.00
Base roof	6,638	N/A
Dual removable roof panels	5,640	$950.00
Air conditioning (dual zone)	26,572	$365.00
Manual air conditioning	N/A	N/A
Luggage shade and parcel net	16,549	$50.00
Base suspension	26,835	N/A
Sport suspension	4,249	N/A

Federal emissions	25,272	$0.00
Selective real time damping	8,374	$1,695.00
Rear axle ratio, 3.15	13,416	$100.00
Performance axle ratio	13,331	$100.00
Rear axle ratio, 2.73	10,562	N/A
Rear axle ratio, 3.42	7,106	N/A
Active handling	5,356	$500.00
Six-speed manual transmission	7,106	$815.00
Sport custom wheels	1,425	N/A
Automatic transmission	23,978	N/A
Fog Lamps	29,310	$69.00
Delco-Bose stereo system with CD player	18,213	$100.00
Remote CD changer	16,513	$600.00
Front license plate frame	16,087	$15.00
Performance handling package	4,249	$350.00
California emission test	N/A	$170.00
Massachusetts/NY emission test	N/A	$170.00
Mexico	N/A	N/A
Export	N/A	N/A

Exterior Colors	Qty
Navy Blue	14
Light Pewter Metallic	3,276
Light Carmine Red Metallic	1,567
Sebring Silver Metallic	4,637
Arctic White	3,346
Black	6,597

Exterior Colors	Qty
Fairway Green Metallic	223
Torch Red	8,767
Bright Blue Metallic	1,098
Gold	15
Majestic Amethyst Metallic	381
Radar Purple Metallic (Indy Pace Car option)	1,163

Interior Colors	
Black	18,338
Light Gray	5,871
Firethorn Red	5,450
Light Oak	1,425

Convertible Top Colors	
Black	8,630
White	843
Light Oak	2,376

1999 Corvette

Total Produced: 33,270   **List Price**

Base Corvette Coupe	18,078	$39,171.00
Base Corvette Convertible	11,161	$45,579.00
Base Corvette Hardtop (fixed-roof)	4,031	$38,777.00

Dimensions

Weight	3,250.0 lb.	Front Tire Size	EMT P245/45ZR17
Length	179.7 in.	Rear Tire Size	EMT P275/40ZR18
Width	73.6 in.	Front Track	62.00 in.
Height (convertible)	47.7 in.	Rear Track	62.10 in.
Height (coupe)	47.8 in.		
Height (hardtop)	47.9 in.		

Engines

350 cid/345 hp V-8 (standard, no options)

Options	Qty	Price
Destination charge	N/A	$580.00
Power tilt/telescopic steering wheel	16,847	$350.00
Twilight Sentinel w/ automatic ext. lamp*	18,895	$60.00
Heads-up display	19,034	$375.00
Lighting package (hardtop)	3,037	$95.00
Sport magnesium wheels	2,029	$3,000.00
Preliminary invoice	N/A	$2.00
Active handling system	20,174	$500.00
Memory package*	23,829	$150.00
Electronic dual-zone AC*	25,672	$365.00
Six-speed manual transmission***	13,729	$825.00
Body side moldings	19,348	$75.00
Dual halogen fog lamps	28,546	$69.00
Six-way power driver seat (hardtop)**	3,716	$305.00
Six-way power passenger seat*	27,089	$305.00
Adjustable seat with lumbar support*	24,573	$625.00

Dual removable roof panels (coupe)	6,307	$950.00
Removable roof panel, blue transparent (coupe)	5,235	$650.00
Stereo with cassette player and Bose speakers**	N/A	$100.00
Bose speakers package (hardtop)	3,348	$820.00
Stereo with CD player and Bose speakers	20,442	$100.00
Stereo with twelve-disc CD changer and Bose speakers**	16,997	$600.00
Performance handling package***	10,244	$350.00
Real time damping*	7,515	$1,695.00
Luggage shade and parcel net (coupe)	18,058	$50.00
Parcel net (hardtop)	2,738	$15.00
Floor mats	32,706	$25.00
Performance axle ratio, 3.15	14,525	$100.00
Front license plate frame	17,742	$15.00
MA, NY, CT, DC, DE, MD, NH, NJ, PA, RI, VA emission test	N/A	$170.00
California emission test	3,336	$170.00
Magnetic Red paint*	2,733	$500.00
Corvette Museum delivery	N/A	$400.00

  * Not available on hardtop

 ** Standard on coupe and convertible

*** Standard on hardtop

Exterior Colors	Qty	Exterior Colors	Qty
Magnetic Red Metallic	2,733	Black	7,235
Light Pewter Metallic	6,164	Torch Red	8,361
Sebring Silver Metallic	3,510	Nassau Blue Metallic	1,034
Arctic White	2,756	Navy Blue	1,439

Interior Colors		Convertible Top Colors	
Black	N/A	Black	N/A
Light Gray	N/A	White	N/A
Firethorn Red	N/A	Light Oak	N/A
Light Oak	N/A		

(hardtop only available in black)

2000 Corvette

Total Produced: 33,682

		List Price
Base Corvette Coupe	18,113	$39,475.00
Base Corvette Convertible	13,479	$45,900.00
Base Corvette Hardtop (fixed-roof)	2,090	$38,900.00

Dimensions

Weight	3,250.0 lb.	Front Tire Size	EMT P245/45ZR17
Length	179.7 in.	Rear Tire Size	EMT P275/40ZR18
Width	73.6 in.	Front Track	62.00 in.
Height (convertible)	47.7 in.	Rear Track	62.10 in.
Height (coupe)	47.8 in.		
Height (hardtop)	47.9 in.		

Engines

350 cid/345 hp V-8 (standard, no options)

Options	Qty	Price
Destination charge	N/A	$580.00
Power tilt/telescopic steering wheel	22,182	$350.00
Twilight Sentinel w/ automatic ext. lamp*	23,508	$60.00
Lighting package (hardtop)	1,527	$95.00
Heads-up display	26,482	$375.00
Sport magnesium wheels	2,652	$2,000.00
Preliminary invoice	N/A	$2.00
Active handling system	22,668	$500.00
Memory package*	26,595	$150.00
Electronic dual-zone AC*	29,428	$365.00
Six-speed manual transmission***	13,320	$815.00
Body side moldings	18,773	$75.00
Dual halogen fog lamps*	31,992	$69.00
Six-way power driver seat**	1,841	$305.00

Six-way power passenger seat*	29,462	$305.00
Adjustable seat with lumbar support*	27,103	$700.00
Dual removable roof panels (coupe only)	6,280	$1,100.00
Removable roof panel, blue transparent (coupe)	5,605	$650.00
Stereo with cassette player and Bose speakers**	N/A	$100.00
Stereo with CD player and Bose speakers	24,696	$100.00
Stereo with twelve-disc CD changer	15,809	$600.00
Bose speaker and amplifier system (hardtop only)	1,766	$820.00
Performance handling package***	7,775	$350.00
Real Time Damping*	6,724	$1,695.00
Luggage shade and parcel net*	15,689	$50.00
Parcel net (hardtop)	938	$15.00
Floor mats	33,188	$25.00
Performance axle ratio, 3.15	14,090	$100.00
License plate frame	17,380	$15.00
California Emission test	3,628	$0.00
Corvette Museum delivery	N/A	$400.00
Deluxe high-polish wheel	15,204	$895.00
Lighting package (hardtop)	1,527	$95.00
Millennium Yellow with tint coat	3,578	$500.00
Magnetic Red Metallic paint (coupe, convertible)	2,941	$500.00

   * Not available on hardtop
  ** Standard on coupe and convertible
*** Standard on hardtop

Exterior Colors (Coupe, Convertible)	**Qty**	
Millennium Yellow	3,578	
Dark Bowling Green	1,663	
Magnetic Red II Metallic	2,941	($500.00 extra cost)
Light Pewter Metallic	5,125	
Sebring Silver Metallic	2,783	

Arctic White	1,979	
Black	5,807	
Torch Red	6,700	
Nassau Blue Metallic	851	

Exterior Colors (Hardtop)

Millennium Yellow	N/A	($500.00 extra cost)
Dark Bowling Green	N/A	
Magnetic Red II Metallic	N/A	($500.00 extra cost)
Light Pewter Metallic	N/A	
Arctic White	N/A	
Black	N/A	
Torch Red	N/A	
Nassau Blue Metallic	N/A	

Interior Colors (Hardtop only available in black)

Torch	N/A
Black	N/A
Light Gray	N/A
Firethorn Red	N/A
Light Oak	N/A

Convertible Top Colors

Black	N/A
White	N/A
Light Oak	N/A

2001 Corvette

Total Produced: 35,627   **List Price**

Base Corvette Coupe	15,681	$40,475.00
Base Corvette Convertible	14,173	$47,000.00
Base Corvette Z06 Hardtop	5,773	$47,500.00

Engines	Qty	Price
350 cid/350 hp V-8 (standard)	N/A	—
350 cid/385 hp V-8 (Z06)	N/A	N/A

Dimensions

Weight	3,250.0 lb.	Front tire size	EMT P245/45ZR17
Length	179.7 in.	Rear tire size	EMT P275/40ZR18
Width	73.6 in.	Front track	62.0 in.
Height (convertible)	47.7 in.	Rear track	62.1 in.
Height (coupe)	47.8 in.		
Height (hardtop)	47.9 in.		

Options	Qty	Price
Destination charge	—	$645.00
Preferred Equipment Group: Sport Coupe (1SB)	2,514	$1,639.00
Preferred Equipment Group: Convertible (1SB)	1,710	$1,769.00
Preferred Equipment Group: Sport Coupe (1SC)	11,558	$2,544.00
Preferred Equipment Group: Convertible (1SC)	11,881	$2,494.00
Memory package (Z06 hardtop)	4,780	$150.00
Power six-way driver seat (hardtop only)	N/A	$305.00
Parcel net (hardtop only)	N/A	$15.00
Floor mats	34,907	$25.00
Body side moldings	20,457	$75.00
Removable roof panel, blue tint	4,769	$650.00

Dual removable roof panels	5,099	$1,100.00
Electronic monochromatic mirrors (Z06)	4,576	$120.00
Six-speed manual transmission	16,019	$815.00
Steering column: power telescope, manual tilt	N/A	$350.00
Sport magnesium wheels	1,022	$2,000.00
Customer pick up at the Corvette Museum	457	$490.00
Deluxe high-polish wheel	22,980	$895.00
Delco-Bose stereo system with CD player	28,783	$100.00
Remote CD changer (all models)	14,198	$600.00
Front license plate frame	18,935	$15.00
Performance handling package	7,817	$350.00
Millenium Yellow with tint coat	3,887	$600.00
Magnetic Red metallic paint (coupe and convertible)	3,322	$600.00

1SA—Corvette Convertible Base Equipment Group

- 1SB option package includes everything above 1SA plus: $1,769.00
  Custom adjustable sport bucket seats
  Power passenger seat
  Dual-zone electronic AC
  Front fog lamps
  Drivers memory package
  Rear luggage shade/parcel net
  Electrochromic inside and left-side outside mirrors

- 1SC Option Package includes everything above 1SB plus: $2,494.00
  Heads-up display
  Twilight Sentinel
  Power telescoping steering column

1SA—Corvette Coupe Base Equipment Group

- 1SB option package includes everything above 1SA plus: $1,639.00
  Custom adjustable sport bucket seats
  Power passenger seat
  Dual-zone electronic AC
  Front fog lamps
  Drivers memory package
  Rear luggage shade/parcel net

- 1SC option package includes everything above 1SB plus: $2,544.00
  Electrochromic inside and left-side outside mirrors
  Heads-up display
  Twilight Sentinel
  Power telescoping steering column

Exterior Colors	Qty	
Light Pewter Metallic	3,462	
Quicksilver Metallic	4,822	
Navy Blue Metallic	2,587	
Speedway White	2,465	
Black	6,971	
Torch Red	7,192	
Millennium Yellow Clear Coat	3,887	$600 option w/ tint
Magnetic Red-II Clear Coat	3,322	$600 option w/ tint
Dark Bowling Green Metallic	919	

Convertible Top Colors	
Black, with black liner	N/A
White, with black liner	N/A
Light Oak, with black liner	N/A

2002 Corvette

Total Produced: 35,767

		List Price
Base Corvette Coupe	14,760	$41,450.00
Base Corvette Convertible	12,710	$47,975.00
Base Corvette Z06 Hardtop	8,297	$50,150.00

Dimensions

Weight	3,250.0 lb.	Front Tire Size	EMT P245/45ZR17
Length	179.7 in.	Rear Tire Size	EMT P275/40ZR18
Width	73.6 in.	Front Track	62.00 in.
Height (convertible)	47.7 in.	Rear Track	62.10 in.
Height (coupe)	47.8 in.		
Height (hardtop)	47.9 in.		

Engines

	Qty	Price
350 cid/350 hp V-8 (standard)	N/A	—
350 cid/405 hp V-8 (Z06)	N/A	N/A

Options

	Qty	Price
Destination charge	—	$645.00
Preferred Equipment Group: Sport Coupe (1SB)	1,359	$1,700.00
Preferred Equipment Group: Convertible (1SB)	1,379	$1,800.00
Preferred Equipment Group: Sport Coupe (1SC)	11,136	$2,700.00
Preferred Equipment Group: Convertible (1SC)	10,964	$2,600.00
Memory package (Z06 hardtop)	7,794	$150.00
Body side moldings	21,422	$75.00
Removable roof panel, blue tint	4,208	$750.00
Dual removable roof panels	5,079	$1,200.00
Electrochromic mirrors	7,394	$120.00
Selective real time damping, electronic	4,773	$1,695.00
Performance axle ratio, 3.15:1	9,646	$300.00

Six-speed manual transmission	8,554	$815.00
Sport magnesium wheels	114	$2,000.00
Customer pick up at the Corvette Museum	371	$490.00
Deluxe high-polish wheel	22,597	$1,200.00
Delco-Bose stereo system with cassette player	4,210	$100.00
Remote twelve-disk CD changer	13,725	$600.00
Front license plate frame	19,948	$15.00
Performance handling package	6,106	$350.00
Millenium Yellow with tint coat	4,040	$600.00
Magnetic Red Metallic paint	3,298	$600.00

1SA—Corvette Convertible Base Equipment Group

- 1SB option package includes everything above 1SA plus: $1,800.00

  Custom adjustable sport bucket seats

  Power passenger seat

  Dual-zone electronic AC

  Front fog lamps

  Drivers memory package

  Rear luggage shade/parcel net

  Electrochromic inside and left-hand outside mirrors

- 1SC option package includes everything above 1SB plus: $2,600.00

  Heads-up display

  Twilight Sentinel

  Power telescoping steering column

1SA—Corvette Coupe Base Equipment Group

- 1SB option package includes everything above 1SA plus: $1,700.00

  Custom adjustable sport bucket seats

  Power passenger seat

  Dual-zone electronic AC

  Front fog lamps

  Drivers memory package

  Rear luggage shade/parcel net

- 1SC option package includes everything above 1SB plus: $2,700.00
  Electrochromic inside and left-side outside mirrors
  Heads-up display
  Twilight Sentinel
  Power telescoping steering column

Exterior Colors	Qty	
Light Pewter Metallic	2,650	
Quicksilver Metallic	4,618	
Electron Blue Metallic	5,407	
Speedway White	1,763	
Black	7,129	
Torch Red	6,862	
Millennium Yellow Clear Coat	4,040	$600 option w/ tint
Magnetic Red-II Clear Coat	3,298	$600 option w/ tint

Convertible Top Colors	
Black, with black liner	N/A
White, with black liner	N/A
Light Oak, with black liner	N/A

2003 Corvette

Total Produced: 35,469

		List Price
Base Corvette Coupe	12,812	$43,895.00
Base Corvette Convertible	14,022	$50,370.00
Base Corvette Z06 Hardtop	8,635	$51,155.00

Dimensions

Weight	3,250.0 lb.	Front Tire Size	EMT P245/45ZR17
Length	179.7 in.	Rear Tire Size	EMT P275/40ZR18
Width	73.6 in.	Front Track	62.00 in.
Height (convertible)	47.7 in.	Rear Track	62.10 in.
Height (coupe)	47.8 in.		
Height (hardtop)	47.9 in.		

Engines

	Qty	Price
350 cid/350 hp V-8 (standard)	N/A	—
350 cid/405 hp V-8 (Z06)	N/A	N/A

Options

		Qty	Price
1SB	Preferred Equipment Group: Sport Coupe	7,310	$1,200.00
1SB	Preferred Equipment Group: Convertible	6,643	$1,200.00
1SC	50th Anniversary Edition: Sport Coupe	4,085	$5,000.00
1SC	50th Anniversary Edition: Convertible	4,085	$5,000.00
AAB	Memory Package (Z06 hardtop)	8,241	175.00
AG1	Power six-way driver seat (standard on Z06)	N/A	305.00
AN4	Child seat tether CRAS	N/A	$0.00
AP9	Parcel net (hardtop only)	N/A	$0.00
B4	Floor mats	N/A	$25.00
B84	Body side moldings	22,243	$150.00
C2L	Dual removable roof panels (coupe)	5,184	$1,200.00
CC3	Removable roof panel, blue tint (coupe)	3,150	$750.00
CV3	Mexico export	N/A	$0.00

Code	Description	Qty	Price
DD0	Electrochromic mirrors (Z06)	8,227	$120.00
EXP	Export option	N/A	N/A
FE1	Base suspension	N/A	—
FE3	Sport suspension (included with Z51)	N/A	N/A
FE9	Federal emission test	N/A	$0.00
F55	Magnetic selective ride control (coupe, convertible)	14,992	$1,695.00
G92	Performance axle ratio, 3.15:1, (auto., coupe, convertible)	9,785	$395.00
GU2	Standard axle ratio, 2.73:1, MXO Auto	N/A	—
GU6	Standard axle ratio, 3.42:1, six-speed	N/A	—
LS1	Standard 5.7-liter SFI aluminum V-8	N/A	$0.00
MN6	Six-speed manual transmission (coupe, convertible) (with 1YY37, $0.00)	8,590	$915.00
MX0	M30-automatic transmission (includes G92 performance axle ratio)	N/A	$0.00
NB8	CA/Northeast emission override	N/A	$0.00
N37	Steering column, power telescope/manual tilt	N/A	$350.00
N73	Magnesium wheels (coupe, convertible)	293	$1,500.00
NC7	Federal emission override	N/A	$0.00
NG1	MA/NY emission test	N/A	$0.00
R8C	Customer pick up at Corvette Museum	787	$490.00
R6M	New Jersey surcharge (mandatory in NJ)	N/A	$0.00
QD4	Domestic standard five-spoke wheel	N/A	—
QF5	Polished aluminum wheels (coupe, convertible)	10,290	$1,295.00
U1S	Remote 12-disc CD changer (coupe, convertible)	15,979	$600.00
UL0	Delco-Bose stereo cassette (coupe, convertible)	4,664	$0.00
V49	Front license plate frame	20,605	$15.00
XGG	Front tire, P245/45ZR17 BW SBR	N/A	N/A
YGH	Rear tire, P275/40ZR18 BW SBR	N/A	N/A
YF5	California emission test	N/A	N/A

Z49	Canadian options	N/A	N/A
Z51	Performance handling package (larger diameter sway bars than previous years; included with FE3 sports suspension; includes power steering fluid cooler) (coupe, convertible)	2,592	$395.00
79U	Millenium Yellow with tint coat	3,900	$750.00
86U	Magnetic Red Metallic paint (coupe, convertible)	N/A	$600.00

Exterior Colors	**Qty**	
Light Pewter Metallic	2,650	
Quicksilver Metallic	4,618	
Electron Blue Metallic	5,407	
Speedway White	1,763	
Black	7,129	
Torch Red	6,862	
Millennium Yellow Clear Coat	3,900	$750 option w/ tint
Magnetic Red-II Clear Coat	3,298	$600 option w/ tint

Convertible Top Colors	**Qty**
Black, with black liner	N/A
White, with black liner	N/A
Light Oak	N/A

2004 Corvette

Total Produced: N/A

Base Corvette Coupe	N/A	$44,535.00
Base Corvette Convertible	N/A	$51,535.00
Base Corvette Z06 Hardtop	N/A	$52,385.00

Dimensions

Weight (coupe)	3,246.0 lb.	Front Tire Size (coupe, convertible)	EMT P245/45ZR17
Weight (convertible)	3,248.0 lb.		
Weight (Z06)	3,118.0 lb.	Front Tire Size (Z06)	Asym. tread P265/45ZR17
Length	179.7 in.	Rear Tire Size (coupe, convertible)	EMT P275/40ZR18
Width	73.6 in.		
Height (coupe)	47.7 in.	Rear Tire Size (Z06)	Asym. tread P295/35ZR18
Height (convertible)	47.8 in.		
Height (Z06)	47.7 in.	Front Track (coupe, convertible)	61.9 in.
		Front Track (Z06)	62.4 in.
		Rear Track (coupe, convertible)	62.0 in.
		Rear Track (Z06)	62.6 in.

Engines

	Qty	Price
350 cid/350 hp V-8 (standard)	N/A	—
350 cid/405 hp V-8 (Z06)	N/A	N/A

Options

		Qty	Price
1SB	Preferred Equipment Group: Sport Coupe	N/A	$1,200.00
1SB	Preferred Equipment Group: Convertible	N/A	$1,200.00
1SB	Commemorative Edition Package: Z06	N/A	$4,335.00
1SC	Commemorative Edition Package: Sport Coupe	N/A	$3,700.00
1SC	Commemorative Edition Package: Convertible	N/A	$3,700.00
AAB	Memory package (Z06 hardtop)	N/A	$175.00
B84	Body side moldings	N/A	$150.00
C2L	Dual removable roof panels (coupe)	N/A	$1,400.00

CC3	Removable roof panel, blue tint (coupe)	N/A	$750.00
DDO	Auto-dimming mirrors (Z06 hardtop)	N/A	$160.00
F55	Magnetic Selective ride control (coupe, convertible)	N/A	$1,695.00
G92	Performance 3.15 axle (auto, coupe, convertible)	N/A	$395.00
MN6	Six-speed manual transmission (coupe, convertible)	N/A	$915.00
N73	Magnesium wheels (coupe, convertible)	N/A	$995.00
QF5	Polished aluminum wheels (coupe, convertible)	N/A	$1,295.00
R8C	Corvette Museum delivery	N/A	$490.00
UL0	Delco stereo cassette (coupe, convertible)	N/A	$0.00
UlS	Remote twelve-disc CD changer (coupe, convertible)	N/A	$600.00
V49	Front license plate frame	N/A	$15.00
Z51	Performance handling package (coupe, convertible)	N/A	$395.00
79U	Millennium Yellow with tint coat	N/A	$750.00
86U	Magnetic Red Metallic II	N/A	$750.00

Exterior Colors

	Qty	
Arctic White	N/A	
Le Mans Blue	N/A	
Black	N/A	
Machine Silver	N/A	
Torch Red	N/A	
Millenium Yellow Clear Coat	N/A	$750 option
Magnetic Red II	N/A	$750 option
Medium Spiral Gray Metallic	N/A	

Convertible Top Colors

Black, with black liner	N/A
White, with black liner	N/A
Light Oak, with black liner	N/A
Shale, with black liner	N/A

Appendix 2:
Suppliers and Services

Al Knoch Interiors
P.O. Box 484
9010 North Desert Blvd.
Canutillo, TX 79835
phone: 800-880-8080
fax: 915-886-4767
www.alknochinteriors.com
specialty: *interiors*

American Custom Industries
5035 West Alexis Rd. (SR 184)
Sylvania, OH 43560-1600
phone: 419-882-2091
fax: 419-885-5161
www.acivette.com
specialty: *accessories*

American Stamp Collectibles
RR 12, Box 180, Donohoe Road
Greensburg, PA 15601
phone: 724-837-8810
fax: 724-837-0444
www.framedstamps.com
specialty: *Corvette postage stamps*

Borla Performance Industries, Inc.
5901 Edison Drive
Oxnard, CA 93033
phone: 877-462-6752
www.borla.com
specialty: *exhaust systems*

Breathless Performance Products, Inc.
2070-F Tigertail Blvd., Building 2
Dania, FL 33004
phone: 954-925-7725
www.breathlessperformance.com
specialty: *performance improvements*

Busch Enterprises, Inc.
908 Cochran St.
Statesville, NC 28677
phone: 704-878-2067
fax: 704-878-9221
specialty: *wheel and metal care*

Carlisle Productions, Inc.
1000 Bryn Mawr Road
Carlisle, PA 17013-1588
phone: 717-243-7855
fax: 717-243-0255
www.carsatcarlisle.com
specialty: *Corvette and other car shows*

Chicago Corvette Supply
7322 S. Archer Road
Justice, IL 60458
phone 800-872-2446
fax: 708-458-2662
www.chicagocorvette.com
specialty: *restoration parts*

Contemporary Corvette
2705 Old Rogers Road
Bristol, PA 19007
phone: 800-367-8388
www.contemporarycorvette.com
specialty: *Corvette boneyard*

Corsa Performance Company
80 Helwig Street
Berea, OH 44017
phone: 440-891-0999
www.corsaperf.com
specialty: *performance improvements*

Corvette America
a division of Auto Accessories of America
Rt. 322, Box 427
Boalsburg, PA 16827
phone: 800-458-3475
fax: 814-364-9615
www.corvetteamerica.com
specialty: *restoration parts, accessories*

Corvette Central
CC Industries L.L.C
5865 Saywer Road
Sawyer, MI 49125
phone: 800-345-4122
fax: 616-426-4108
www.corvettecentral.com
specialty: *restoration parts, accessories*

Corvette Clocks by Roger
24 Leisure Lane
Jackson, TN 38305
phone: 800-752-3421
fax: 731-664-1627
www.corvetteclocks.com
specialty: *clock, radio and gauge restoration and sales*

Corvette Club of America
CCA–P.O. Box 9879
Bowling Green, KY 42102-9879
phone: 270-737-6022
www.corvetteclubofamerica.com
specialty: *Corvette association*

Corvette Mike
1133 North Tustin Avenue
Anaheim, CA 92807
phone: 800-327-VETT (327-8388)
fax: 714-630-0777
www.corvettemike.com
specialty: *preowned Corvette sales*

Corvette Mike New England
151 Samoset Street
Plymouth, MA 02360
phone: 508-747-VETT (747-8388)
fax: 508-747-0016
www.corvettemikenewengland.com
specialty: *preowned Corvette sales*

Corvette Rubber Company
10640 W. Cadillac Road
Cadillac, MI 49601
phone: 888-216-9412
www.corvette-rubber.com
specialty: *restoration parts and weatherstripping*

Custom Autosound Manufacturing, Inc.
1030 W. Williamson Way
Fullerton, CA 92833
phone: 800-888-8637
www.custom-autosound.com
specialty: *retro-look stereo sound systems and CD changers*

Davies Corvette Parts
7141 U.S. 19
New Port Richey, FL 34652
phone: 800-236-2383
fax: 727-846-8216
www.corvetteparts.com
specialty: *restoration parts, accessories*

Design Specialties Custom Products
121 Vanderbilt Court
Bowling Green, KY 42103
phone: 270-796-3000
fax: 270-796-3093
www.designspec.com
specialty: *accessories*

DeWitts Reproductions, Inc.
11672 Hyne Road
Brighton, MI 48114
phone: 810-220-0181
fax: 810-220-0182
www.dewitts.com.
specialty: *correct date-coded aluminum radiators and cooling system components*

Doug Rippie Motorsports
5767 State Highway 55 SE
Buffalo, MN 55313
phone: 763-477-9272
fax: 763-477-9277
www.dougrippie.com
specialty: *performance improvements*

Dr. Rebuild
P.O. Box 6263
25 Wells Street
Bridgeport, CT 06606
phone: 800-866-9362
fax: 203-576-0715
www.docrebuild.com
specialty: *restoration parts, accessories*

DR Vette Brake Products
Corvette Stainless Steel Brakes, Inc.
14364 SW 139 Court
Miami, FL 33186
phone: 800-262-9595
fax: 305-253-3641
www.cssbinc.com
specialty: *brake and suspension products*

Eastwood Company, The
263 Shoemaker Road
Pottstown, PA 19464
phone: 800-345-1178
www.eastwoodcompany.com
specialty: *restoration tools and supplies*

Ecklers Corvette Supplies
5140 S. Washington Avenue
Titusville, FL 32780
phone: 800-327-4868
fax: 321-383-2059
www.ecklers.com
specialty: *restoration parts, accessories*

Edelbrock Performance Parts
2700 California Street
Torrance, CA 90503
phone: 310-781-2222
fax: 310-320-1187
www.edelbrock.com
specialty: *performance improvements*

Ertl Corporation
(Ertl Racing Champions Die Cast)
800 Veterans Parkway
Bolingbrook, IL 60440
phone: 630-790-3507
www.ertltoys.com
specialty: *die cast models*

Dana Forrester Watercolors
17611 48th Terrace Court South
Independence, MO 64055
phone: 888-755-8388
fax: 816-478-2405
www.danaforrester.com
specialty: *limited edition lithographic prints of original Corvette watercolors*

Franklin Mint Precision Models
Franklin Center, PA 19091
phone: 877-843-6468
www.franklinmint.com
specialty: *die cast models*

Guldstrand Engineering & Motorsports
912 Chestnut Street
Burbank, CA 91506
phone: 818-558-1499
www.guldstrand.com
specialty: *performance improvements*

Hi-Tech Software
10 Little Tarn Court
Hardystown, NJ 07419
phone: 973-827-0339
www.htsoftware.com.
specialty: *Corvette Anthology and Corvette Ads CD-ROMs, other automotive CD-ROMs*

HotRod Hardware, Inc.
29929 Clemens Road,
Westwood Centre 1E
Westlake, OH 44145
phone: 800-575-1932
fax: 440-899-8045
www.genuinehotrod.com
specialty: *Corvette accessories, furniture, clocks and automobilia*

IBIZ, Inc.
750E. Sample Road, Bldg. 7, B-7
Pompano Beach, FL 33064
phone: 800-FOR-R-WAX (367-7929)
fax: 954-783-7131
www.ibiz-inc.com
specialty: *cleaning, waxing and car care products*

Kerbeck Corvette
430 N. Atlantic Avenue
Atlantic City, NJ 08401-1315
phone: 609-344-2100
www.kerbeck.com
specialty: *new Corvette sales*

Lingenfelter Performance Engineering
1557 Winchester Road
Decatur, IN 46733
phone: 260-724-2552
fax: 260-724-8761
www.lingenfelter.com
specialty: *performance improvements*

Long Island Corvette Supply
1445 Strong Ave S.
Copiague, NY 11726
phone: 800-466-6367
fax: 631-225-5030
www.licorvette.com
specialty: *Mid-year-only parts and accessories*

Mallet Cars, Ltd.
484 Geiger Street
Berea, OH 44017
phone: 440-243-8550
www.malletcars.com
specialty: *performance improvements*

Mattel, Inc.
(Hot Wheels Die Cast)
333 Continental Boulevard
El Segundo, CA 90245-5012
phone: 310-252-2000
fax: 310-252-2180
www.mattel.com
specialty: *die cast models*

Michael Bruce Associates, Inc.
Post Office Box 396
Powell, OH 43065-0396
phone: 614-430-8118
www.corvetteblackbook.com
specialty: *Corvette Black Book*

Mid America Motorworks
P.O. Box 1368
Effingham, IL 62401
phone: 800-500-1500
fax: 217-347-2952
www.madvet.com
specialty: *restoration parts, accessories*

Muskegon Brake and Distributing
848 East Broadway Avenue
Muskegon, MI 49444
phone: 800-442-0335
www.muskegonbrake.com
specialty: *brake and suspension products*

**National Corvette Museum &
NCM Store**
350 Corvette Drive
Bowling Green, KY 42101-9134
phone: 800-53VETTE (538-3883)
fax: 270-781-5286
www.corvettemuseum.com
specialty: *official Corvette museum and
merchandise outlet*

National Corvette Restorers Society
Cincinnati, OH 45252
24-hour fax line: 513-385-8554
email: info@ncrs.org
www.ncrs.org
specialty: *Corvette restoration association*

National Council of Corvette Clubs, Inc.
327 Baywood Drive
Campobello, SC 29322-9049
phone: 800-245-VETT (245-8388)
www.corvettesnccc.org
specialty: *Corvette association*

Paddock, The
12399 Belcher Road, Suite 160
Largo, FL 33773
phone: 800-338-0167
www.paddockparts.com
specialty: *restoration parts, accessories*

Paragon Reproductions
8040 South Jennings Rd.
Swartz Creek, MI 48473
phone: 800-882-4688
fax: 810-655-6667
www.corvette-paragon.com
specialty: *restoration parts, accessories*

Playing Mantis, Inc.
(Johnny Lightning Die Cast)
3618 Grape Road
Mishawaka, IN 46545
phone: 800-MANTIS-8 (626-8478)
www.playingmantis.com
specialty: *die cast models*

Ssnake-Oyl Products, Inc.
114 N. Glenwood
Tyler, TX 75702
phone: 800-284-777
fax: 903-526-4501
www.ssnake-oyl.com
specialty: *seat belt restoration and accessories*

Stainless Steel Brakes Corporation
11470 Main Road
Clarence, NY 14031
phone: 800-448-7722
fax: 716-759-8688
www.stainlesssteelbrakes.com
specialty: *brake and suspension products*

K. Scott Teeters Illustrations
18 Stanwood Court
Medford, NJ 08055
phone: 800-858-6670
www.illustratedcorvetteseries.com
specialty: *hand-drawn Corvette illustrations*

Thompson Astro Tops & Performance Products
1422 Huntsville Road
P.O. Box 2002
Florence, AL 35630
phone: 800-239-2659
www.astrotops.com
specialty: *removable transparent tops and accessories*

Trim Parts
2175 Deerfield Road
Lebanon, OH 45036
phone: 513-934-0815
fax: 513-934-0816
www.trimparts.com
specialty: *restoration trim parts and accessories*

Vanacor's Corvette Parts, Inc.
P.O. Box 701 (17272 Hwy. 90 West)
Des Allemands, LA 70030
phone: 800-225-6508
fax: 985-758-2777
www.vanacorvette.com
specialty: *fiberglass replacement parts and accessories*

Vette Brakes & Products
7490 30th Avenue North
Saint Petersburg, FL 33710-2304
phone: 800-237-9991
fax: 727-347-4818
www.vettebrakes.com
specialty: *brake and suspension products*

Zip Products
8067 Fast Lane
Mechanicsville, VA 23111
phone: 800-962-9632
www.zip-corvette.com
specialty: *restoration parts, accessories*

Magazines

Corvette Magazine
Ross Periodicals, Inc.
42 Digital Drive #5
Novato, CA 94949
phone: 415-382-0580
fax: 415-382-0587

Corvette Capers
CCA–P.O. Box 9879
Bowling Green, KY 42102-9879
phone: 270-737-6022
www.corvetteclubofamerica.com

Corvette Enthusiast
Amos Automotive Publishing
4265 New Tampa Highway, Suite 3,
Lakeland, FL 33815
phone: 863-688-2881
www.corvetteenthusiast.com

Corvette Fever
Subscription Fulfillment Department
PO Box 503
Mount Morris, IL 61054-7999
phone: 815-734-6026
www.corvettefever.com.

Corvette Journal
1525 Aviation Blvd., Suite 375
Redondo Beach, CA 90278

Corvette Quarterly
P.O. Box 2063
Warren, MI 48093-2063
phone: 586-753-8338
fax: 248-447-7566
www.chevrolet.com/corvette/
enthusiast.htm

Vette Magazine
McMullen Argus, division of PriMedia
2400 E. Katella Ave., 11th Floor
Anaheim, CA 92806
phone: 714-939-2400
fax: 714-978-6390
www.vetteweb.com

Vette Vues
P.O. Box 741596
Orange City, FL 32774
phone: 386-775-8454
fax: 386-775-3042
www.vette-vues.com

Acknowledgments

A very special and heartfelt thank-you goes out to these individuals (alphabetically listed) whose generosity, help and contributions helped to make this book all that it is:

Janet Barnes (my acquisitions editor at Bentley Publishers)

Carl Bessey (fellow Corvette nut and "hands" model)

Jerry Burton (fellow author and *Corvette Quarterly* Editoral Director)

Tom DeWitt (DeWitt's Reproductions)

James Garner (actor and AIR)

Jim Hall (Chaparral Cars)

Mark Havilland (Fujifilm U.S.A.)

Jim Hegadorn (Fujifilm U.S.A.)

Harry W. Ilaria (Hi-Tech Software)

Davey Jordan (AIR driver)

George Kerbeck (Kerbeck Corvettes)

Jennifer Knightstep (GM Media Archives)

Bobbie Jo Lee (National Corvette Museum)

Dave McLellan (fellow author and Corvette's second Chief Engineer)

Richard Newton (fellow author and my technical editor)

Bob Radke (SFO)

Jonathan A. Stein (my editor)

Mike Yager (Chief Cheerleader of Mid America Motorworks and my foreword author)

Fred Yeakel (Cheetah)

and numerous others whose help, encouragement, advice and humor all helped to make this book a reality.

Art Credits

All artwork is courtesy of the author, except as noted below:

Big Picture Agency: 14, 27

Dennis Boyer: 143 (bottom)

Peter Brock: 24

Callaway Cars: 31 (all), 32, 33 (all), 190

Carlisle Events: 101, 127, 128

Rich Chenet: 167

Creative Communication: 183

Bill Evitts: 146 (right)

Dana Forrester: 73

Karen Gale: 78

GM/Wieck: 28, 29 (top), 69 (bottom left, bottom right)

GMAC: 121 (all), 122

GMMA: 4, 10, 11 (all), 17, 19, 22, 29 (bottom), 38 (all), 39 (all), 44, 49 (all), 65, 77, 81 (all), 88, 89, 141, 142, 146 (left), 154, 171, 174, 178, 180, 201, 205, 206, 207 (all), 210, 213, 214, 215, 216

Winston Goodfellow: 147, 169 (bottom)

Jim Hall Collection: 40

John Heinricy: 90

Hi-Tech Software: 48

Hooker Headers, a division of Holley Performance Products, Inc.: 25 (bottom)

Lingenfelter Performance Engineering (LPE): 116

Ludvigsen Library: 85 (bottom left), 117

Dave McLellan Collection: 47, 54, 137 (all), 159 (right)

National Corvette Museum: 3, 9, 30, 43, 62, 70, 84, 93, 103 (bottom left), 125, 129, 130, 133, 134, 143 (top), 145, 170, 173, 177, 186 (right)

Penske Racing: 144

Richard Prince: 106

Bob Radke: 7, 67, 68

Greg Rager: 209 (top right)

Randy Rippie: 157 (all)

Road America: 162

Carroll Shelby: 42

Jonathan A. Stein: 26, 53, 61, 95, 119, 159 (left)

Kevin Suydam: 13, 209 (bottom left), 211

K. Scott Teeters: 109, 185

Bon Tronolone: 85 (top right)

Fred Yeakel: 41

Zora Arkus-Duntov Collection: 1

Cover Art Credits

Tom Benford:
Front cover—1963 C2 (left, 2nd from top)
Back cover—Quad lights (top)

Rich Chenet:
Front cover—C5R at Sebring (top right)

GMMA:
Front cover—1961 C1, 1978 C3, 1991 C4, 2003 C5, 2004 C6 (left, top to bottom); cavalcade of 1954 Corvettes (right, 2nd from top); steering wheel and dash (right, 3rd from top); 2003 5.7L V-8 LS6 (right, bottom)
Back cover—ZL1 engine (middle); Corvette SS (bottom)

Zora Arkus-Duntov Collection:
Front cover—Zora and Bill Mitchell (right, 4th from top)

About the Author

A freelance writer and editor for more than 30 years, Tom Benford has written hundreds of articles. His by-line has appeared in publications including *Oui, Harley-Davidson Enthusiast, Lens, New Jersey Business, New Jersey Living, New Jersey Monthly*, the *New York Times*, the *Wall Street Journal* and *USA Today*. He is also a frequent contributor to *Vette, Corvette Fever, CorvetteMagazine.com, Corvette Enthusiast, Cars & Parts Corvette* and *Cars & Parts* magazine.

An award-winning writer and dedicated Corvette historian, Tom is the author of *Corvette Performance Projects 1968–1982* (MBI), *The Street Rod* (MBI), and *The Complete Idiot's Guide to Restoring Collector Cars* (Alpha/Penguin Books). He also shares author credit with Randy Leffingwell on *Corvette: Five Decades of Sports Car Speed* (Crestline Books).

In addition to his automotive writing, Tom has authored three books on computer science published by MIS: Press, a division of Henry Holt and Company: *Welcome To...CD-ROM, Welcome To...PC Sound, Music and MIDI* and *Introducing Desktop Video*.

Also a published songwriter, he has recorded two albums.

The Benford stable of vintage cars includes six Corvettes from the 1963 through 1981 years, a 1933 Dodge coupe street rod and a recent addition, a 1998 C5 triple-black convertible. An avid enthusiast and member of the National Corvette Restorers Society, Tom does much of his own restoration work.

Tom lives in New Jersey with Liz, his wife of 25 years, and their German Shepherd, Wolf.

Selected Books and Repair Information From Bentley Publishers

Driving

The Unfair Advantage
Mark Donohue
ISBN 0-8376-0073-1 (hc);
0-8376-0069-3 (pb)

Going Faster! Mastering the Art of Race Driving *The Skip Barber Racing School* ISBN 0-8376-0227-0

A French Kiss With Death: Steve McQueen and the Making of *Le Mans Michael Keyser*
ISBN 0-8376-0234-3

Sports Car and Competition Driving *Paul Frère* with foreword by *Phil Hill* ISBN 0-8376-0202-5

The Technique of Motor Racing *Piero Taruffi* ISBN 0-8376-0228-9

Engineering/ Reference

Maximum Boost: Designing, Testing, and Installing Turbocharger Systems *Corky Bell* ISBN 0-8376-0160-6

Supercharged! Design, Testing, and Installation of Supercharger Systems *Corky Bell*
ISBN 0-8376-0168-1

Bosch Fuel Injection and Engine Management *Charles O. Probst, SAE*
ISBN 0-8376-0300-5

Road & Track Illustrated Automotive Dictionary
John Dinkel ISBN 0-8376-0143-6

Alfa Romeo

Alfa Romeo All-Alloy Twin Cam Companion 1954–1994
Pat Braden ISBN 0-8376-0275-0

Alfa Romeo Owners Bible™
Pat Braden ISBN 0-8376-0707-8

Audi

Audi A4 Service Manual: 1996–2001, 1.8L turbo, 2.8L, including Avant and quattro *Bentley Publishers* ISBN 0-8376-0371-4

Audi A4 1996–2001, S4 2000–2002: Official Factory Repair Manual on CD-ROM *Audi of America* ISBN 0-8376-1072-9

BMW

BMW 3 Series Enthusiast's Companion™ *Jeremy Walton* ISBN 0-8376-0220-3

BMW 6 Series Enthusiast's Companion™ *Jeremy Walton* ISBN 0-8376-0193-2

The BMW Enthusiast's Companion *BMW Car Club of America* ISBN 0-8376-0321-8

BMW 3 Series (E46) Service Manual: 1999–2001, 323i, 325i, 325xi, 328i, 330i, 330xi Sedan, Coupe, Convertible, Sport Wagon *Bentley Publishers* ISBN 0-8376-0320-X

Chevrolet

Zora Arkus-Duntov: The Legend Behind Corvette *Jerry Burton* ISBN 0-8376-0858-9

Corvette from the Inside: The 50-Year Development History *Dave McLellan* ISBN 0-8376-0859-7

Corvette by the Numbers: The Essential Corvette Parts Reference 1955–1982 *Alan Colvin* ISBN 0-8376-0288-2

Corvette Fuel Injection & Electronic Engine Management: 1982–2001 *Charles O. Probst, SAE* ISBN 0-8376-0861-9

Corvette 427: Practical Restoration of a '67 Roadster *Don Sherman* ISBN 0-8376-0218-1

Chevrolet by the Numbers: The Essential Chevrolet Parts Reference 1965–1969 *Alan Colvin* ISBN 0-8376-0956-9

Camaro Exposed: 1967–1969 *Paul Zazarine* ISBN 0-8376-0876-7

Ford

The Official Ford Mustang 5.0 Technical Reference & Performance Handbook: 1979–1993 *Al Kirschenbaum* ISBN 0-8376-0210-6

Ford Fuel Injection and Electronic Engine Control: 1988–1993 *Charles O. Probst, SAE* ISBN 0-8376-0301-3

Jeep

Jeep CJ Rebuilder's Manual: 1946–1971 *Moses Ludel* ISBN 0-8376-1037-0

Jeep CJ Rebuilder's Manual: 1972–1986 *Moses Ludel* ISBN 0-8376-0151-7

Jeep Owner's Bible™ *Moses Ludel* ISBN 0-8376-1117-2

Porsche

Porsche: Excellence Was Expected *Karl Ludvigsen* ISBN 0-8376-0235-1

Porsche 911 (964) Enthusiast's Companion: Carrera 2, Carrera 4 and Turbo, 1989–1994 *Adrian Streather* ISBN 0-8376-0293-9

Porsche 911 Carrera Service Manual: 1984–1989 *Bentley Publishers* ISBN 0-8376-0291-2

Volkswagen

Volkswagen Sport Tuning for Street and Competition *Per Schroeder* ISBN 0-8376-0161-4

New Beetle Service Manual: 1998–2002 1.8L turbo, 1.9L TDI diesel, 2.0L gasoline *Bentley Publishers* ISBN 0-8376-0376-5

Golf, GTI, Jetta 1999–2004, Jetta Wagon 2001–2004: Official Factory Repair Manual on CD-ROM *Volkswagen of America* ISBN 0-8376-1081-8

Passat Service Manual: 1998–2004, 1.8L turbo, 2.8L V6, 4.0L W8, including wagon and 4motion *Bentley Publishers* ISBN 0-8376-0369-X